7/18/85

D0890176

LANDSCAPE FORESTRY

LANDSCAPE FORESTRY

STEPHEN G. BOYCE

JOHN WILEY & SONS, INC.

New York · Chichester · Brisbane · Toronto · Singapore

This text is printed on acid-free paper.

This publication is designed to provide accurate and
authoritative information in regard to the subject
matter covered. It is sold with the understanding that
the publisher is not engaged in rendering legal, accounting,
or other professional services. If legal advice or other
expert assistance is required, the services of a competent
professional person should be sought.

Library of Congress Cataloging in Publication Data:
Boyce, Stephen G.
    Landscape forestry /   Stephen G. Boyce.
        p.   cm.
    Includes bibliographical references (p. 000) and index.
    ISBN 0-471-00784-6 (Cloth : acid-free paper)
    1. Forest landscape management. 2. Forest landscape management-
    -Simulation methods. I. Title.
    SD387.L35B69   1995
    634.9′2—dc20   94-22898

Printed in United States of America

10 9 8 7 6 5 4 3 2 1

To all who benefit from forested landscapes.

PREFACE

Forested landscapes are rearranged continually for new kinds of benefits and environments. Every forested landscape bears evidence of human interventions over many thousands of years. History records how human societies benefit by arranging forested landscapes to provide wood for cooking and heating, forage and shelter for domestic animals, habitats for hunting and fishing, trees for timbers and fiber, glades for solitude and ceremony, and trails for aesthetics and recreation. This book is written for all who benefit from forested landscapes.

One purpose for this book is to help managers and landowners rearrange forested landscapes to fulfill the changing demands of consumers. A second purpose is to help consumers understand why forested landscapes produce baskets of benefits in the aggregate rather than as separate items in a grocery cart. A third purpose is to provide ways for consumers and managers to jointly simulate the consequences of rearranging forested landscapes before changes are made. A fourth purpose is to help growing populations arrange forested landscapes for living the way they want to live.

This book begins four decades ago at North Carolina State University with Professor B. W. Wells telling me about systems as described by Norbert Wiener. I modified these concepts in combination with system dynamics methods, as described by Jay Forrester, to direct forested landscapes. My modifications are based on operational procedures described in the 1920s by P. W. Bridgman, Professor Emeritus of Physics at Yale University. My intent in documenting these methods is to give managers and consumers procedures to repeat experiences and confirm or change suppositions about consequences expected from rearranging a forested landscape.

Many more people than I can list here helped me adapt system concepts to directing forested landscapes. Many employees in the USDA Forest Service gave me encouragement and helped me shape procedures that were published by the USDA Forest Service. Faculties in the School of Forestry and Environmental Studies at Yale University and the School of the Environment at Duke University gave me opportunities to critically examine concepts in academic environments. Employees of state and industrial organizations contributed to making procedures useful in many different situations.

Attempts to satisfy hundreds of inquisitive and challenging students led me to abandon as much traditional terminology as possible. Much older terminology helped people of past eras live the way they wanted to live. New generations are changing the way they want to live, and new terminology describes new demands for forested landscapes. The posture for this book is to help people decide what is wanted from forested landscapes and how to obtain those wants.

To the hundreds of people who helped me shape, test and prune the information presented here, I offer my sincere thanks and gratitude.

STEPHEN G. BOYCE

ACKNOWLEDGMENTS

Apple and Macintosh are trademarks of Apple Computer, Inc. registered in the United States and other countries.

The DYNAMO Editor is copyrighted by Pugh-Roberts Associates, 41 William Linskey Way, Cambridge, MA 02142.

Professional DYNAMO and Professional DYNAMO Plus are trademarks of Pugh-Roberts Associates, 41 William Linskey Way, Cambridge, MA 02142.

STELLA and STELLA II are trademarks of High Performance Systems, Inc., 45 Lyme Road, Suite 300, Hanover, NH 03755.

CONTENTS

LANDSCAPE FORESTRY

1

PEOPLE AND LANDSCAPE FORESTRY

THIS BOOK

People demand fuel and timber more than any other benefits from forested landscapes. Incident to filling market demands, benefits, such as aesthetics, habitats, and biological diversity, are produced by landowners and forest managers. As world populations grow, more fuelwood and timber are demanded, fewer incidental benefits are produced, and more people become concerned about changes in the mix of market and incidental benefits. Changes in consumer demands are changing conservation and use of forested landscapes from structuring stands for fuelwood and timber to ordering stands across landscapes to enhance aesthetics, habitats, and biological diversity. Landscape forestry provides methods, concepts, and analytic procedures for shifting management from traditional to landscape forestry.

Incidental benefits do not compete with fuelwood and timber for cash flow. People do not purchase aesthetics, a kind of habitat, or a unit of biological diversity from forest owners. Yet, increasing numbers of people want landowners to conserve aesthetics, habitats, and biological diversity. These demands require diverting some solar energy from fuelwood and timber to benefits with no market values. Managers are reluctant to make these diversions because cash flow is reduced. In response to this situation, an increasing number of people are using procedures other than markets to encourage managers to change the use and conservation of forested landscapes. This book is concerned with simulating consequences of changing management from traditional forestry to landscape forestry or some other course of action.

After 1960, concerns of an increasing number of people for aesthetics, habitats, and biological diversity brought laws and regulations to limit the harvest of forests for fuelwood and timber. Public concerns stimulated national and international institutions to encourage and coerce governments and industries in many countries to increase efforts to conserve aesthetics, habitats, and biological diversity. A recent approach to conserving nonmarket values involves "certifying" forested landscapes as "sustainable forests" and labeling forest products as "environmentally friendly." A supposition is that consumers will purchase products labeled "environmentally friendly" in preference to products without labels. Labels are to identify products from forested landscapes managed to jointly produce desirable mixes of aesthetics, habitats, fuelwood, timber, cash flow, and biological diversity into the distant future. Managers are expected to want forested landscapes "certified" as a way to increase sales. One effect may be increased cost to consumers for wood products to pay for aesthetics, habitats, and biological diversity.

This book presents procedures to compare cash flows for producing and marketing different combinations of benefits in the aggregate. This book is a contribution toward helping consumers and managers find acceptable ways to fulfill demands for joint productions of many different combinations of benefits.

People Use Forested Landscapes

Fuelwood, houses, paper, and furniture are physical products demanded by consumers. The beauties of a wild bird, a scenic view, a wreath of dried plants, a glass of water, a period of solitude, and a glade of spring flowers represent kinds of consumer demands. Wildfires, mud slides, erosion, and loss of habitats, timber, and fuelwood are consequences of the way forested landscapes are used. Consumers determine how forested landscapes are to be used today and conserved for productions into the distant future (Huggett 1993; Tangley 1988; Martin et al. 1993a,b).

Managers and owners, including public and nonprofit owners, view use and conservation of forested landscapes in relation to personal desires for benefits, such as producing a livelihood for self and family. Personal desires are compromised by the demands of consumers, who continually change the mix of goods, services, and effects purchased in markets or indirectly paid for through taxes and gifts. Differences in opinions between consumers and producers result in continual negotiations, altercations, and confrontations. Benefits from forested landscapes are so important to the livelihood of humankind that issues spill into the highest levels of government and sometimes dominate social, political, economic, and legal events. For many reasons, there will never be harmony between consumers of forest benefits and managers and owners (Egan 1994).

Consumer demands are expressed, many times, with emotional and ideological phrases that confuse, irritate, and pose uncertainties for managers skilled in producing measurable benefits, such as wood for houses, paper, and furniture. Managers and owners are concerned with limiting changes in use and conservation practices that may place additional burdens on them. For example, consumers often carry mental models of forested landscapes as biologically balanced and harmonious communities of plants and animal working together to keep the world in an equilibrium state. This kind of mental model suggests to some consumers that removing human interventions will produce more desirable baskets of benefits than culturing forested landscapes. In contrast to balanced, harmonious equilibrium models, managers carry mental models of aimless changes from state to state in unmanaged flower gardens, cornfields, and forested landscapes. Cultural practices enhance the beauty in flower gardens, increase food production from cornfields, shape scenic values of forested landscapes, conserve biological diversity, and increase timber values for paper and furniture.

Demands of human populations for aesthetics, habitats, fuelwood, timber, and biological diversity far exceed biological potentials of unmanaged forest to fulfill demands. It is fortunate for humankind that enhanced productions of aesthetics, habitats, and biological diversity depend on management, the harvest of fuelwood and timber, to culture forested landscapes. It is as if, from a flower garden, the pulled weeds were edible. There is no way humanity can sustain livelihoods for current populations without applying cultural practices to gardens, farmlands, orchards, and forested landscapes.

Much energy and many resources are consumed by different factions working to get forested landscapes managed to their self-interest. Millions of people contribute to special-interest groups that maintain their attractiveness by implying or claiming destruction of forested landscapes by managers and owners. It is true that cultural practices, when used without concern for future consequences, can reduce and destroy productions of forest benefits. So can every useful tool. Axes and hammers damage some feet and fingers. Professor R. C. Lewontin makes the point that humans do not have the aimless, destructive properties of other organisms, but do have a unique property for scheduling actions, such as culturing flower beds and forested landscapes, and for mentally perceiving and evaluating future consequences. Lewontin (1993) suggests that energy and resources can be conserved if people turn their attentions to deciding how they want to live and how to arrange it so they can live that way. When I apply all these thoughts to the use and conservation of forested landscapes, what emerges is landscape forestry.

Landscape Forestry is an Art

Landscape forestry is the art of organizing forested landscapes to produce baskets of benefits that require two or more kinds of stands ordered over space and time. This concise statement needs a lot of explanation. This book provides illustrations, explanations, methods, principles, and theorems to help readers understand and apply landscape forestry. In this introduction, the art is described briefly.

Landscape forestry is management. It is the art of organizing forested landscapes to capture and pipe solar energy to the production of desired goods, services, and effects. For example, many animals require stands of one age class or type for feeding and stands of other age classes and types for shelter, escape, and reproduction. Aesthetics and wilderness values are related to patterns of stands. Scenic quality is related to order and diversity of stands dispersed over time and space. Proximity of stands for travel, escape, and migration are important for some animals and for seed dispersion. Areas of stands affect feeding, escape, and travel opportunities. Biological diversity is enhanced by a variety of stands interspersed in time and space by type, age, and area classes. The model for landscape forestry says changes in states of organization of forested landscapes change the availability of benefits.

Landscape forestry is an art based on personal experiences, results of managerial actions, research results, and understanding of the dynamics of biological systems. The art is following and adjusting, step by step, courses of action found by experience to result in acceptable productions of desired benefits.

Landscape foresters schedule rates of harvest of stands to bring about patterns, linkages, and distributions of stands to enhance habitats, aesthetics, timber production, cash flow, and biological diversity. The purpose of harvesting stands is to organize landscapes with a full range of stands classified by type, age, and area classes and to continually generate these classes in perpetuity over space and time. Every state of organization is dynamic. A stand classified into one type, age, and area class changes over time to a different class. Harvest schedules are designed to direct these changes toward states of organization that product sustainable baskets of desired benefits.

A chosen state of organization produces a particular mix of benefits. Changes in states of organization are directed by choosing rates of harvest of stands, sizes of canopy openings formed by harvesting stands, and kinds of regeneration to be encouraged.

Cash flow is an item in every basket of benefits. All benefits, including positive cash flow, are produced incident to goals for organizing forested landscapes. No single benefit, such as timber or wilderness, is produced at maximum rates with disregard for other values. Harvests of stands proceed, step by step, for the purpose of moving the forested landscape toward a sustainable state that produces desired baskets of benefits (Boyce 1975b, 1977, 1985, 1986; Boyce and McNab 1994; Bacon and Dell 1985; Diaz and Apostol 1992; Lucas 1991; McDonnell and Pickett 1993; Gomez-Pompa and Kaus 1992; Oliver 1992; Hunter et al. 1992; Martin et al. 1993a,b; Hunter 1990; O'Hara and Oliver 1992; Oliver et al. 1992).

The Purpose of This Book

This book is written as a textbook for consumers, students, managers, landowners, and faculty involved in studying, teaching, conserving, using, and managing forested landscapes. The minimum requirement for reading this book is experience or education in natural resources, such as forestry, wildlife management, geology, watershed management, agriculture, landscape ecology, silviculture, land management, landscape design, environmental management, or resource economics. This book is suitable for introductory and continuing education courses in the conservation and use of natural resources. Methods and concepts are well within educational and personal experiences of policy makers, members of environmental organizations, and professionally trained managers. Specialized words and technical terms are kept to a minimum, and explanations of concepts begin with observations familiar to most people.

Readers will find information about using forested landscapes for many benefits, including aesthetics, habitats, fuel, timber, and biological diversity. People concerned with developing policies for the conservation, use, and management of natural resources will find useful ideas, principles, theorems, and controls for implementing policy.

Advanced courses are developed around this book by adding a laboratory section to include design and construction of models to simulate options for real landscapes. Requirements for advanced students include experience in the use of computers; software for designing and constructing simulation programs; and access to inventories, economic variables, wildlife, watershed, aesthetic, and biological functions. Software such as STELLA for Macintosh machines and DYNAMO for DOS-based machines are effectively used in advanced courses. Other computer languages may be used. This book does not include instructions for using software, constructing computer models, or using the models mentioned in the text.

Six Classes of Benefits

This book centers on managerial concepts to meet the demands of consumers for baskets of habitats, aesthetics, timber, fuelwood, cash flow, and biological diversity. These six classes include thousands of different kinds of goods, services, and effects. There are too many different kinds of benefits to attempt discussion of each in a book of this scope. An assumption is that this classification includes most benefits produced by forested landscapes. Illustrations provide readers with methods that can be modified for specific benefits.

Aesthetics   include scenic views, the beauty of individual plants and animals, the beauty of communities of oganisms, the structure of forest stands, and outdoor recreation of many kinds. Aesthetics include enjoyment of hiking, camping, hunting, fishing, swimming, boating, and many other recreational activities provided by forested landscapes. For some people, aesthetics may be a satisfied feeling that desired states of organization of a forested landscape are being conserved in desired states into the distant future.

An operational definition of aesthetics is sometimes what is not measured rather than what is measured. For example, aesthetics may be the absence of noise, disturbance, or human activities that limit the enjoyment of beauty, tranquility, and serenity. Forested landscapes may be places for individuals to escape demands from civilization. The absence of these responsibilities is an operational measure of aesthetics. Operational measures are procedures others can use to repeat experiences and evaluate consequences that support decisions.

Habitats   include situations to enhance the livelihood of all endemic plants and animals, including endangered species. The number of possibilities for simulating individual habitats may be in the millions. Habitats include places to live for game animals, habitats of aquatic organisms associated with forested landscapes, and livelihood for nongame animals and plants. Habitats include places for people to spend time working, playing, hunting, hiking, fishing, and other activities. Picnic facilities, camping areas, boat ramps, hunting areas, and cabins are examples of human habitats.

Habitats are operationally measured by observing how organisms use different stands for getting food, escaping an enemy, reproducing, and other purposes (Bailey 1984; Hunter 1990; Elton 1949).

Fuelwood   is the end product of more than half of all wood harvested in the world (FAO 1993). Fuel wood is operationally measured as any wood-based material oxidized for heat. This definition includes wood collected for cooking and heating homes, camps, campfires, and industrial use of waste materials.

Relationships for fuelwood production vary from one part of the world to another. There is no way to design a single model that simulates the use of by-products of wood and wood-based materials to produce heat and electric energy in manufacturing plants and production of fuelwood in parts of the world where other forms of fuel may be scarce or very expensive. Specific situations determine how simulation models are to be designed to guide use of forested landscapes for fuels.

Timber   includes trade, manufacturing, jobs, marketing, and production of hundreds of wood-based products to support human livelihood. The operational measure is the harvest for processing into useful products of wood, gums, resins, bark, fruits, and other materials that require removing parts of standing or felled trees (Schniewind 1989). Fuelwood is excluded from the definition of timber because fuelwood is very different from lumber, veneers, fibers, and chemicals.

Cash Flow   is operationally measured with any number of economic indicators (Clark et al. 1979; Fleischer 1984; Gunter and Haney 1984). Net present value is used in this book, but other economic indicators may be more useful to some people.

Biological Diversity   is operationally measured as the number of individuals classified by species in a defined area. Biological diversity includes elements related to differences in biological systems. Such elements may include forest types, soil conditions, topographic variables, genetic variables, morphological variables, and physiological situations. Measurements of characteristics are to distinguish elements that are meaningful for providing benefits and for management decisions (Boyce and Cost 1978; Wenger 1984).

Biological diversity means differences in elements and numbers of items, such as individuals, in a classification of species. Taxonomic works are the basis for operationally defining species of organisms and for measuring biological diversity based on species. As used in this book, the word *species* refers to one kind of element. The common names used in this book are taken from the cited publications because I have no way to consult original studies on which the publications are based. Two primary sources of many common names are Martin et al. (1993a,b) and Radford et al. 1968).

The benefit called biological diversity includes organizing forested landscapes to provide potential livelihoods for most, and possibly all, endemic species to evolve and become extent. There is no way to remove human intervention from conservation, use, and enjoyment of biological diversity. This classification involves design and construction of many different forms of managerial models.

Every choice of a course of action requires partitioning captured solar energy among all six classes of benefits. There is no way to restrict solar energy to any one of the classes without changing productions of one or more benefits in all other classes. There is no way to preserve nesting and escape cavities in trees that must be burned to cook meals. There are ways to jointly produce nesting and escape cavities in combination with fuelwood. This book tells how to organize forested landscapes for joint productions of benefits. It is written to help people decide what they want from forested landscapes and how to organize landscapes to fulfill those wants for today and into the distant future.

WHY USE LANDSCAPE FORESTRY?

Our ancestors spent all but the last 20,000 years subsisting on collections of wild animals and plants produced with little or no management (Hill and

Hurtado 1989; Lewin 1988). Extensive areas of forest and grasslands were required to support relatively small human populations. Livelihood often remained at subsistence levels. People had few ways to counter destructive events such as storms, floods, and fires (Weiss et al. 1993). A long-held mental model was that natural forests, grasslands, oceans, and streams were common property from which benefits could be taken with little concern for future events (Schenck 1897, 1974; Fernow 1891, 1893; Gomez-Pompa and Kaus 1992; Ludwig et al. 1993).

As tools improved and management procedures evolved, people developed concepts such as sustained yield, regeneration of harvested lands, and scheduled rates of harvest. Traditional forestry evolved to match productions of wildlife and timber with consumer demands (Terminology Committee 1917; Marcin 1993).

Consumer demands change ways forests are used and conserved. After 1950, landscape forestry gained emphasis as consumers increased demands for aesthetics, habitats, and biological diversity in combination with productions of wood for fuel, houses, furniture, and paper (McArdle 1962; Cliff 1962; Steenberg 1972). Words and phrases that appealed to many people in this era included "sustained yield," "the greatest good for the greatest number," "ecosystem," "ecosystem management, "even flow," "regulated forests," "living in harmony with nature," and "multiple use." Political and social debates centered on "multiple use," defined at the time as the deliberate and planned integration of various forest uses so that users interfere with each other as little as possible (McArdle 1962). In the 1990s, the new terms include "forest health," "eco-label," and "sustainability."

Increased demands for aesthetics, biological diversity, and habitats are documented in the Multiple Use Sustained Yield Act of 1960. The National Forest Management Act of 1976 (NFMA) repeated some of the phrases (USDA Forest Service 1983). This act and later legislation encourages forest managers to shift emphasis from structuring stands for timber and cash flow to organizing stands across landscapes for aesthetics, habitats, and biological diversity. Increased demands for more and different kinds of benefits increased requirements for allocating solar energy to produce different mixes of benefits.

All forested landscapes are used directly or indirectly by humans. Growing world populations are increasing demands for more kinds and amounts of forest resources. Mental models for traditional forestry are changing. The amount of photosynthetic area per person is decreasing, and some kind of management is required to direct productions toward satisfying demands for fuel, timber, habitats, aesthetics, and biological diversity. As demands change, management must change. Four reasons are given for shifting traditional forestry toward landscape forestry (Bowler 1992; Marcin 1993; Ehrlich and Ehrlich 1990; Meadows et al. 1992; Kennedy 1993; Norse 1990; Schneider 1993; Egan 1993a,b, 1994; USDA 1993).

To Fill Baskets with Diverse Benefits

Landscape forestry is a way to fulfill diverse demands from consumers and a way to change the mix of benefits over time. New generations demand different ways for using forested landscapes. For example, timber and water are recorded as consumer preferences for the 1890s; grazing, timber, and water for the 1920s; wilderness, game habitats, soil erosion, and timber in the 1930s; economics, timber, and aesthetics in the 1940s; plant habitats, outdoor recreation, timber, and water in the 1950s, endangered species and biological diversity in the 1960s; old-growth stands in the 1970s; and sustainability in the 1990s (Conrad 1889; James 1897; Leopold 1933; Duerr 1949; Duerr et al. 1979; Martin et al. 1951; Norse 1990; Martin et al. 1993a,b; *Journal of Forestry* 1993).

Unlike shelves in a grocery store, stands in forested landscapes cannot be quickly reorganized to fulfill rapidly changing consumer demands. Because of biological constraints on rates of growth of plants and animals, productions of benefits from forested landscapes always lag, by a decade or more, changes in consumer demands. Yet landscape forestry offers a way to conserve a dispersion of stands so that the lag time between states of organization and production of benefits is reduced. The method is to use superimposed rotations to organize forested landscapes with stands representing all forest types, age classes from seedlings to old growth, and a variety of canopy openings. This variety of states contributes to current demands and is a flexible basis for change to meet new demands.

Since we know not tomorrow's mix of demands, it is irrational to establish standards for sustained yields of benefits demanded by today's consumers. Consumer demands are always changing. A rational approach is to organize forested landscapes to fulfill today's demands within the limits of conserving the landscapes for future uses, which are unknown. Analytic procedures, described in later chapters, illustrate how landscape forestry is used to guide tradeoffs between use and conservation.

Consumer demands today include baskets of timber, biological diversity, recreation, wilderness, old growth, habitats, and aesthetic values. In a decade, concerns could be different. One effect of changing demands is to extend silviculture from culturing stands as unrelated units to culturing stands as elements within organized landscapes. Professors in schools of forestry are concerned with making these kinds of changes in curricula and with educating students to adapt practices to providing baskets of benefits (P. G. Smith 1993; Probst and Crow 1991; Bachiel 1992; Payne et al. 1992; Cordell and Hendee 1982; Kessler et al. 1992; Sharitz et al. 1992; Hornbeck and Swank 1992; Swanson and Franklin 1992).

An area of activity related to landscape forestry is landscape ecology. Landscape ecology is a primary source of information about landscape structures, processes, functions, and interactions between and among organisms and environments. Widespread interest in landscape ecology documents the concerns of many informed people about conserving, using, and managing forested landscapes for benefits that require different kinds of stands ordered over space and time. Landscape forestry uses information from landscape ecology to analyze options and to help managers make choices that include relationships from ecology (Forman and Godron 1981, 1986; Harris 1984; Pickett and White 1985; Boyce 1977, 1985; Diaz and Apostol 1992; Oliver 1992; Risser et al. 1984).

To Provide a Platform for Common Goals

Another reason for using landscape forestry is to provide a platform for individuals with different interests to search for ways to jointly product baskets of benefits rather than wasting energy competing for special interests. Landscape forestry does not resolve conflicts. Landscape forestry provides a physical model for scrutiny by all interested parties, for proposed changes, and for adjustments in actions to compromise on issues. Procedures provide explicit displays of mental models, displays of consequences simulated for different courses of action, and controls that can be adjusted for jointly produced baskets of benefits (Probst and Crow 1991; Schneider 1993; Egan 1993a,b).

Many natural resource educators, ecologists, environmentalists, students, and consumers want forest managers to be caretakers and stewards of the earth so that future generations will have the opportunity to enjoy and use its resources. There is repeated demand for partnerships and cooperation among groups such as academicians and practitioners, environmentalists and industrialists, researchers and land managers. There is strong interest in structuring curricula toward meeting the demands of the current social and political environment to strengthen interdisciplinary competency and to view the whole forested landscape as an object for management rather than managing disciplinary islands. A theme expressed by many students, faculty, and practitioners revolves around recognition that traditional forestry, based on sustained yield of timber, does not satisfy current demands for habitats, aesthetics, and biological diversity (Norse 1990; Whaley 1993; Peterson 1993; Hosner 1993; Gilbert et al. 1993; Ellefson 1993; Norris 1993; Wilcox 1987).

The previous paragraph documents fragmentation of demands for forest benefits into islands of special interest, such as habitats, aesthetics, timber, water, biological diversity, biological conservation, wildlife management, landscape ecology, and resource economics. Members of each special-interest group perceive that others "do not understand us." Conflict develops between groups inside management organizations and between institutions that lobby for special kinds of benefits and management actions. Three decades of confrontation between managers and special-interest groups are stimulating many consumers to request more cooperation. Few conflicts, such as habitats for spotted owls and timber harvest, are resolved quickly and effectively. Landscape forestry provides a platform for many interest groups to examine the consequences of their demands in the context of other demands. This kind of analysis may contribute to a search for common goals in the use and conservation of forested landscapes (P. G. Smith 1993; Whaley 1993; Egan 1993a,b; Raines 1993).

Landscape forestry is a platform for examining consequences of options. Landscape forestry is not a procedure for resolving conflicts between parties that desire different options. Conflict resolution is beyond the limits for this book. If and when conflicts are resolved, landscape forestry provides managers and others with tools to jointly produce baskets of goods, services and effects.

To Help Managers Make Tradeoffs among Uses

Landscape forestry provides managers and consumers with ways to favor a basket of desired benefits and a way to reduce undesirable consequences with tradeoffs. Tradeoffs between desirable and undesirable consequences are displayed for scrutiny by all interested parties. Options can be simulated to examine ways to limit adverse effects and minimize undesirable events. Landscape forestry is a way for managers to analyze and trade off the consequences of use to produce acceptable, not necessarily ideal, baskets of benefits.

Conservation, use, and management of forested landscapes vary from one part of the world to another. Yet states of organization in every kind of forest affect consequences, both desirable and undesirable. These relationships are grounded in flows of solar energy, amounts of solar energy trapped in forested landscapes, and flows of materials through the landscapes. Regardless of differences in climate, geology, and species, methods for organizing forested landscapes are grounded in certain fundamental principles, theorems, and controls. These fundamentals are described in this book and are used to relate the organization of landscapes to consequences. The methods are useful for analyzing tradeoffs in any part of the world.

Examples of Tradeoffs   All uses are dependent on access and on the presence of an infrastructure to support people. People who hike, gather firewood, harvest timber, fish, hunt, and gather fruits require roads, trails, sanitary facilities, waste containers, protection, housing, rescue, information, maps, water, and food. As populations of people increase and more people demand more kinds and amounts of forest uses, more infrastructure and more management is required. In North Carolina, Shinning Rock Wilderness is adjacent to the Blue Ridge Parkway, near mile post 418. Blacktop trails provide access to millions who want to enjoy the aesthetics of this forested landscape (Fig. 1.1).

Every year, millions of people visit forested landscapes around Shinning Rock Wilderness, Mt. Pisgah, and the Pisgah National Forest. Roads, restaurants, overlooks, maps, trails, and other infrastructures provide people opportunities that would be denied if infrastructures were poorly developed. Access is essential for conservation, use, and management. Blacktop trails are a symbol of many kinds of tradeoffs that must be made to conserve productivity and biological diversity as demands for use increase. Over the next 40–50 years, a short time in the life of forested landscapes, human populations may double and demands for use may require many tradeoffs.

A tradeoff worth special attention is a mile-long, elevated walkway that provides thousands of people, of all ages and conditions, access to an old stand of western red cedar in Glacier National Park, Montana (Fig. 1.2).

The stand of cedars is on Going to the Sun Road at Avalanche Creek. The walkway protects soils, roots, herbaceous plants, and other organisms from

Figure 1.1   A blacktop trail protects the landscape and provides access to thousands of people who want to walk from the Blue Ridge Parkway, near mile post 418, into Shinning Rock Wilderness, which is part of the Pisgah National Forest in North Carolina.

trampling; permits a natural flow of water, nutrients, and materials through the stand; and provides experiences for many people who could not otherwise visit such a stand. Consequences include damage to trees next to the walkway and damage to soils and roots during construction. These are some of the tradeoffs to be considered by managers.

Roads are an essential part of the infrastructure for any forested landscape. In North Carolina, near mile post 411 on the Blue Ridge Parkway, an exit to Scenic Highway US 276 provides access to towns and villages on both sides of Pisgah Ridge, and onto the Pisgah National Forest. Protection of the resources and service to users requires rapid access and supporting restaurants, sanitary facilities, camping areas, waste collection, and other services. West of Shinning Rock Wilderness, the Parkway leads to Great Smoky Mountain National Park and the Cherokee Reservation at mile post 469. Infrastructures in many areas are well developed, although some are in poor condition because of use by millions of people. Throughout the world, many scenic attractions are framed by forested landscapes that are managed for many kinds of goods, services, and effects.

All infrastructures change the state of organization of forested landscapes and change the availability of benefits. An example is a part of the Pisgah

Figure 1.2 An elevated walkway protects the landscape and provides access to thousands of people who want to see an old stand of western red cedar at Avalanche Creek in Glacier National Park, Montana.

National Forest near Brevard, North Carolina. Near mile post 410 on the Parkway, Scenic Highway US 276 leads south to campgrounds and to the Cradle of Forestry Visitor Center. Thousands of visitors come here to see a Climax steam locomotive and logging tools from 100 years ago. At lower elevations, Sliding Rock, Looking Glass WaterFalls, Davidson River, the ranger station, and the North Carolina State Fish Hatchery are favorites of thousands. Tall yellow poplars and dense stands of oaks, birches, beeches, hickories, ashes, hemlocks, and white pines enclose the roads and overlap many hiking trails, campgrounds, and trout streams. From the Parkway, a discerning viewer can often find openings in the forest canopies where sprouts and seedlings are rapidly growing to replace harvested trees. The dense growth provides areas for many species of plants and animals that cannot find a livelihood in older stands. Biological diversity is increased and wood is produced by judicious use of timber harvesting to organize the forested landscapes. Millions of people experience this area because the state of organization provides a variety of habitats and a related infrastructure for management, protection, conservation, and use.

In April and May, silver bell, flame azalea, fire cherry, shadbush, rhododendron, yellow poplar, bloodroot, violets, and many other plants are in flower on Pisgah Ridge. The diversity of habitats, herbaceous plants, animals, and trees attracts students and faculty from many colleges and universities. Game lands, managed by the North Carolina Wildlife Resources Commission, protect game and endangered species and provide hunting and fishing opportunities for thousands of state residents and visitors. Endangered peregrine falcons nest on Looking Glass Rock; black bears take advantage of a bear reserve; bobcats, raccoons, white-tailed deer, and skunks are present. Migrating hawks are common in spring and fall; migrating warblers thrill birders in the spring and fall; and, in the spring, many wintering birds from Central and South America come to nest.

Jobs and cash flow are consequences related to changes in states of forest organization. Jobs are created from automobile, food, and housing services for visitors. Many people earn a living from harvesting and processing timber for paper, housing, and furniture. Others earn a living from construction and maintenance of roads, trails, tables, and recreation areas. Still others have jobs removing trash and keeping recreation areas clean and inviting for users. Management of these forested landscapes provides jobs that are tradeoffs against exclusion of people from any use or intervention in natural events.

To Emulate Natural Events

Landscape forestry focuses on emulating natural events to achieve desired states of organization. Natural mortality is emulated with scheduled rates of harvest of stands; natural gaps are emulated by scheduling sizes of canopy openings; and regeneration is emulated by encouraging natural regeneration and planting when natural regeneration fails. Emulation of natural processes requires tradeoffs between optimal flows of cash and timber and conservation of biological diversity, habitats, and aesthetics. Landscape forestry is a way to help managers find a course of action that produces positive, not optimal, cash flow in combination with productions of other values.

MANAGEMENT WITH MENTAL MODELS

The argument in this book says every management action is an option simulated with a mental model (Norman 1981). If we analyze our mental models, we find a similar sequence of events is used to drive automobiles, choose clothing, play golf, and work. We sense a situation, structure a policy, pose a question, design a mental model to simulate options, consider the consequences of different options, and choose a course of action. This intrinsic procedure is used in this book. The procedure is expanded to include conversion of mental models into physical models, such as maps, diagrams, equations, and computer programs, in order to display information from our mental models.

Physical models help us relate large numbers of complex relationships and help us link and interrelate mental models from different people. Physical models, such as computer programs, simulate consequences produced by many variables changing simultaneously. Computers and equations help us document our mental models in formats that enhance communication with colleagues, collaborators, and workers. Documentation provides for all interested parties to scrutinize analyses and contribute to managerial decisions. Physical models may become objects for most of our efforts and for guiding our actions. Yet all physical models are aids, not replacements, for our mental models. Every choice of a course of action is still a choice made from a mental model.

Managers use mental and physical models to schedule trash removal, maintenance of roads and trails, timber harvests, wilderness protection, and recreational developments. People develop mental models for harvesting, processing, transporting, and marketing goods, services, and effects from forested landscapes. Some mental models include services to support swimming, hiking, hunting, birding, exploring, nature study, skiing, restaurants, motels, and maintenance of travel vehicles. Mental models underlie all actions and perceptions of situations. When mental models become complex due to many variables changing simultaneously, physical models are applied as tools. Yet it is important to repeat that final decisions are derived from mental models.

Development of Mental Models

One persistent concept in the literature that relates to landscape forestry is the deeply held mental model that people can and must live in harmony with nature. This mental model includes perceptions of aesthetic, social, and biological values derived from forested landscapes. Demands for harvest of wood for fuel, paper, houses, and furniture conflict with perceptions of aesthetic, social, and biological values. Out of these demands for conflicting uses of forested landscapes, landscape forestry evolved slowly over many years. The model for landscape forestry is based on the observations and experiences of many people over many decades (Evelyn 1664; Marsh 1964; Leopold 1933; Conrad 1889; James 1897; Gomez-Pompa and Kaus 1992; McArdle 1962; Cliff 1962; Steenberg 1972; Schenck 1897, 1974; Fernow 1891; Boyce 1977, 1985, 1986; Boyce and McNab 1994; Oliver 1992; Hunter et al. 1992; Martin et al. 1993a,b; Bacon and Dell 1985; Diaz and Apostol 1992; Burns 1989; McDonnell and Pickett 1993; Loomis 1993; Waring and Schlesinger 1985; Huggett 1993; Bowler 1992).

Mental models for landscape forestry say that habitats, aesthetics, timber, fuelwood, cash flow, and biological diversity are determined by states of organization of forested landscapes. A number of writings express this model in different ways. H. A. Smith (1936) wrote, "We are attempting to develop landscape art in order to express beauty through nature." Forrester (1961) linked an understanding of the structure of systems to effective and efficient management. Bridgman (1927) used procedures for measuring structure to give one person a basis for comparison of experiences with those recorded by others. Bruner (1960) noted that grasping the structure of a subject is the first step in understanding functions and in linking functions to management. Our understanding of structure, linkage of parts, and states of organization underlie our ability to use and conserve complex systems, such as forested landscapes.

Mental models use information about structure and functions to design forested landscapes. Managers have long perceived forested landscapes as stands distributed across space and changing over time. This model is used by Frothingham (1917, 1931) in describing states of organization of forested landscapes in the Southern Appalachians. Frothingham described the landscape in terms of stands classified by forest habitats, ages, and crown cover. "Habitats," as used by Frothingham, are essentially equivalent to "stands" as used in this book. Crown cover is essentially the size of canopy openings, which establish area classes for new stands. Frothingham and earlier workers (Evelyn 1664; Miles 1967) knew that the state of organization of forested landscapes determined the availability of all goods, services, and effects. This perception is the basis for landscape forestry.

Failure of Mental Models

Many managerial mistakes are related to deeply held, incorrect mental models. Mental models may be in error because of inadequate, incorrect, or discarded information. Many people learn to recognize errors in mental models and to deal with inadequate and incorrect information. Others have difficulty scrutinizing traditional beliefs that may be held by large numbers of people. When situations are complex, people tend to ignore or discard information as a way to reduce complexity. Ignoring and discarding conflicting information is a way for managers to avoid admitting past mistakes. Yet ignoring or discarding new information to favor traditional beliefs may produce poor decisions (Horridge 1977; Senge 1990; Kahneman et al. 1982; Beer 1966, 1975; Bowler 1992).

Consider a deeply held mental model about preserving pristine situations in old-growth forests, wilderness, and other kinds of forest reserves. One mental model argues for no intervention into natural events and no actions to manage aesthetics, habitats, and biological diversity. Such deeply held mental models may be appropriate for some situations. In different situations, the same mental model may limit managerial actions until failures become intolerable and corrective actions become very costly. For example, some mental models for pristine conditions in a wilderness may lead to arguments against constructing blacktop trails and boardwalks (see Figs. 1.1, 1.2). Yet without blacktop trails or some other kinds of managerial intervention, aesthetics, habitats, and biological diversity may be damaged (Fig. 1.3).

Readers of this book learn to question mental models. Throughout this book, mental models about the dynamics of forested landscapes are challenged by comparing them with observations, personal experiences, scrutiny

Figure 1.3   Photograph, taken near the trail shown in Figure 1.1, is of an eroded trail in Shinning Rock Wilderness, Pisgah National Forest, NC. Erosion of trails is one kind of undesirable consequence that results when managers cannot intervene to provide access for thousands of people and simultaneously manage forested landscapes for asesthetics, habitats, and biological diversity.

by others, and research results. Whenever possible, descriptions use operational definitions. Such definitions frame meanings of words and phrases with procedures that help others repeat experiences and evaluate consequences that support decisions. For example, others can repeat observations supported by photographs (Figs. 1.1–1.3) and suggest changes in interpretation and in proposed managerial actions.

THE POSTURE FOR THIS BOOK

Millions of people claim membership in conservation and environmental organizations. In the United States 42 national organizations, each with more than 10,000 members, represent more than 15.7 million members. In addition to national groups, hundreds of additional organizations are concerned with protecting forested landscapes in cities, counties, and states (Hendee and Pitstick 1992).

Most members of environmental organizations are not landowners and are not trained or experienced as professional managers of forested landscapes. Yet through their actions as consumers and interested parties, these members influence policies for management and use of forested landscapes (Hendee and Pitstick 1992; Stern 1993; Holland et al. 1991; Probst and Crow 1991; Martin et al. 1993a,b; McDonnell and Pickett 1993; Bowler 1992).

The two largest organizations of professional conservationists, namely the Soil and Water Conservation Society and the Society of American Foresters, reported a combined membership of 32,000 in 1991. These two societies represent managers trained and experienced in directing the use and conservation of most forested landscapes in the United States. For many decades, professional conservationists have directed forested landscapes with the relatively simple policy of maintaining a positive cash flow and producing raw materials to support the national economy. To this policy, millions of consumers are adding habitats for all kinds of plants and animals, aesthetics, and biological diversity.

The posture for this book is to help society decide what is wanted from forested landscapes and how to obtain those wants. The goal is to help managers, consumers, environmentalists, and other interested parties choose a desired state of organization for a forested landscape and agree on courses of action.

This book makes no claim to the development of policies and takes no particular policy position. The supposition is that policies are made from simulations in mental and physical models. This book presents systematic procedures to convert mental models to physical models that are used to communicate with others, adjust suppositions about futures, and evaluate consequences before imposing management schemes. Operational definitions frame mental models with procedures that help others evaluate management schemes. Recognition of states of organization of forested landscapes as the common denominator for diverting solar energy to productions of desired goods, services, and effects is an effort to reintroduce into management of forested landscapes a sense of unity that is lost in the fragmentation of systems into disciplines.

Managers and owners will find ways to change states of organization of forested landscapes to produce baskets of benefits in the aggregate. Consumers will find ways to discover how demands rearrange forested landscapes and change baskets of benefits in the aggregate, not as single items tossed into a grocery cart. Environmentalists will find ways to simulate the consequences of human existence as systems of interlocking natural events, demands of consumers, and directed rearrangement of forested landscapes.

2

OPERATIONAL DEFINITIONS

Operational definitions frame meanings of words and phrases with procedures that help others repeat experiences and evaluate consequences that support decisions. To say a tree is 12 cm dbh (diameter at 1.37 m above ground) is to use an operational definition that helps others repeat the measurement (Avery and Burkhart 1983). When measurements cannot be repeated, complexity, ambiguity, confusion, and arguments arise. Without operational definitions, managers have no way to relate consequences to managerial actions, no way to compare outcomes with policy, and no basis for adjusting managerial actions to fulfill consumer demands.

This chapter examines some ways for consumers and managers to use operational definitions to explicitly convey mental models to others. The method is many decades old (Bridgman 1927). Whenever available, operational definitions are described and used in this book.

SOME DEFINITIONS FOR THIS BOOK

The intent of operational definitions is to help others repeat experiences, evaluate consequences, agree with suppositions, or suggest changes. Operational definitions are essential for understanding the behavior of complex systems and for directing systems toward desired states of organization. Without operational definitions, scientists and managers struggle against confusion of thought and terms. A change in meaning of words and phrases is often an improvement over fuzzy connotations and established traditions of thought. Yet well-meaning people are often attracted to words and phrases that carry mysterious and fuzzy meanings. Use of ambiguous phrases contributes to

21

confusion in communications and in the design and use of mental models. Fuzzy words and phrases find their way into the scientific literature and into managerial terminology (Benjamin 1955; Ashby 1973; Bridgman 1927; Beer 1966, 1975; Forrester 1961; *Journal of Forestry* 1993; Tansley 1935; Oreskes et al. 1994).

Sunlit Canopy

Sunlit canopies are the photosynthetic surfaces of a stand that capture more than half of the received solar radiation during the growing season. Sunlit canopies are measured as the proportion of a stand area covered by a canopy of photosynthetic surfaces during a growing season. Sunlit canopies may be categorized by species and elevation above the ground. Measurements may be made from aerial photographs, satellite images, or from the ground.

As trees age, crowns change in size and composition. Old parts of crowns die and fall to the ground, and some parts are eaten by animals and fungi. New branches, flowers, fruits, and leaves form to continue the flow of solar energy trapped in sunlit crowns. Crowns expand in height and width to fill sunlit spaces. Dominant and codominant trees are defined as those that fill sunlit spaces, close canopies and limit opportunities for shaded trees to grow and penetrate the sunlit canopy. Sunlit canopies capture most of the solar energy used in a stand, influence stand structure and determine most of the pathways for use of solar energy by animals, trees and other plants. Typically, trees with sunlit canopies form more valuable boles for timber, more aesthetically pleasing shapes of crowns and boles, more flowers, and more fruits than shaded trees. Understory trees produce fewer carbohydrates, grow more slowly, and are more susceptible to insect and disease attacks than sunlit trees. Shaded plants are exposed by canopy openings created by natural deaths of sunlit trees and harvest of trees (Belsky and Canham 1994).

Stand

A stand is an area of two or more contiguous trees delimited by measurable or observable features, such as roads, streams, kinds of dominant trees, sizes of dominant trees, age class of dominant trees, and physical characteristics of soil and topography. Stands are classified by forest type, age class, understory vegetation, density of trees, biomass, depth of litter, physical features of the landscape, and habitat characteristics. Boundaries of stands are arbitrarily identified and located to fit conservation, use, and management requirements. Stands are often numbered or given names, for identification in records and on maps. Stands are generally considered part of a larger forested landscape, but a stand and a landscape can cover the same area of ground.

Stands are convenient units for management. Boundaries are arbitrarily selected to provide operational units that can be named, measured, documented, cultured, harvested, and regenerated. Boundaries are not permanent and are not surveyed and documented with permanent markers. Areas and sizes are estimated carefully but with minimum effort (Avery and Burkhart 1983). Harvest, regeneration, thinning, fire, and road construction are examples of events that change stand boundaries. Maps of stands are temporary models of a situation. Maps of stands are changed as states of organization of forested landscapes change. The important observation is that stands are fundamental units of landscapes managed for producing different kinds of goods, services, and effects.

For many classification systems, the smallest hierarchical units fit definitions for stands and communities. Borders of the smallest units of every classification may coincide with one feature, such as aspect, slope, geology, growth rate, solar radiation, or age, but borders rarely coincide with all features of a classification scheme. Stands are defined here the same as they were 100 years ago. The concept is well established in the literature of many professions. The concept of *stand* is commonly used by silviculturists, ecologists, landscape designers, forest designers, forest managers, wildlife biologists, geologists, hydrologists, engineers, and other resource managers. The stand is the common denominator for linking forested landscapes to other forms of land classification (Martin et al. 1993a,b; Mengel and Tew 1991; Terminology Committee 1917; Bailey 1988, 1989).

Stands Are Landscape Units

Stands are convenient units of landscapes for analysis, planning, and implementing courses of action. Although mental models may vary in some characteristics from one to another functional discipline, the word *stand* conveys a mental model of a unit of landscape. Criteria for defining stands almost invariably include terms that imply forest type, stand age, and area. The concept of *stand* is the common denominator for communication among functional disciplines (Boyce 1977, 1985, 1978; Thomas 1979; Forman and Godron 1981; Barnes et al. 1982; Harris 1984; D. M. Smith 1986; Oliver and Larson 1991; McNab 1987, 1991; Mengel and Tew 1991; Bacon and Dell 1985; Diaz and Apostol 1992).

Forest Type

A forest type is a group of stands with sufficient similarity in biological and physical features to be consistently identified by different observers. Forest types are defined by species of dominant and codominant trees and sometimes by species of understory trees. Names of forest types, such as oak-hickory type, use names of dominant and codominant trees. Adjectives, such as *dry, mesic, upland, cove, northern, mixed, black water, bog,* and *wet,* are used in combination with names of dominant species. Names of understory plants are used in some forest type names. Other names used in classification systems may include consideration of topographic features, soils, animals, and the potential for rates of growth. Forest types vary geographically and within a forested landscape in relation to human use and natural events.

Canopy Openings

Canopy openings are formed when sunlit trees die or are removed by harvests. Natural events and harvesting produce openings as small as the crown areas of single dominant trees, about 0.05 ha, and as large as hundreds of hectares. Crowns of trees adjacent to canopy openings expand laterally and fill parts of sunlit spaces. Surfaces of sunlit canopies appear from a distance to be formed of trees of about equal height and of the same or similar species. Closer inspection reveals stands with trees of different heights and with holes in the sunlit canopy. Fleeting flecks of sunlight penetrate canopies and contribute to survival of understory species. Flecks of sunlight rarely provide understory plants with enough energy to challenge dominant trees in the sunlit canopy. Although some seedlings, trees and sprouts in the understory live for many decades, most understory plants are starved because of low rates of photosynthesis. Most understory plants are distorted in shape, often infested with disease and insects, and are closer to death than to becoming a member of the sunlit canopy (Wahlenberg 1960; Sheffield and Thompson 1992; Lorimer and Frelich 1994; Merz and Boyce 1956; Boyce 1951; Shorrocks and Swingland 1990; Belsky and Canham 1994).

When canopy openings are small, that is, equivalent to the area of the crowns of one or two trees, growth of understory plants is slow; little, if any, new regeneration survives; few seeds, stored in the forest floor, germinate; flowering and fruiting of shrubs and herbaceous plants are increased little if any; and chances are small of any understory tree penetrating the sunlit canopy. Small canopy openings tend to encourage replacement of the sunlit canopy with trees that can survive long periods in suppression in the understory. Suppressed trees are rarely desirable as future trees for timber because of poor health and vigor, distorted shapes, and injuries suffered from diseases and insects (Frothingham 1917; Boyce 1951; Wahlenberg 1960; Runkle 1981, 1982; Uhl et al. 1988; Lorimer 1980).

Willison (1981) presents some consequences 20 years after circular canopy openings were made in a forested landscape on the Vinton Furnace Experimental Forest in southeastern Ohio. Sizes of canopy openings were 0.05, 0.1, 0.2, 0.405, 1.2, and 2 ha repeated 6 times. Willison reported the consequences of letting the new stands grow for 20 years without any silvicultural treatments. Openings were located on a good site with a site index for black oaks of greater than 23 m at age 50, and on an average site with a site index of less than 23 m for black oaks. At the time of harvest, all trees taller than 1.37 m were cut. After 20 years, the general conclusions are: New stands form quickly from seedlings and sprouts on both good and average sites for all canopy openings of 0.05 to 2 ha. In 20 years, the sunlit canopies rise from less than 1.37 m to more than 17 m on good sites and to more than 14 m on average sites. Openings larger than 0.2 ha on good sites favor development of large trees. In openings larger than 0.2 ha, sunlit trees have more basal area than shaded trees, which are mostly in the understory (Fig. 2.1).

Basal area is the square meters of cross-sectional area per hectare of all trees larger than 11.4 cm dbh. Basal area is a function of the diameter and number of trees and is related to volume and the sunlit crown area. Sunlit trees in openings 0.2 ha and larger have more basal area than shaded trees (Fig. 2.1), but there are many more shaded trees than sunlit trees (Fig. 2.2).

Stands of varying age, and thus heights of sunlit canopies, provide a variety of habitats, aesthetics, biological diversity, timber, and recreation values. Sunlit canopies are shifted to suppressed trees when dominant trees are harvested or die. When suppressed, many trees exhibit slow growth; injuries from diseases, insects, and other animals; distorted stems; and limited root systems. When dominant canopies are removed, some suppressed trees may die and others may increase in growth rates. An alternative to leaving suppressed trees is to remove all trees larger than about 2 cm dbh. This transfers the sunlit canopy to seedlings and sprouts and creates habitats to favor many kinds of organisms that survive poorly under high canopies.

When canopy openings are large, that is, 5 to 10 ha or more, lateral expansion of adjacent trees fills small fractions of openings and the sunlit canopy is shifted to trees formerly in the understory and to shrubs, seedlings,

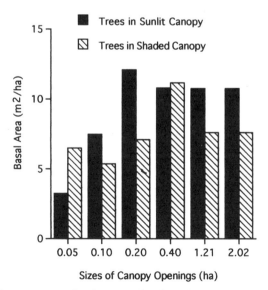

Figure 2.1   Twenty years after harvest of upland hardwood stands in Ohio, growth of sunlit and shaded trees is faster in canopy openings larger than 0.2 ha than in smaller openings. (Data for this illustration was used with permission of the Northeastern Forest Experiment Station, USDA Forest Service, Delaware, OH.)

sprouts, and herbaceous plants. The consequences of large openings include increased growth of formerly suppressed trees, increased flowering and fruiting of shrubs and herbaceous plants, increased germination of seeds stored in the forest floor, increased survival of new seedlings, increased availability of browse for many animals, and formation of a dense layer of plants less than 1.37 m above the ground. For many forested landscapes, canopy openings as large as 0.5 to 5 ha provide habitats that vary in characteristics from the margins to the center of the openings (Willison 1981; Phillips and Shure 1990; Shure and Phillips 1987; Buckner and Shure 1985; Holland et al. 1991; D. M. Smith 1986; Oliver and Larson 1990).

Phillips and Shure (1990) describe changes in canopy openings one and two growing seasons after openings are made in a hardwood forest near Highlands, NC, in Jackson County. Openings are 0.016, 0.08, 0.4, 2, and 10 ha. Trees larger than about 2.5 cm dbh are removed. Solar radiation, soil temperature, and air temperature are higher in the larger openings than in the smaller ones. The openings contain more slash, stumps, and logs than does uncut forest. Increased germination of seed and sprouting result in many more live stems in openings than in adjacent stands. Standing crop biomass increases with increasing size of openings (Fig. 2.3).

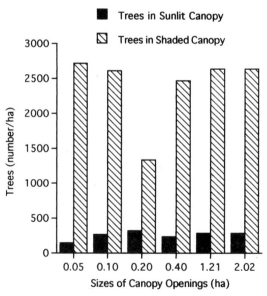

Figure 2.2   Twenty years after harvest of upland hardwood stands in Ohio, a few, fast-growing sunlit trees dominate canopy openings and reduce growth rates of large numbers of shaded trees. (Data for this illustration was used with permission of the Northeastern Forest Experiment Station, USDA Forest Service, Delaware, OH.)

Size of canopy openings formed by natural events and by harvesting changes the capture and distribution of solar energy in forested landscapes. Tree seedlings and sprouts capture more solar energy, typically, than understory species of shrubs, vines, and herbaceous plants. As sunlit canopies increase in height, rates of net primary production (NPP) shift increasingly from understory species to trees. Phillips and Shure (1990) found that NPP increases with size of openings for trees and for understory plants (Fig. 2.4).

Sizes of canopy openings affect the microenvironment, stream flow, plant and animal species composition over space and time, litter fall patterns across the openings, nutrient relationships, small-mammal populations, insect grazing patterns, arthropod populations, and chemistry of plants. Sizes of canopy openings affect habitats, aesthetic values, timber production, and biological diversity (Phillips and Shure 1990; Shure and Phillips 1991; Shure and Wilson 1993; Buckner and Shure 1985; Wilson and Shure 1993; Shure and Phillips 1987; Bruce and Boyce 1984; Willison 1981; Strom 1985; Douglas 1983).

Natural events form canopy openings that expose understory plants, animals, and litter to a changed environment. Changes include solar radiation, moisture, and temperature. Plants and animals respond to the new environment in attempts to maintain essential variables in their bodies within limits for survival. Trees surrounding canopy openings increase in growth rates. Grape vines, sprouts, and understory plants grow faster in canopy openings

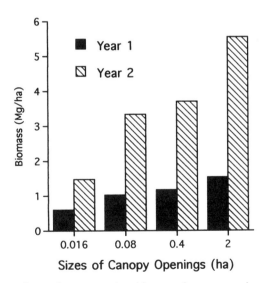

Figure 2.3   Rates of growth, measured as biomass, increase as sizes of canopy openings increase. (Data for this illustration was used with permission of the Southeastern Forest Experiment Station, USDA Forest Service, Asheville, NC and Highlands Biological Station, Highlands, NC.)

than under canopies of adjacent stands. Amounts of litter deposited by falling leaves and branches change in relation to size of canopy openings. Decomposition of litter changes. Some species of plants and animals increase in numbers, and other species decrease in numbers. Environments in canopy openings continue to changes over time as tree crowns close the openings with a high canopy. Animals and plants continue to respond in their own particular ways as sunlit canopies rise above the ground to maximum heights (Willison 1981; Runkle 1981, 1982; Shure and Phillips 1987, 1991; Phillips and Shure 1990; Shure and Wilson 1993; Wilson and Shure 1993; Pickett and White 1985; Bruce and Boyce 1984; Holland et al. 1991; Oliver and Larson 1990; D. M. Smith 1986; Clinton et al. 1993).

Traditional forestry forms canopy openings incident to structuring stands to maintain a balance of age classes within a range of optimum timber harvests. Landscape forestry forms canopy openings incident to organizing landscapes in time and space to produce baskets of benefits. A variety of sizes of canopy openings, from about 0.016 to 10 ha, provide for many kinds of habitats, aesthetics, biological diversity, and amounts of fuel and timber.

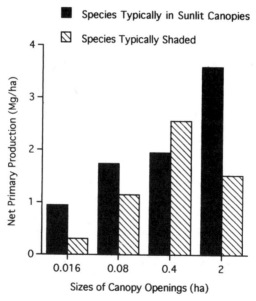

Figure 2.4   As size of canopy openings increases, net primary production shifts more and more to species typically in sunlit canopies and less and less to species typically shaded. (Data for this illustration was used with permission of the Southeastern Forest Experiment Station, USDA Forest Service, Asheville, NC and Highlands Biological Station, Highlands, NC.)

Habitat

Habitats are operationally defined by observing how organisms use different stands for getting food, escaping enemies, reproducing, and other purposes. The only way to operationally define a habitat is to observe consistent use of a situation by an organism. An assumption is that the organism requires that kind of situation for some aspect of its livelihood (Bailey 1984; Shaw 1985).

This operational definition is in agreement with concepts presented in Elton's essay (1949). A habitat is an area that seems to possess a certain uniformity with respect to physiography, vegetation, or other features. A habitat is a kind of stand considered important for the livelihood of an organism. The livelihood of an organism may require two or more stands of different forest types, ages, or areas.

In a forested landscape, a stand classified by forest type, age, and area class is a habitat by Elton's definition. An organism may use many habitats in a day, season, year, or life. Organisms may move from one to another habitat to find food, shelter, and mates. Habitats change as plants and animals grow, die, and are replaced by others. Animals and plants that depend on young stands may decrease to small numbers or disappear from landscapes as young stands grow into old stands. As habitats change from one to another forest type, age, and area class, the potential livelihoods of plants and animals change, and biological diversity of the forested landscape changes (Thomas and Radtke 1989).

There are many possible combinations of stands classified by forest type, age, and area classes. The greater the number of combinations distributed over space and time, the greater the probability that habitats will be provided for large numbers of endemic organisms. There is no way to assure that any particular organism or any number of organisms will be present for a given combination of stands. From observation of the kinds of stands frequented by organisms for a purpose, such as feeding or nesting, we can develop habitat indices. The indices indicate our mental models about requirements for the livelihood of a species but do not indicate the presence of a particular organism (Thomas and Radtke 1989; Martin et al. 1993a,b; Hunter 1990).

Livelihood

Potential livelihood of organisms is determined by the arrangement of stands, which are classified by forest type, age, and area and distributed over time and space. Thus, potential livelihood is determined by change in states of organization of forested landscapes (Thomas and Radtke 1989; Hunter 1990).

Space and Time

Colors, shadows, and edges of stands are dynamic. Some changes occur in minutes; other changes require many years. Some changes occur over space as well as time. Color, texture, shapes, shadows, and edges change in relation to solar radiation, topography, geologic formation, cloud cover, fog, harvest of timber, road construction, streams, wetlands, natural succession of trees, and seasonal changes in leaf and flower formation. Every day a forested landscape looks different from past days, and a new day brings visual distinctions never before observed and never again observed. Each small change contributes to aesthetic values, wildlife habitats, timber production, stream flow, and other values. Benefits fall on a continuum in time and space (Boyce 1977, 1985; Thomas 1979; Thomas and Radtke 1989; Litton 1984).

Spatial scales of activity range from the smallest organism to the limit of area for a landscape. Solar energy, trapped by photosynthesis, flows from canopies into boles, branches, roots, soil, animals, fungi and eventually flows out of the landscape to the rest of the universe as heat. Scientists fragment this continuum into disciplines as a way to reduce complexity and investigate areas of interest. Soil science, entomology, zoology, botany, and taxonomy are examples of disciplines that concentrate on fragments of forested landscapes. There is no way managers can interrelate all fragments of knowledge in management plants. Management works by using manipulating controls that change states of organization (Fig. 3.1). Complexity is matched by changes in states of organization of the managed system (Ashby 1973; Beer 1975; Forrester 1961). Landscape forestry matches complexity by changing states of organization of stands over spatial and temporal scales (Allen and Starr 1982; O'Neill et al. 1986; Payne et al. 1992).

Temporal scales of activity in landscape forestry range from seed and seedlings to the oldest age classes of stands. Harvest schedules are superimposed for the purpose of directing the distribution of stands over time for a variety of habitats in all endemic forest types. Harvests of the oldest stands are superimposed on harvests of younger stands, and different age classes are intermixed and connected over the landscape. The purpose is to provide habitats for all endemic species. Different kinds of habitats are maintained over time and within travel distances for organisms that require two or more kinds of stands to complete their life cycles. Stands are harvested for the purpose of organizing the landscape for baskets of benefits and not for optimal production of a good, service, or effect (Boyce 1977; Franklin et al. 1981).

Ecosystem Model

The original ecosystem model dates to 1935, when Tansley first published a definition. The original definition had no operational procedures. Tansley apparently used the word *ecosystem* to help him counter what he called "The Use and Abuse of Vegetational Concepts and Terms," which is also the title of his paper (Tansley 1935). Most professional ecologists modify the concept of *ecosystem* to make the term operational. Some modifications separate organisms from environments and define an ecosystem as an interacting system including all the component organisms in a space together with the nonliving environment. Some writers describe ecosystems as complex communities of organisms and their environments functioning as an ecological unit in nature. Odum (1983) defines an ecosystem as a collection of communities and non-living environments functioning together. The word *ecosystem* seems appealing to large numbers of people because it is interpreted by some people to mean holism and to infer mysticism in the organization and response of communities to disturbances (Hansen 1962; Art and Bormann 1993; Evans 1976; Andrewartha and Birch 1954).

Tansley's intent was to counter mysticism in mental models of communities as expressed by terms such as *complex organism* and *biotic community*. Tansley wanted to turn ecological studies toward scientific methods as described by Levy (1932) for physics. Tansley (1935) wrote

> The whole method of science, as H. Levy has most convincingly pointed out, is to isolate systems mentally for the purposes of study, so that the series of isolates we make become the actual objects of our study, whether the isolate be a solar system, a planet, a climatic region, a plant or animal community, an individual organism, an organic molecule or an atom. Actually the systems we isolate mentally are not only included as parts of larger ones, but they also overlay, interlock and interact with one another. The isolation is partly artificial, but is the only possible way in which we can proceed.

To this mental model, Tansley applied the term *ecosystem* when the system included organisms because "we cannot separate them from their special environment, with which they form one physical system."

Tansley (1935) applied the term *ecosystem* to "all forms of vegetational expression and activity," including "so-called 'natural' entities—and expressions of vegetation now so abundantly provided us by the activities of man." From Tansley's statements, forested landscapes, stands, communities, populations, regions, single organisms, and any other biological systems in combination with the associated physical environment are ecosystems. Ecosystem is an abstract concept applying to any system that includes an organism. The earth is an ecosystem, but there are no ecosystems on the moon, the sun, Venus, or any known solar body because organisms are not known to be on these bodies (Hagen 1992).

Ecosystem Management

About 1970, the phrase "ecosystem management" began to appear in publications of environmental organizations. As used in the literature, the phrase seems to imply a philosophy designed to compliment deeply held mental models that embrace land stewardship and naturalism rather than theorems and procedures for providing goods, effects, and services. Descriptions of ecosystem management reflect deeply held institutional, social, and personal mental models (Hagen 1992; Sample 1992; USDA Forest Service 1988,

1991b, 1992a,b; Blackmon 1992; Rowe 1991; Kessler et al. 1992; Swanson and Franklin 1992; Odum 1983; Jamison 1993; McKibben 1989; Norse 1990; National Research Council 1986).

One definition labels ecosystem management as "the skillful, integrated use of ecological knowledge at various scales to produce desired resource values, products, services, and conditions in ways that also sustain the diversity and productivity of ecosystems" (USDA Forest Service 1992b). "It means that we must blend the needs of people and environmental values in such a way that the National Forests and Grasslands represent diverse, healthy, productive, and sustainable ecosystems" (USDA Forest Service 1992a). The phrase "ecosystem management" is used by Sample (1992) without definition. Norse (1990) says ecosystem management mimics natural disturbances. Faculty are concerned with how to teach ecosystem management, which is not defined in academic terms (Blackmon 1992). Some people are concerned with ecological divisions of land for resource management (Bailey 1988, 1989). Rowe (1991) and Andrewartha and Birch (1954) call attention to the difficulty of different people consistently defining boundaries of ecosystems for management purposes.

If we use Tansley's definition of ecosystems, ecosystem management is the management of any system containing an organism. The space shuttle Columbia, when an organism is aboard, is a managed ecosystem. Natural reserves, cash-flow forestry, traditional forestry, and landscape forestry are examples of ecosystem management. All agriculture, gardening, wildlife management, and range management is ecosystem management. If these suppositions are acceptable, then procedures described in this book provide operational definitions of and a systematic approach to ecosystem management.

Old-Growth Forests

After 1980, the concept of *old-growth forests* began to emerge. Definitions of old growth are based on measures of the physical structure of old stands. Definition of old growth for Douglas-fir and western hemlock forests in Washington and Oregon include measures of size and age of long-lived trees, number of layered canopies, amounts of dead organic matter on the ground, and amounts of standing, dead boles of large trees. From these measures, operational definitions are developed to define mental models of old growth. Studies of physical structure in old-growth forest reveal varieties of stands dispersed over time and space. The physical structure from stand to stand differs according to size of live trees, age of trees in sunlit canopies, presence of dead trees, and number of dead trees on the ground. Some stands have dense sunlit canopies with many species in the understories. As pointed out by Franklin (1993a), it is this structural complexity that supports an array of specialized species. States of organization of forested landscapes determine the availability of habitats, esthetics, fuelwood, timber, and biological diversity (Franklin et al. 1981; Franklin and Spies 1991; Tammi et al. 1983; Franklin 1993a,b; Lippke and Oliver 1993).

Harvest of Trees Regulates Capture of Solar Energy

Scheduled harvests of stands distribute sunlit canopies across landscapes by forest type, age, and area classes. Every combination of type, age, and area class traps solar energy at a different rate. A state of organization of a forested landscape is an indirect measure of rates of capture of solar energy.

Mass flows of solar energy, carbon dioxide (CO_2), and water (H_2O), flood forested landscapes (Fig. 2.5).

In the process of photosynthesis, solar energy traps and transforms CO_2 and H_2O into carbon compounds. Solar energy in these compounds drives the construction of plants and animals and activities in forested landscapes. Trees in sunlit canopies are a primary trap for solar energy, CO_2, and H_2O. Trapped energy is stored for short periods in many structures, such as cellulose in wood, fat in nuts, starch in roots, and sugar in fruits. Organisms are warehouses of carbon compounds. Organisms without chlorophyll, such as humans, consume plants and animals to obtain energy and materials. Digestion reduces organic compounds to heat, which dissipates to the universe; to CO_2, which disperses in the atmosphere; and to H_2O, which disperses to the atmosphere, soil, and oceans. Mortality and oxidation of organic compounds releases solar energy to continue its journey into the universe.

Landscape forestry is a way to organize landscapes to collect and pipe solar energy toward production of many kinds of benefits. Trees provide humankind with the largest active reservoir of solar energy because there are

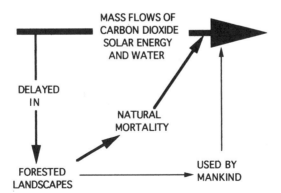

Figure 2.5   Forested landscapes capture solar energy from mass flows and store this energy in many forms that benefit humankind. Rates of capture of solar energy peak at stand ages of less than 50 years for most of the world's forested landscapes.

no chemical and physical methods for removing and storing carbon from the atmosphere in amounts greater than that captured and stored by forests (Aresta and Forti 1986). Boles of trees are bundles of solar energy that can be harvested and stored for fuel, building materials, and paper. These same trees provide shelter and food for many plants and animals and contribute to aesthetics and biological diversity. Harvesting of stands is the primary tool for directing the capture and flow of solar energy to produce desired benefits.

Solar Energy and Biological Diversity

Research and observation show that canopies below the browse line of animals, usually less than 1.37 m off the ground, support different kinds of organisms than high canopies. Removal of high canopies, those above 1.37 m, by natural events and timber harvesting, shifts the primary place for the capture of solar energy from a relatively few species of trees and a relatively few individuals to thousands of shrub, tree, and herbaceous species with low canopies (Figs. 2.1–2.4). A variety of plants in low canopies is a source of energy for a variety of animals that cannot feed in high canopies. Biological diversity, measured as numbers of species, may not be greater in a young, low-canopy stand than in an adjacent, 80-year-old, high-canopy stand. But biological diversity is different between the two stands, and total biological diversity of the two stands is greater than either alone (Bruce and Boyce 1984).

An important observation is that every age class and every different area of canopy opening makes a different contribution to biological diversity. Every age class and every different size of canopy opening provides flows of solar energy in different forms and at different distances above and below ground. Each age and area class of a canopy opening provides a different physical structure for shelter and different temperature and moisture gradients. In young, low canopies, flowering and fruiting are profuse until high canopies close and reduce flows of solar energy, water, and nutrients to herbaceous plants and shrubs. In high canopies, leaves and twigs, which are far above the reach of deer and rabbits, are eaten by many kinds of insects, which are eaten by other animals. Dead bodies of animals, droppings from worms, and dead trees, leaves, branches, flower parts, bark, and fruits pass energy to organisms on the ground. Dominant and codominant trees in high canopies trap most of the energy used by forest animals, bacteria, and fungi. Most of the energy captured in high canopies is eaten by organisms that can feed on leaves, wood, bark, roots, flowers, and fruits of the relatively few species of canopy trees. Every year, in every stand, kinds of food available change, and changes in kinds of food change kinds of consumers.

Biomass, a Measure of Trapped Solar Energy

Trapped energy is estimated by measuring accumulations of organic carbon or biomass. Data for organic carbon, averaged for forest stands in the continental United States (Birdsey 1992), provide insights into how harvest schedules influence energy flows (Fig. 2.6).

Average carbon/ha is 177 Mg (One megagram (Mg) equals 1000 kg, or 1 metric tonn). The largest single accumulation, 59 percent excluding roots, is in the soil. This accumulation takes place over 50 to 100 or more years. Carbon accumulates in soils in many chemical forms, and many forms are resistant to oxidation.

Above ground, the largest single reservoir of solar energy is in boles of trees, specifically, standing live and dead trees larger than 12.7 cm dbh and up to a top diameter of 10 cm. Boles store an average of 16 percent of accumulated carbon (Fig. 2.6). This accumulation in boles may take 80–100 years.

Canopies include leaves, flowers, fruits, twigs, and branches smaller than 10 cm. Average carbon in canopies is 10 percent. Carbon flows from high canopies, those above 1.37 m, out of forested landscapes and to forest floors and soils. As animals eat leaves, flowers, fruits, nectar, and twigs, these items and droppings are distributed across the landscape.

Under high canopies, little carbon accumulates in the understory (Fig. 2.6). This situation changes with the death of trees in sunlit canopies. The single most important effect of timber harvest is to shift sunlit canopies to less than 1.37 m from the ground. For the next 5–10 years or more, carbon accumulations are dispersed among many plant species, and the carbon accumulations are available to a different group of animals than carbon trapped in high canopies. As sunlit canopies rise above the ground with an increase in stand age, storage of carbon in the understory is reduced to about 1 percent of

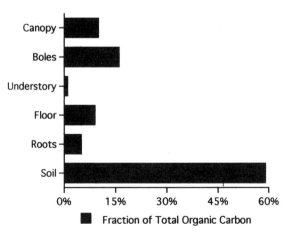

Figure 2.6   Forested landscapes accumulate and store large amounts of organic carbon in boles of trees, which are an important source of energy and raw materials for humankind. (After Birdsey 1992.)

accumulations. Animals dependent on carbon from low canopies decrease in numbers, and animals dependent on carbon from high canopies increase in numbers. For the production of landscape benefits, these effects of timber harvest are much more important than the amounts of carbon removed as merchantable timber.

When trees in the sunlit canopy are harvested, it is important to create canopy openings larger than 0.2 ha and fell all residual trees in the opening that are taller than 1.37 m. The purpose is to shift the sunlit canopy to production of food and shelter for organisms that live near the ground. Browse for insects, mammals, and other animals is increased. When exposed to full sunlight, many plants below 1.37 m in height produce more flowers and fruit than when under high canopies. Removal of all trees in a canopy opening increases biological diversity and increases potential livelihood for organisms that survive in very low numbers under high canopies.

Harvest and Flows of Solar Energy

A typical harvest of merchantable timber removes about two-thirds of the carbon stored in boles. This removal is about 10 percent of the total and is about equal to amounts of carbon stored in average canopies. During harvest, carbon in high canopies is moved to the forest floor. Site preparation, burning, and other cultural practices may remove much of this carbon. Cultural practices are intended to regenerate harvested areas with minimum loss of carbon from soils and forest floors.

Carbon escapes forested landscapes as gaseous carbon dioxide and as particulates in smoke. Erosion of soil carries carbon compounds from forests. Wood and other organic materials of carbon are carried from forest by people and animals. Conversions of carbon from one to another form and oxidation of carbon to carbon dioxide converts solar energy to heat, which is dissipated to the universe. Some carbon is retained in forest floors and soils. Much of the canopy and bark falls to the forest floor annually and biennially. Changes in chemical composition in the forest floor add carbon to this huge soil reservoir. Harvest schedules change flows of carbon and related solar energy in many ways. The single most important change is the shift in rates of capture of solar energy brought about by maintaining age classes older than the age for the maximum accumulation of carbon.

The primary guidelines managers use in scheduling harvest rates for stands are by forest type, age, and area class. These three actions, applied in a variety of combinations, direct flows of solar energy in many different ways and provide for joint productions of habitats, aesthetics, timber, cash flow, and biological diversity. Since flows of energy through forested landscapes are not easily measured, effects of harvest schedules are monitored in terms of dispersion of stands over time and space by type, age, and area classes. These variables are measured directly, are related to aggregated baskets of benefits, and are used to simulate consequences for different harvest schedules.

STATES OF ORGANIZATION DETERMINE BENEFITS

A stand of trees with sunlit canopies near the ground provides worms and insects for turkeys and browse for deer. A stand of trees with sunlit canopies 10 to 30 m above the ground provides little food for turkeys and deer but does provide food for woodpeckers and wood borers and cover for many herbaceous plants. As stands age, kinds of plants and animals living in a stand change. No single age class provides habitat for all endemic organisms. A dispersion of stands by forest type, age, and area classes provides a variety of habitats to support a diversity of organisms. A particular dispersion of stands is the state of organization of a landscape.

States of organization determine ways solar energy is captured and used in productions of benefits. In forests throughout the world, stands 1–5 years old capture less solar energy per hectare than stands 30–40 years old. Stands 300 years old capture less solar energy than any younger age classes. Every change in proportions of stands distributed by age classes changes rates of capture of solar energy and how that energy is piped to different mixes of benefits. It is differences in capture and the use of solar energy by different states of organization that underly the use of landscape forestry to produce desired combinations of benefits.

Productions of kinds and amounts of benefits are related to different rates of capture of solar energy by sunlit canopies at different elevations above the ground, different sizes of canopy openings, and different species that occupy sunlit canopies as stands age. These relationships underlie decisions in landscape forestry to schedule rates of harvest of stands, sizes of canopy openings formed, and kinds of regeneration encouraged. These controls are scheduled to systematically bring about steady-state rates of change in stands and to produce desired combinations of benefits into the distant future.

Events that bring about natural mortality are not scheduled. Natural mortality does not bring about steady-state rates of change in stands. Natural mortality changes forested landscapes in aimless directions. Unscheduled occurrences of fires, storms, insects, and diseases shift states of organization without goals. Events that bring about natural mortality incidentally produce combinations of habitats, aesthetics, timber, cash flow, and biological diversity. There is no evidence for negative feedback scheduling fires, storms, and other events to order forested landscapes for a purpose (Sheffield and Thompson 1992; Lorimer and Frelich 1994).

In contrast to events that bring about natural mortality, harvest schedules are developed to fulfill policies. Policies vary from one to another landscape because of different desires of owners, demands of consumers, political edicts, climate, soils, and other factors. Regardless of differences in policies, the basic methods for management are essentially identical.

OPERATIONAL DEFINITIONS AND MENTAL MODELS

Operational definitions are used to frame mental and physical models for the purposes of simulating consequences that appear to be "true." Since there is no way to verify or prove a future event, decisions are based on mental models as modified by outcomes from physical models and other sources of information. The argument for landscape forestry says all managerial decisions are based on mental models.

The mental model for landscape forestry says that changes in the distribution of stands over time and space and by forest type, age, and area classes determine the availability of benefits. It is the state of organization of the landscape at any given moment of time that determines the availability of habitats, aesthetics, timber, cash flow, and biological diversity. The role of managers is to change forested landscapes from an initial state of organization, state by state, toward a state that provides acceptable baskets of benefits.

Acceptability of Mental Models

Models are acceptable whenever simulated states of organization are explicit and outcomes provide a rational basis for making decisions. No mental or physical models are valid in the sense of predicting future events or duplicating events of the real world. Models are valued for underlying assumptions that clearly expose relationships better than any other procedures. Decisions are made with mental models, as argued in this book, because mental images of how systems are ordered are more acceptable to a manager than decisions made by physical models (Gauch 1993; Warren 1986; Forrester 1961).

Acceptability is related to preconceived and deeply held mental models derived before analyses for a particular landscape. Operational procedures provide individuals opportunities to repeat experiences or procedures and to sort their mental models into degrees of acceptability. Management of a watch is used to illustrate some basic concepts of acceptability of both mental and physical models.

Mental models perceive time. A watch, which is a physical model, is acceptable when the locations of hour and minute hands are explicit and the location of the hands provides a rational basis for making decisions about time. States of organization of a watch simulate states of a standard timekeeping machine. Use of a watch does not require duplication or linkage to the standard machine. Acceptable simulations of standard time-keeping machines make watches useful physical models that are managed by millions of people.

An acceptable watch is driven by energy, such as a spring or battery, to change states of organization according to rules built into the watch. Positions of the hour and minute hands relative to marks on the face of the watch simulate states of the standard machine. Owners interpret each state of organization as a different index of time. Watches do not make decisions. Watches can only change from state to state and provide information which is used by owners to make decisions about time.

A watch cannot know if its state of organization is in or out of agreement with that of a standard time machine. A watch cannot adjust itself to fulfill goals of the owner. An owner's policy is for a watch to simulate a standard time. Owners observe the state of a watch, in this case the position of the hands, and compare the watch's state with a standard, such as "correct" time provided by a telephone service. Owners make adjustments by changing controls, such as moving the hands, winding a spring, or replacing a battery.

According to built-in rules, each watch changes from state to state as long as energy is available. There is no decision mechanism to seek a goal, such as simulating states of a standard time machine, changing a battery and winding a spring. The longer the watch runs without management, the greater the difference between the state of the watch and the state of the standard time-keeping system. Without a manager, the watch is an aimless system.

Without a manager, models for landscape forestry are aimless systems that change from state to state according to rules built into mathematical equations, maps, and computers. Every rule is a supposition even if based on scientific results. Scientific conclusions are past events that become suppositions when applied to future events. Suppositions are limited by lack of information and by the inability of our mental models to manipulate all facets of complex systems at one time. Attempts to improve mental models by adding more information merely increases confusion and constrain decisions. Highway maps that include every curve, hill, roadside sign, bump, exit, and bridge confuse drivers. Mental models function most efficiently when information is reduced to explicit relationships and organized to construct mental images of options (Gauch 1993; Warren 1986).

Physical models for landscape forestry display relationships as physical elements, such as tables of numbers, plots, and maps, which reveal internal contradictions, fuzzy suppositions, and clouded images. Acceptable physical models help us understand consequences, evaluate mental models, and improve our mental images of a desirable course of action.

Physical Models Document Mental Models

Physical models document and display mental models. Displays help us understand relationships when many variables are changing simultaneously. Displays and documentation help others to scrutinize our suppositions and offer changes. Physical models help us expose flaws in our underlying suppositions, exchange ideas with others, manipulate variables, and perceive consequences of actions. Mental models help managers instruct workers and help institutions coordinate efforts to achieve common goals. Yet it is the mental model that is used by managers to choose a course of action.

3

MANAGEMENT OF FORESTED LANDSCAPES

Mental models underlie management decisions because there is no way to jump into the future, verify a future event, jump back to the present, and make a decision. Research conclusions, opinions, and experiences are used by mental models to form policies for directing systems. Policies set objectives, constraints, and goals for managers. This chapter places landscape forestry in the context of management concepts and relates policies for landscape forestry to policies for forest reserves and for traditional forestry (Beer 1966; Armstrong 1985; Senge 1990).

MANAGEMENT TO FULFILL POLICIES

Babies design mental models to manage parents. Kicking, screaming, crying, smiling, and waving arms are used to obtain wants. Over time, babies grow and form mental models to relate various controls to driving automobiles, choosing clothing, scheduling a day's activities, and selecting food. Every day, each of us designs hundreds of mental models that simulate consequences of actions as a basis for choosing courses of action. After use, models are discarded. New models are designed for new situations. Every manager of natural resources extends this well-developed and well-known procedure to design mental models for directing forested landscapes.

A physical form of the generalized mental model, as applied to forested landscapes, is illustrated in Fig. 3.1. Thick lines represent flows of energy and materials through forested landscapes. Thin lines represent linkages that direct flows of information among component parts. Information is driven by very small amounts of energy relative to amounts of energy flowing through the landscape.

An information network forms a closed loop that connects a forested landscape to managers (Fig. 3.1). Information, called inventories, flows from the landscape to inform managers of changes in states of organization. Consequences are simulated with mental or physical models. A difference between simulated consequences and benefits desired by policy is the basis for managers to issue changes in a course of action. An important observation is that benefits desired and consequences are matched by changing the states of organization of the managed system. There is no way a manager can direct production of a single benefit without changing the state of organization of the forested landscape. A change in the state of organization changes productions of all benefits. The course of action is a set of instructions for supervisors, workers, and other interested parties.

Policy determines how a forested landscape is to be used and conserved. Policy statements are translated into objectives, constraints, goals, and desired benefits. Managers fulfill policy by monitoring and changing states of organization of forested landscapes and adjusting courses of action in an attempt to provide desired benefits. Policy changes when owners change what they want from the forest and when consumers change demands. Every change in policy stimulates managers to adjust the course of action. This is done by using mental or physical models to simulate new sets of consequences and to adjust the course of action. Managers are continually making adjustments to keep changes in forested landscapes on a desired course.

Noise, such as cost of capital, stumpage prices, cost of labor, storms, fire, government regulations, and other unexpected events, increases the uncer-

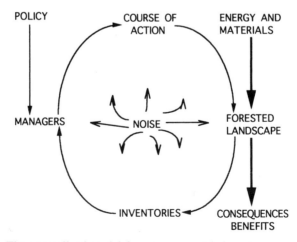

Figure 3.1   The generalized model for management is based on a negative feedback loop.

tainty about future productions. Noise occurs in every information channel in the managerial loop (Fig. 3.1). Some noise, such as fire and insect attacks, can be suppressed, but noise is rarely if ever eliminated. An important managerial response is to monitor the effects of noise and to adjust courses of action to compensate. Managers can simulate consequences relative to noise. Physical models can be used to simulate the consequences of a fire, an insect attack, a change in cost of capital, or an increase in labor cost. Outcomes are used in the manager's mental model to help in the choice of a course of action.

Management decisions are concerned with relating consequences to changes in states of organization of the forested landscape. Consequences of concern to managers include those related to policy statements, unexpected events, and potentially adverse situations. One intent of management is to change states of organization, step by step, to fulfill policy. A secondary role of management is to inform owners, consumers, and governments about noise that may inhibit fulfillment of a proposed policy. In this way, managers influence policy but do not control it.

All forested landscapes are directed by scheduling rates of harvest of stands, sizes of canopy openings, and species regenerated. Policies for forest reserves permit all of these controls to operate as natural events. Natural mortality, insects, diseases, fires, storms, and other unscheduled events change states of organization without human intervention. With forest reserves, benefits are incident to aimless changes in states of organization (Engelberg and Boyarsky 1979). Policies for both traditional and landscape forestry schedule rates of harvest, sizes of canopy opening, and kinds of regeneration to systematically order the landscape to produce desired benefits.

Managers cannot move stands around a landscape at will, cannot instantly convert young stands to old stands, and cannot direct the behavior of each organism. These constraints are related to many variables, including geology, suitability of species to a landscape, initial state of organization, climate, fires, and insects. Because of these constraints, fulfillment of changes in policy require years and decades. Physical models help managers extend mental models to landscapes and help managers reduce the complexity of choosing a course of action. Simulations for periods covering many decades provide managers with a basis for fulfilling consumer demands today and conserving states of organization to fulfill demands into the distant future.

Managing forested landscapes is viewed as analogous to driving an automobile. The desire of a driver to travel from one to another place is independent of the process of directing the automobile. Noise in the automobile system includes laws, the location of police cars, the state of traffic lights, positions of other vehicles, and the state of the highway. The intent of the driver is to bring about desired states of organization of the automobile in order to fulfill a policy for travel. It is changes in states of organization of the automobile relative to the highway situation that produces desired benefits. Mental models are used by drivers to simulate consequences of manipulating the steering wheel, brakes, gear shift, and accelerator as uncertain events unfold. A driver is continually designing mental models, simulating consequences, and choosing a course of action. This procedure is analogous to procedures for directing forested landscapes.

An automobile is a complex machine made up of electrical, fuel, hydraulic, mechanical and other systems. Drivers cannot direct the firings of each spark plug, injections of fuel, or mixtures of fuel while driving on a busy highway. Rather, automobiles are designed to be managed with four controls. Large numbers of people learn to manipulate the steering wheel, gear shift, brakes, and accelerator without knowing anything about spark plugs and carburetors. In an analogous way, managers of forested landscapes learn to manipulate rates of timber harvest, sizes of canopy openings, and kinds of regeneration without knowing the habitat requirements of each species. In fact, attempts to manipulate habitat requirements for even a dozen species while managing a forest would be as impossible as scheduling the firing of six spark plugs while driving an automobile on a busy highway.

The management of forested landscapes and other complex systems requires reduction of complexity to a few controls that can be manipulated simultaneously. From more than a hundred years of experience, resource managers discovered the controls for directing forested landscapes to be (1) rates of timber harvest (D. M. Smith 1977), (2) sizes of canopy openings formed by harvesting (Boyce 1985; Belsky and Canham 1994), and (3) kinds of regeneration encouraged in the canopy openings (D. M. Smith 1986). All other managerial actions, such as thinning, adding fertilizer, pruning, and using genetically improved trees, enhance the consequences of the three basic controls. For example, when the three basic controls are not used, as for forest reserves, there are no advantages to thinning, pruning, adding fertilizer, or developing genetically superior trees.

This book argues that all management decisions are based on simulations made with mental models. Physical models, such as doodles, maps, blueprints, mathematical equations, and computer outputs, are sources of information for mental models. The final choice of a course of action is derived from mental models that use information from physical models.

Astute managers document their mental models. Documentation has several purposes: to inform others of what is to be done, to examine complex relationships, to document legal events, and to record the logic of decisions. Examples of documented mental models include files of information and decisions, diagrams, blueprints, spreadsheets of data, maps, mathematical equations, charts, and computer programs. Documented models are called *physical models*. Physical models provide for scrutiny by others and for enhanced communication. Physical models help managers gain insights and increased understanding of complex systems. Yet mental models are used to choose a course of action.

Mass Flows Drive Forested Landscapes

Forested landscapes trap energy and materials from mass flows of solar radiation, water, carbon dioxide, oxygen, suspended particles, soils, and materials weathered from rocks (see Fig. 2.5). Most mass flows are driven by solar radiation, which originates millions of miles away. Storms are generated thousands of miles away from forested landscapes. Water vapor formed many miles away falls as liquid water. Effervescence on oceans is a primary source of mass flows of salts (Boyce 1954). Mass flows of energy change temperatures that affect rates of photosynthesis, formation of ice, rates of respiration, rates of rock and soil erosion, transpiration and evaporation of water, and many other chemical reactions that in turn affect the livelihood of organisms.

Bodies of organisms are constructed from mass flows of solar energy, water, oxygen, carbon dioxide, and nutrients. Each organism functions by using mass flows to keep essential variables within the limits of life. There is no evidence that mass flows are scheduled and directed by some centralized control system for the purpose of producing, directing, maintaining, and stabilizing forested landscapes. Rather, mass flows act to cause responses called *positive feedback* (Ashby 1973).

Positive Feedback Systems

Mass flows of energy and materials drive positive feedback systems to the limits of available resources without any decision-making mechanism or goal for the system. Positive feedback systems have no goals and no decision-making mechanisms to direct actions of the system. Systems using positive feedback are sometimes referred to as growth-producing, liquidating, or self-reinforcing systems. Positive feedback systems are characterized by amplification of change as change progresses (Fig. 3.2).

Mass flows of solar energy, water, carbon dioxide, food, shelter, and nutrients amplify rates of reproduction of organisms to the limits of available resources. As a population of trees increases, the number of seeds produced increases, the number of rodents and birds eating and burying seeds increases, the number of seeds germinating increases, the mortality of seedlings increases, and the number of mature trees increases. Each element in the loop continues in one direction without a central decision mechanism to negate amplifications of changes. Systems amplified with positive feedback are halted as resources are consumed or as the energy driving the mass flows is dissipated. Two positive feedback systems working against each other may appear to maintain a steady state. But appearance of these kinds of systems can be misleading because there are no decision-making mechanisms and no goal to direct behavior of the elements (Getz and Haight 1989).

Bacteria in a confined culture grow exponentially until energy and materials for life are dissipated. With mass flows of energy and materials, numbers of organisms quickly decline or all die. Positive feedback in biological systems, driven by the availability of energy and materials, can be found in both small and large systems. An example of positive feedback in a large system is the rate of increase in human populations. The number of people on the earth are estimated to have increased from 0.5 billion in 1650 to 1.6 billion in 1900, to 3.6 billion in 1970, and to 5.4 billion in 1991 (Meadows et al. 1992). If these rates are plotted over time, the resulting curve is exponential. That is, the curve can be expressed as the initial size of the system raised to some power. When food, space, and other resources are not limiting, all biological populations grow as positive feedback systems. Populations of predatory birds, such as owls and hawks, increase when food is abundant and decrease when food is scarce. The systems are sometimes said to be population-dependent, size-dependent, or density-dependent (Begon and Mortimer 1986).

The Lotka-Volterra equations in population ecology are examples of mathematical models that simulate positive feedback systems (Begon and Mortimer 1986). The models increase or decrease a population relative to changes in states of organization until resources, which set the carrying capacity, limit changes in population size. These equations demonstrate positive feedback but are not good equations to describe community structure (Roughgarden et al. 1989). Positive feedback loops have no goals, are not self-organizing in relation to an external environment, and do not direct flows of energy and materials. Positive feedback systems are driven by aimless, mass flows of energy and materials.

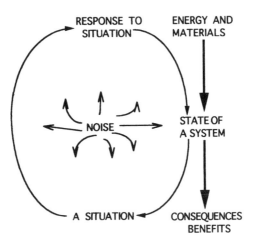

Figure 3.2 Positive feedback systems have no goals and no decision-making mechanisms to direct the actions of the system.

So far, only examples of positive feedback systems in which quantities increase have been given. An example of a positive feedback loop reducing something is the depreciation of a mortgage with constant annual payments. As the mortgage decreases in size, the amount of the annual payment allocated to interest decreases and the amount allocated to principal increases. This system functions until the mortgage is depleted or some force outside the system changes the state of organization. For example, interest rates could change or a third party could purchase the mortgage.

Forested landscapes, without management, are naturally organized as positive feedback loops. Populations of plants and animals grow exponentially in size until one or more resources, such as rain, limit, terminate, or disturb the system. The forested landscape has no control and no influence over mass flows, rates of regeneration, or rates of mortality of any plants or animals. An important observation is that without management, states of organization of forested landscapes change aimlessly from state to state.

Conversion of a forested landscape into a forest reserve results in states of organization of the landscape changing aimlessly. Exponentially growing populations are not directed by a decision-making mechanism to fulfill a goal, such as to provide habitats, aesthetics, timber, cash flow, or biological diversity. Productions of benefits are incident to exponential growth and mortality of populations that change aimlessly in relation to mass flows of energy and materials. Aimless systems are converted to directed systems by adding information networks to create negative feedback systems (Engelberg and Boyarsky 1979).

Management Uses Negative Feedback Systems

Negative feedback systems direct flows of energy and materials to achieve a goal. Managers use negative feedback to convert aimlessly changing forested landscapes into directed systems (Fig. 3.1). Over centuries of time, humankind has learned to use negative feedback to direct the behavior of aimless systems and thereby enhance potentials for survival. Examples include agriculture, animal industry, radios, television sets, and robots.

Managers of forested landscapes are decision-making mechanisms that function to negate deviations from goals (Fig. 3.1). Managers seek to move forested landscapes from an initial state toward a state that fulfills policies for use and conservation. The name *negative feedback* is given to this kind of system because amplifications from positive feedback are negated to achieve a goal (Wiener 1961, 1967). Wiener viewed negative feedback systems as analogous to the behavior of a steersman who guides a boat by turning the bow to starboard or port to achieve a goal. A landscape forester changes rates of timber harvest, sizes of canopy openings, and kinds of regeneration to achieve desired states of organization. The concept of *negative feedback* underlies cybernetics, robotics, artificial intelligence, and automation.

Negative feedback systems are characterized by the presence of a central decision-making mechanism and a goal established outside the system. The behavior of negative feedback systems depends on the presence of implementation mechanisms and information networks. The presence of a negative feedback system is indicated by decisions that regulate a system by comparing the immediate past state of organization with a goal and directing adjustments to move the system toward the goal (Fig. 3.1). For example, a fox chasing a mouse exhibits behavior characteristic of negative feedback systems.

Failures in negative feedback systems may involve delays if information is inaccurate, sensing mechanisms are slow to detect changes, or information networks are inefficient. Delays between times of sensing a state and making changes to adjust differences may cause oscillations in behavior. Negative feedback systems dampen oscillations and move directed systems toward steady states (Getz and Haight 1989). This characteristic is used in traditional forestry to plan for sustained yields of timber and in landscape forestry to plan for baskets of benefits into the distant future. In forest reserves, there are no negative feedback systems to dampen oscillations or achieve steady states.

Management Plans Are Feed-Forward Systems

Feed-forward systems are variations of negative feedbck systems. Feed-forward behavior is characterized by the presence of anticipatory mechanisms. As used in this book, feed-forward systems describe procedures used by managers to design plans for managing forested landscapes. A management plan may be designed to choose a course of action for 50 years. But, in practice, actions are adjusted as states of organization of the managed system change, possibly at 3- to 5-year intervals (Fig. 3.3).

Feed-forward systems require humanlike intelligence. Managers use past events to make suppositions about events never before encountered (Fig. 3.3). Suppositions establish directions for action but do not predict exact, future events. This procedure is to change courses of action as uncertain events unfold. Simulations of feed-forward suppositions help managers identify limits for taking action. Feed-forward loops are limited by errors in forecasts. Forecast errors are kept to a minimum with frequent inventories and constant adjustment of courses of action (Armstrong 1985).

Management of Self-Organizing Systems

Negative feedback behavior is observed in both single- and multicelled organisms (Koshland 1977; Horridge 1977; Okada and Shimura 1990). Decision-making procedures seem to be both mechanical and chemical. Evidence suggests that organisms are able to self-organize, to change behavior in relation to a goal for survival, to change information flows internally, and change states of organization to adjust to events never before encountered. A mouse, chased by a fox, self-organizes as uncertain movements of the fox unfold.

Organisms self-organize; that is, they change their states of organization to fulfill self-interests as environments change over time (Ashby 1973; Wiener 1961, 1967; Kauffman 1993). This self-organizing ability results from negative feedback loops that pipe information about states of the organism to a decison-making mechanism that changes the organism in an attempt to keep essential variables within the limits of life. Physical systems such as robots and computers are constructed with feedback loops, but the behavior and self-organization of the physical systems are limited by mathematical rules built in to the physical systems (Denning 1988). Physical systems process symbols without regard to their meanings. Organisms process symbols with regard to their meanings, which often vary from situation to situation. It is the ability of human managers to respond to situations never before encountered and not described in their past experiences that makes human decisions different from computer decisions (Fig. 3.1).

An important difficulty for human managers of forested landscapes is the ability of organisms to self-organize. Animals learn to eat foods not normally a part of their past diets. In comparison with organisms, physical systems such as the solar system can be described in relation to physical forces with much greater accuracy than can the behavior of a hawk, a fox, or a tree in relation to changes in their environments. Forested landscapes are composed of organisms with decision-making mechanisms that cannot be consistently described by mathematical and physical rules. A manager cannot mathematically program every event in a forested landscape. Managers must adapt to

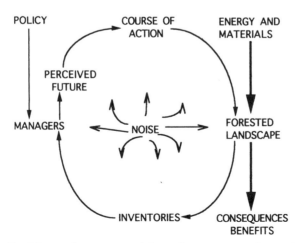

Figure 3.3   Feed-forward systems anticipate future states of organization and are used to design management plans.

uncertain responses of organisms by continually sensing consequences and adjusting courses of action (Fig. 3.1).

The self-organization of organisms in forested landscapes increases uncertainty in forecasting responses of organisms to managerial actions. Managers can develop new habitats similar to those in which the organisms live, but there is no assurance the organisms will use the new habitats. Organisms may abandon past habitats in favor of developed ones, such as bird feeders, hiking trails, and harvested areas. Conclusions about behavior of organisms in managed landscapes contain uncertainty because organisms are self-organizing.

Managerial Organizations

Implementation of a course of action requires an organization of people supported with an infrastructure of capital, information networks, sensing and action procedures, equipment, and learning procedures. Management organizations must be systems of people, that is, teams that learn and adapt to situations never before experienced as uncertain environments unfold. Discussion of management organizations falls outside the scope of this book. For more information see Senge (1990), Beer (1966, 1975), Forrester (1961) and Armstrong (1985).

Multiple Managerial Loops

Once managers choose a course of action (Fig. 3.1), implementations to change states of organization of forested landscapes depend on people. The method is to develop a shared vision that serves the interests of each involved person. Shared visions include (1) defining a course of action, (2) explaining the needs for adjusting procedures, (3) providing training and demonstrations, and (4) monitoring actions for quality and timing. Each of these decisional areas involves a managerial loop (Fig. 3.1). An important observation is that management is layers of interlocking managerial loops, which link flows of information and materials for directing forested landscapes, people, equipment, materials, facilities, and capital investments. Elaboration of these actions is beyond the limits of this book (Forrester 1961; Ashby 1973; Beer 1966, 1975; Boyce 1985; Kepner and Tregor 1965; Meadows et al. 1992; Richardson and Pugh 1981; Senge 1990; Wiener 1961, 1967).

Compliance with Laws and Regulations

Managers are concerned with keeping management actions within the bounds of laws and regulations, such as the National Environmental Policy Act and the Endangered Species Act. Legislation may place constraints on the use of forested landscapes or provide incentives to produce benefits perceived to be in the public's best interest. Regulations, such as those published in the *Federal Register,* are more often constraints than incentives. Court actions that place constraints on the use and conservation of forested landscapes are a major concern for managers. Descriptions of laws and regulations that affect management are beyond the scope of this book.

HARVEST SCHEDULES ORGANIZE FORESTED LANDSCAPES

Forested landscapes are directed by scheduling harvest rates for trees and stands. This practice channels solar energy into kinds of stands that produce habitats, aesthetics, timber, cash flow, and biological diversity. The basic process is to schedule rates of mortality. This process is used in weeding a garden, planting flowers, maintaining a lawn, harvesting hay for animals, thinning bean plants, growing corn, and tending potted plants on a window sill. Scheduling the rates of mortality in biological systems favors organisms desired for food, clothing, and shelter, and other benefits. Culturing biological systems shifts flows of solar energy, water, nutrients, and growing space from undesirable toward desirable organisms. The practice of organizing biological systems by scheduling rates of mortality reduces uncertainties of production, which are inherent in natural biological systems.

Traditional foresters learned centuries ago to intervene in natural rates of mortality to structure forest stands for timber products (D. M. Smith 1977, 1986). Every cultural action schedules rates of mortality of one or more populations. Every culture action to favor an endangered species directs the mortality rates of one or more populations in the affected habitats. Every forest area reserved for wilderness is a choice between the uncertainties of production associated with natural rates of mortality versus dependable rates of production associated with scheduled rates of mortality.

When harvesting stands is prohibited, there are no ways to direct or enhance productions of benefits, including aesthetic values, habitats, biological diversity, timber, and scenic values. Policy statements typically include desires for a harvest schedule that produces specified benefits, including aesthetics, biological diversity, timber, and habitats. Harvest schedules to fulfill policies are dependent on changing forest type, age, and area relationships.

Landscape forestry schedules harvest of forest stands to organize landscapes. Each state of organization, measured by the distribution of stands classified by type, age, and area class, determines the benefits available. This relationship is analogous to the benefits available from scheduling rates of harvesting farm crops. The gain in values of landscape forestry over traditional forestry is the fulfillment of human demands for biological, economical, political, and social values that cannot be produced in single stands (Boyce 1977, 1985).

Harvest to Organize Age Classes

Publications for the past 200 years have documented relationships between age and average heights of trees, average diameters at 1.37 m from the ground (dbh), basal areas in m²/ha, volumes in m³/ha without bark, and numbers of trees per hectare. Data are collected from measurements of different stands rather than from periodic measurements of single stands. Since no two stands behave exactly the same way, stands are classified by forest type, age, area, and *site index,* which is height expected at a reference age such as 25 or 50 years. Values are averaged using regression analyses. Regressed averages are assumed to reflect the average growth of a stand that occurs in the same type and site class (Clutter et al. 1983). These relationships show approximately the same waveforms, though not the same values, for stands in all kinds of forests (Wenger 1984).

A typical example of these relationships is illustrated with data for oak stands in and near the Appalachian Mountains in the eastern United States (Schnur 1937). Dominant trees in the stands are oaks. Canopies are closed or nearly closed, site class for these data is 21.3 m at age 50, and stand ages are those of dominant oaks. The data are for all trees larger than 1.5 cm dbh (Table 3.1). Data in this table are specific to the stands measured, but trends of the relationships are characteristic of all forests. Values are normalized and plotted on identical scales to display trends and waveforms (Fig. 3.4).

TABLE 3.1   An Example of Typical Relationships Between Age of Dominant Trees and Average Heights, Diameter at 1.37 m dbh, Basal Area, Volume, and Number of Trees Per Hectare. All Data are for Trees 1.5 cm dbh and Larger, for Oak Types and Site Class 21.3 m at 50 Years (Schnur, 1937)

Age (years)	Height (m)	dbh (cm)	Basal Area (m²/ha)	Volume (m³/ha)	Trees (no/ha)
10	6.4	4.1	9.9	28.7	7759
15	8.8	5.6	13.3	48.6	5362
20	11.0	7.4	16.3	68.2	3707
25	12.9	9.7	18.4	87.5	2545
30	14.6	11.7	20.2	106.7	1836
35	16.5	13.7	21.1	126.0	1428
40	18.3	15.2	22.0	145.2	1166
45	19.8	16.8	23.0	164.4	1021
50	21.3	18.3	23.9	182.6	924
55	22.6	19.8	24.8	200.8	830
60	23.8	21.1	25.7	218.0	751
65	24.7	22.4	26.6	234.4	677
70	25.3	23.6	27.5	250.2	623
75	25.9	24.9	28.5	265.5	581
80	26.5	25.9	29.4	279.9	554
85	27.1	26.9	30.3	294.2	531
90	27.4	27.9	31.2	307.9	512
95	27.7	29.0	31.9	321.5	489
100	28.0	29.7	32.8	334.5	474

The number of trees per hectare has been normalized by dividing by 7759. Mean annual increment is the volume per hectare divided by the age and normalized. The volume per tree is the volume per hectare divided by the number of trees per hectare and normalized. Waveforms may vary among forests, yet the trends are found in all forests.

For this illustration, mean annual increment is the average annual rate of accumulation of wood in boles larger than 1.5 cm dbh. Wood accumulates faster before than after age 50. Rates of mortality are faster before than after age 50. In stands with closed canopies, as in this example, mortality is essential if wood is to be accumulated on residual trees. Fifty years is the age for culmination of mean annual increment. After age 50, rates of mortality decline and rates of wood accumulation decline. The volume per tree increases to 100 years of age. After age 50, the mortality of a few large trees can remove wood from stands faster than residual trees grow.

Data are not available for stands older than 100 years for the Craggy Mountain Forested Landscape. Data for a few stands 200 to 300 years old

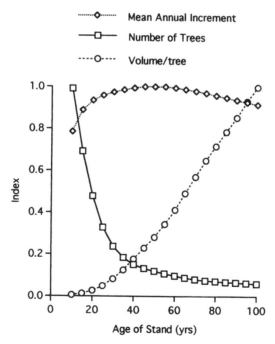

Figure 3.4 As stands age, some relationships have similar waveforms, though not the same values, for all kinds of forests. Because of these relationships, a landscape that is managed to distribute stands across all age classes, in time and space, provides a greater variety of benefits than a landscape that is permitted to accumulate stands in old age classes.

suggest that the volume per tree continues to increase after 100 years but at very slow rates. The mortality of only one large tree produces openings large enough to stimulate increased growth of some understory seedlings and suppressed trees (Runkle 1981, 1982). However, few, if any understory trees become dominants until canopy openings larger than 0.2 ha are formed.

As sunlit canopies are elevated above the ground, the density of leaves and stems betwen the bottom of the canopy and the ground decreases. Suppressed trees and understory seedlings develop from sprouts and seed, grow slowly, die, and are replaced by new individuals. There is continual turnover in understory trees and seedlings. Some trees may compete for a place in the dominant canopy if gaps larger than about 0.2 ha are formed in the dominant canopy. Stands older than 100 years are dominated by a few large trees (Frothingham 1931; Della-Bianca 1983). Unequal rates of mortality between dominant and suppressed trees structures the forest to favor dominant trees that can capture the most solar energy, the most space with spreading and overtopping crowns, and the most water and nutrients with large root systems.

As stands age from one to another age class, land areas in each age class change. The mental model views these changes as flows of land across age classes. Land areas are perceived to cycle through age classes as stands are harvested and regenerated and as stands die and are regenerated by natural events (Fig. 3.5).

These kinds of changes, related to time, are the basis for forecasting future states of forested landscapes. Traditional forestry schedules harvests of stands at ages that produce pulpwood and mature timber. Stands older than mature timber are liquidated.

Landscape forestry superimposes rotations for the purpose of maintaining positive cash flows by harvesting some stands at ages for pulpwood and mature timber and other stands at old-growth age classes (Fig. 3.5). The result is baskets of goods, services, and effects, without maximum production of any one benefit over all others. The mix of benefits in a basket is scheduled by changing the proportion of areas cycling through different ages for harvest, the sizes of canopy openings formed, and the species regenerated (Boyce 1977, 1985).

Effects of Dispersed Age Classes

A dispersion of stands by age classes provides a variety of habitats for many plants and animals that have a low livelihood in a single age class. Young stands, those with canopies below 1.37 m, provide browse, dense understory for shelter and escape, lots of soft mast and very little hard mast, and the capture of solar energy by many species and individuals. Old stands, those with canopies above 1.37 m, provide limited amounts of browse, thin understories for limited shelter and escape, little soft mast and large amounts of hard mast, and the capture of solar energy by few species and few individuals. A dispersion of stands between ages 1 and 100 years provides an annually changing continuum of habitats. The maintenance of this variety of habitats requires harvest schedules that do not permit gaps of more than 1–3 years in age classes (Fig. 3.5).

Many studies document changes in dominant and codominant trees as stands increase in age (Table 3.1). As stands age, trees larger than 2.5 cm dbh rapidly decline in number and individuals sharing the sunlit canopy rapidly decline in number and in species. Very few studies document changes in herbaceous plants, insect populations, small mammals, or other organisms as stands age (Bruce and Boyce 1984). As stand ages and canopy heights increase, the populations of some organisms increase and the populations of others decrease. These changes, called succession, have not been thoroughly studied in relation to harvest schedules. Two examples, one for plants and another for animals, are considered here.

An Example with Plants

In 1955, on the Vinton Furnace Experimental Forest in Ohio and in cooperation with the USDA Forest Service, I established 100 plots, each 4 m², in a canopy opening of 2 ha (Boyce 1955). Harvest in the winter of 1953–1954

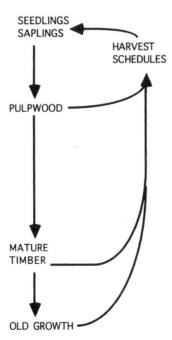

Figure 3.5 Superimposed rotations are used in landscape forestry to distribute stands across all age classes and to schedule harvest rates for desired mixes of benefits.

removed all trees taller than 1.37 m. Dominant trees in the original stand of oaks and some hickories were about 100 years old at the time of harvest. Measures were made of the percentage of ground covered by herbaceous and woody plants less than 1.37 m tall during the second growing season after harvest. The sunlit canopy was close to the ground, about 1.37 m high. Large numbers of plants shared in the capture of solar energy. Many small parts of logs, twigs, and leaf litter covered the area. A few areas of bare soil were exposed by the harvesting operation.

Twenty-five years later, when the canopy opening was 27 years old and the sunlit canopy was about 12 m above ground, Strom (1985) determined the percentage of ground covered by herbaceous plants and trees less than 1.37 m tall. The data collected were comparable for the two ages.

When the canopy opening was 2 years old, I found 58 species of herbaceous and woody plants less than 1.37 m high covering an average of 73 percent of the plots. At 27 years of age, the plots were found by Strom to have 65 species less than 1.37 m tall covering an average of 47 perent of the plots. This difference in cover is illustrated by plotting the cumulative cover over species, which are arrayed from the highest to the lowest cover for the two ages (Fig. 3.6).

During the 25-year period, 21 species found in 1955 were not found in 1980. In 1980, 28 species found were not recorded in 1955. This change of 36–43 percent in species composition is too large to result from errors in

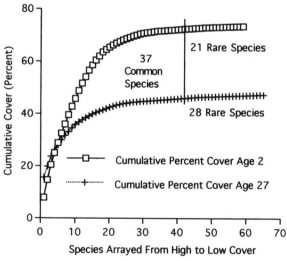

Figure 3.6   As stands age and sunlit canopies rise above the ground, the composition of understory species of plants changes and solar energy is piped to different kinds of leaves, twigs, flowers, fruits, and roots. Changes in flows of solar energy and carbon bring shifts in kinds and numbers of animals inhabiting stands of different ages.

sampling, identification, or measuring. The changes did not occur at random. The changes did occur in the rare and least important species, those that covered the least amount of ground. A vertical line in Fig. 3.6 separates the 37 species common to the opening at 2 and 27 years of age from the 21 rare species recorded at age 2 and the 28 rare species recorded at age 27.

In the 2-year-old canopy opening, the 21 rare and disappearing species contributed 2 percent to the cover. In the 27-year old opening, 28 rare and invading species contributed 4 percent to the cover. Cumulative cover for the 37 common species was 71.5 percent of the plots at age 2 and 45.1 percent at age 27 (Fig. 3.6). In terms of the relative cover, the common species provided 98 percent (71.5/73) of the cover at age 2 and 96 percent (45.1/47) at age 27. None of the species that were most important at age 2 disappeared during 25 years, and none of the species that were most important at age 27 invaded during 25 years. There were changes in relative amounts of cover. The 37 common species were the most important species for covering the ground throughout the 25-year period, but the 49 rare species may have contributed to the livelihood of some organisms that lived in this stand as it aged and as the sunlit canopy moved from about 1 to 12 m above the ground.

The important mental model is this: Two canopy openings, each 2 ha, one 2 years old and one 27 years old, are expected to have greater biological diversity in the aggregate for both plants and animals than either age class alone. Biological diversity is expected to change as stands age and canopies rise above the ground. Changes in biological diversity are expected to occur in the least important and rarest plant and animal species (Bruce and Boyce 1984; Martin et al. 1993a,b; Shorrocks and Swingland 1990). If this were not the case, theorems of evolution and genetic selection would have to be changed (Kauffman 1993).

An Example with Animals

Spiders occupy many different kinds of habitats. On the Nantahala National Forest, near Highlands, NC, Coyle (1981) estimated the number of species of spiders in canopy openings 2–5 years after all trees taller than 1.4 m were harvested and in an adjacent stand older than 80 years. Twenty species were limited to the old stand, 72 species were limited to the young stands, and 42 species were found in both kinds of stands. The total number of species, including genera for some immature forms, found in all habitats was 134 (Table 3.2).

Some species of spiders in all categories occur in both low- and high-canopy stands, for this example, about 30 percent of the recorded taxons. About half of all taxons recorded are found in young stands with sunlit canopies about 1.37 m above the ground. Hunting and trapdoor spiders seem to be favored by this habitat. The variety and large numbers of spiders found in low-canopy stands may be related to the variety of prey associated with the variety of plants in the sunlit canopy. The smallest numbers of spiders were found in the old stands. These small numbers may be related to the difficulty of sampling in high canopies, to flows of solar energy restricted to dominant species, and to limited food supplies in the understory. The important mental model is that a dispersion of age classes over time and space is likely to enhance the biological diversity of spiders and other animal species well above that needed for reducing a forested landscape to young stands with low sunlit canopies or for eliminating timber harvest and keeping almost all of the landscape in old stands with high sunlit canopies. The aggregate production of habitats, biological diversity, and other benefits is related to a dispersion of age classes maintained by scheduled harvesting of stands.

Harvest to Organize Canopy Openings

Traditional foresters learned more than 100 years ago to make canopy openings large enough to encourage the growth of new seedlings and sprouts. Removals included slow-growing, diseased, crooked, and suppressed understory trees. Most suppressed understory trees survive for many years with slow growth and exhibit distorted form and injuries suffered from harvesting operations, insects, and diseases. Suppressed trees, when left standing after the harvest of sunlit canopies, are subject to injury from wind and ice because the shape of the stems and the loss of adjacent supporting trees limits the ability of the trees to bear additional weight on the crown and upper stem (Schenck 1897, 1974; Schnur 1937; James 1897; Evelyn 1664).

Residual, formerly understory trees inhibit the germination and survival of new seedlings, the fast growth of new sprouts, and the formation of new layers of herbaceous plants. These constraints limit development of suitable conditions for many species that require some habitats with sunlit canopies close to the ground to provide food, shelter, and escape cover. The desirable situation is to shift sunlit canopies from maximum heights to near ground level for some fraction of area and time in order to provide suitable conditions for

TABLE 3.2   Numbers of Species of Spiders Found in a Mature Stand and in Seedling Stands of Hardwood Forests in the Nantahala National Forest Near Highlands, NC (Coyle, 1981)

Category of Spiders	Number of Spiders by Kind of Habitat			
	Old Stand	Young Stands	Both Stands	Totals
Litter spiders	4	18	16	38
Hunting spiders	4	39	16	59
Aerial web spiders	12	15	10	37
Totals	20	72	42	134

Source. Data used with permission of the Southeastern Forest Experiment Station, USDA Forest Service, Asheville, NC and Highlands Biological Station, Highlands, NC.

many species to survive and reproduce through space and time (Holland et al. 1991). A convenient and efficient way to do this is to fell, at the time of harvesting, all trees taller than 1.37 m and leave the boles on the ground for food, cover, watershed protection, and protection for new seedlings and sprouts (Hansen and di Castri 1992; D. M. Smith 1986; Holland et al. 1991; Oliver and Larson 1990; Willison 1981).

The inaccurate mental model that appeals to many people is to remove old trees one at a time in the belief that an understory tree is waiting beneath the sunlit canopy to fill the canopy gap. The appealing idea is to keep a closed canopy and a beautiful forest of large trees. This misleading mental model often includes the belief that stands of large, old-growth trees provide for a greater diversity of species than managed stands. Landscape forestry is built on the mental model, supported by research and experience for more than 100 years, which says that biological diversity is enhanced by a variety of stands, dispersed over time and space and by age and area classes. Biological diversity is enhanced by canopy openings large enough to permit sunlit canopies from the time of regeneration to formation of the highest canopy. Sunlit canopies at all heights are essential for growth of a variety of plants that provide habitats for a diversity of animals (Baker 1923; Frothingham 1931; Spaeth 1928; Duerr 1949; D. M. Smith 1986; Oliver and Larson 1990; Merz and Boyce 1956; Sander and Clark 1971; Clark and Boyce 1964; Martin et al. 1993a,b; Hansen et al. 1991, 1993).

TRADEOFFS FOR AESTHETICS AND BIOLOGICAL DIVERSITY

Butterflies and milkweeds are used to illustrate many situations that require tradeoffs between different benefits. Many people agree to removing milkweeds from vegetable gardens to favor bean plants because beans are more edible than milkweeds, which are toxic. Yet many of these same people resent favoring species valuable for fuel and timber and discriminating against other species (Andrewartha and Birch 1954; Ackery and Vane-Wright 1984). Removal of milkweeds and other weeds from gardens, farms, grasslands, and forests directs solar energy toward the production of food, shelter, clothing, and habitats for humankind and preferred animals.

The larvae of the monarch butterfly and many related species feed on milkweeds. Milkweed butterflies, their larvae and pupae, are colorful animals well known in many parts of the world, especially the tropics. Many people enjoy watching, photographing, and studying butterflies. Other people hunt and gather butterflies for collectors and for scientific purposes. Milkweed butterflies represent the kinds of aesthetics and biological diversity requested of forested landscapes by many consumers.

Many species of milkweeds occur as weeds in gardens, farms, pastures, grasslands, and forests (Ackery and Vane-Wright 1984). Milkweed butterflies, pupae, larvae, and the milkweed plant are not known to make important contributions to the food, shelter, and clothing of humans. Yet if enough influential people decide milkweed butterflies are an essential part of humankind's environment, managers will be encouraged to organize gardens, forests, and farms to partition solar energy between food plants, timber, fuelwood, and milkweeds. The values of aesthetics, enhanced by milkweed butterflies, and the values of conserved biological diversity of milkweed butterflies are not questioned. The milkweed question is how to include milkweed habitats in states of organization of gardens, grasslands, deserts, farms, and forests. Butterfly habitats require allocations of portions of sunlit forest canopies to habitats for milkweeds. This can be accomplished with landscape forestry if producers are rewarded for benefits foregone for milkweeds.

Rewards to Producers

Traditional ways to partition solar energy to fulfill human demands are based on some kind of rewards to producers. In many countries, rewards from sales determine kinds of plants that will be favored as food for animals and for humankind. Plants such as milkweeds and thistles are considered undesirable by most producers. When demands are for goods, services, and effects for which managers can capture rewards, productions increase until demands and rewards come to a steady state. An example is the increased sales of wood for fuel in the United States after 1976. After 1976, productions of fuelwood increased until rewards matched demands in about 1982 (Ulrich 1990). Another example is game habitats, which change in relation to payments for hunting leases and for subsidies from governments. Reforestation of retired croplands and harvested forestlands vary with amounts of public subsidies (Vise 1991). The equilibrium for demands without rewards is a production level incident to productions of other benefits.

Requirements for Conservation and Use

Conservation of milkweed butterfies is discussed by Ackery and Vane-Wright (1984). They propose conserving representative biological systems, ranging in size from small nature reserves to large national parks, in as many different parts of the globe as possible. The authors recognize the very large expense of this effort and suggest the problem is more political and economic than biological. Their mental model seems to say that nature reserves and national parks are necessary to enhance aesthetics and conserve biological diversity of selected biological systems, especially those that include milkweed butterflies. The model includes assumptions that most people want to pay taxes and other assessments to fund reserves and parks where some milkweed butterflies may survive. A question not investigated or reported is whether forestlands can be directed to provide habitats of milkweeds and milkweed butterflies in combination with fuelwood, timber, and habitats for species other than butterflies. This last approach, if biologically possible, may not be as costly to taxpayers as reserves and parks.

Traditional mental models for conservation involve removal of human activities. A deeply held belief seems to be that natural events will partition trapped solar energy to best conserve species that evolved under past environments. This supposition should be investigated before options are limited to encouraging taxpayers to fund relatively expensive reserves and parks (Andrewartha and Birch 1954).

Ackery and Vane-Wright (1984) said they did not know what requirement need to be satisfied for continued existence of the many kinds of milkweed butterflies within a fauna. They offer a mental model for minimum requirements. Larvae must have appropriate species of milkweeds. Adults require a pyrrolizidine alkaloid that is produced by a number of plant species. Adults require usable forms of nitrogen, sugar, water, and roosting sites, which are usually stands of trees. All of these conditions can be generated and sustained within forested landscapes by scheduling rates of harvest, sizes of openings, and kinds of regeneration. Simulations with physical models could be used to determine opportunities for tradeoffs between habitats for butterflies, habitats for other species, fuelwood, biological diversity, and timber.

Natural reserves and national parks may be expedient and expensive actions for a few decades. However, no initial or particular combination of habitats can be fixed in time and space by removing human intervention. Management is required to direct landscapes toward states of organization that provide habitats required by the diversity of milkweed butterflies. Procedures for landscape forestry offer ways to organize landscapes to produce, at minimum cost to society, many kinds of benefits, such as milkweed butterflies, that have no market values.

Sales of adult butterflies in markets contribute to the aesthetics experiences of many people who cannot view these animals in natural habitats. Little is known about changes in biological diversity as a consequence of hunting and gathering adult butterflies for markets. There is little evidence that traders make any contributions to managing habitats to conserve the biological diversity of milkweed butterflies.

Minimum Cost for Aesthetics and Biological Diversity

Policies for maximum cash flow, as described by Ackery and Vane-Wright (1984) for the Philippine island of Cebu, eliminate all merchantable trees, eliminate habitat diversity, and produce a single habitat type that discriminates against organisms requiring multiple habitats and stands of trees.

Reserves favor the livelihood of organisms that benefit from accumulations of old stands and discriminate against organisms that require young stands to complete a part of their life cycle. As pointed out by Ackery and Vane-Wright (1984) for milkweed butterflies, very little is known about the requirements for conserving aesthetics and biological diversity. This is a situation in which landscape forestry can be used to choose a course of action, monitor consequences, and change models and actions as uncertain events unfold (Fig. 3.1).

ISSUE OF CASH FLOW

For hundreds of years, the single most important challenge for forest managers is to maintain positive cash flows (Duerr 1949). Without positive cash flows there is no way to employ workers, structure stands, and organize landscapes for flows of habitats, aesthetics, fuelwood, timber, and biological diversity. Forest reserves of all types, including wilderness areas, carry a cost for management. Demands for values that require forest reserves without providing for cash flow strain relationships between consumers and managers (Egan 1993a,b). People in almost every society want habitats, aesthetics, and biological diversity with little or no payment for management of the forested landscape. Some of the benefits, such as scenic values and biological diversity, have no units of measure for use in a market. Direct tradeoffs based on market values are not possible (Evelyn 1664; Schenck 1897; USDA Forest Service 1991b; Schneider 1993).

One policy, proposed for many years, is for government to constrain harvesting of trees on both private and public lands, to set up reserves with no timber harvest, and to let natural events take their course by limiting human intervention to removing only one or a few trees at any one time (Conrad 1889; James 1897; Hecht 1993). A second policy, that of traditional forestry, is to treat timber as a renewable resource to support the necessities of life and to protect, to the extent possible, resources that serve the comforts of society (Fernow 1891, 1893; Schenck 1897, 1974; Duerr 1949; Duerr et al. 1979). Both of these policies evolve over time and appear in different words and phrases in legislation, such as the Multiple-Use, Sustained-Yield Act of 1960, the National Environmental Policy Act of 1969, the Wilderness Act of 1964, and the Endangered Species Act of 1973 (USDA 1983). The predicament of how to harvest stands for timber while keeping old-growth stands of trees for other benefits continues to plague managers (Schneider 1993; Egan 1993a,b; Hecht 1993).

Landscape forestry does not solve the cash-flow dilemma. However, landscape forestry does provide an analytic procedure for examining consequences of tradeoffs among items in a basket of benefits, including cash flow. Landscape forestry uses operational definitions, which provide others with procedures for repeating experiences and confirming or changing relationships. Relationships are displayed as operationally defined indices that are easily understood by others. The method provides a way to evaluate differences in benefits produced by forest reserves, traditional forestry, and landscape forestry. Included in the analytic procedures are ways to assess cash flows, which underlie all uses and conservation efforts.

A Policy for Optimal Cash Flow

This policy seeks a program of uses that promises optimal cash flow in light of all its management goals and values. One example is for a firm to purchase lands and associated timber at prices below the cost of replacement. Accumulated volumes of timber are harvested at rates to liquidate old stands as soon as possible without depressing market prices. This procedure is documented in removals of forests in England hundreds of years ago (Evelyn 1664), harvest of much of the pre-Columbian forests of the United States (Fernow 1891, 1893; Conrad 1889), harvest of some forests today (Egan 1993a,b), and in harvest of forests in the Amazon basin (Hecht 1993).

Optimal cash flow is a policy used by some people who invest in pine plantations in the South. The idea is to purchase pine plantations for which the cost of establishment and growth for 10–15 years are foregone because of government subsidies (USDA 1983, 1993). Stands are held for another 10–15 years, which is a period of rapid increase in volume. At ages from 25 to 35 years, land and trees are sold. Economic benefits include recovery of capital in a decade or two and limited responsibility for the cost of reforestation and for holding lands through periods of slow increases in volume. After timber is harvested, some lands have value for other uses such as pasture, farms, minerals, and home sites. These kinds of policies often produce optimal cash flows (Egan 1993a,b; Hecht 1993).

Landscape forestry, in contrast to policies for optimal cash flow, schedules rates of timber harvests, sizes of canopy openings, and natural regeneration to sustain into the distant future productions of habitats, aesthetic values, timber, cash flow, and biological diversity.

A Policy for Forest Reserves

The desire to establish and conserve forest reserves has been documented over the last several hundred years (Evelyn 1664; H. A. Smith 1936; Marsh 1964). Desires include wilderness, natural areas for research, nature preserves, and many other classifications. Reasons given for reserves include preserving natural states for scientific research; pristine areas for human enjoyment, recreation, and inspiration; and, deeply held mental models for a "return to nature." Carried to an extreme application, forest reserves could and do lead to unrealistic and contradictory tenets in management of forested landscapes (Gomez-Pompa and Kaus 1992). These tenets, if applied as proposed, limit productions of goods, services, and effects to support the livelihood of humankind and many other organisms.

Landscape forestry, in contrast to forest reserves, uses rates of timber harvests, sizes of canopy openings, and natural regeneration to bring about habitats, aesthetic values, timber, and biological diversity to serve humanity and preserve other species. Landscape forestry emulates ways natural events change states of organization. However, unlike the aimless timing of natural

events, landscape forestry systematically organizes landscapes for greater productions of benefits than do natural events. Scheduled harvests of trees and
stands are used by rural populations, based on centuries of experience
(Gomez-Pompa and Kaus 1992). Because of widespread perceptions that the
consequences of natural events are superior to those of humankind's culture
(Hendee and Pitstick 1992), I include in this book simulations of a policy for
forest reserves. Outcomes provide a frame of reference for evaluating the
consequences of using policies for landscape forestry.

The death of trees in sunlit canopies is the single most important event
that changes the way solar energy is trapped and directed through forested
landscapes (Belsky and Canham 1994). Deaths of high canopy trees by natural events such as storms, fire, insects, and disease are very uncertain events.
The primary difference between natural mortality and management is that
management schedules mortality to fulfill policies for use and conservation.
Management uses mortality to enhance the use and conservation of forested
landscapes.

A Policy for Traditional Forestry

Hundreds of years ago, harvesting trees without regard for future supplies of
wood and other forest values stimulated efforts to plant trees and schedule
harvests to remove annual growth without liquidating the growing stock of
trees (Evelyn 1664; Schenck 1974; Fernow 1893). From these early concerns,
a concept called *sustained yield* became intuitively appealing because the
words implied preservation of inherent productivity of the forest and sustained
availability of timber supplies into the distant future (Ludwig et al. 1993).
For more than 200 years, sustained yields of timber have been the goal of all
policies for traditional forestry (Frothingham 1917; Burns 1983, 1989; D. M.
Smith 1986; Buford 1991; Oliver and Larson 1990; Matthews 1991; Spurr
1979). In some parts of the world, sustained yield of timber continues to be
a successful policy. Where sustained yield for timber has failed, it is because
of a change in policy to produce optimal cash flow rather than a failure of
sustained-yield procedures (Egan 1993a,b, 1994).

Traditional forestry is viewed as a mixture of pragmatic and idealistic values, including aesthetics, recreation, habitats, and biological diversity. However, primary concern for sustained yield relates to timber and cash flow
(Duerr et al. 1979; Vardaman 1989; Davis and Johnson 1987). Frothingham
(1917) said the object of traditional forestry is "to produce stands of the
highest economic value attainable in each particular habitat." A more recent
statement of purpose is to structure stands to maintain a balance of age classes
within a range of optimum timber harvests (Davis and Johnson 1987). Regardless of how objectives are stated, the central theme is to produce timber
for some economic purpose, such as supplying raw material to an industry or
increasing cash flow from timber sales. Habitats, aesthetics, and biological
diversity are produced incident to the primary goals of timber and cash flow.

A Policy for Landscape Forestry

Landscape forestry is concerned with providing baskets of goods, services, and effects that require organizing landscapes with a variety of stands classified by forest type, age, and area classes. The management loop for landscapes orders, step by step, the distribution of stands over time and space to fulfill policy (Fig. 3.1). Superimposed rotations are used to distribute stands across all forest types by age classes from seedlings to old ages (Fig. 3.5). The systematic procedure for landscape forestry is called DYNAST, a mnemonic for DYNamic Analytic Systems Technique (Boyce 1977). The procedure is to design mental models, convert the mental models to physical models for scrutiny by other interested parties, simulate options thought to fulfill policy, choose a course of action, monitor consequences, and adjust mental and physical models as unexpected events. Procedures are illustrated by simulating the consequences of landscape forestry, forest reserves, and traditional forestry for selected landscapes.

4

CRAGGY MOUNTAIN FORESTED LANDSCAPE

This chapter illustrates DYNAST, a mnemonic for DYNamic Analytic Systems Technique (Boyce 1977, 1985). A forested landscape in the Craggy Mountains, north of Asheville, NC, is the subject. This area was selected because it is accessible from a number of roads and trails, visited by thousands of people annually, and publicly owned. Information about the area was available, and I had more than 20 years of experience in the area.

STEP 1. DEFINE THE SITUATION

Landscape forestry begins with questions about the situation. What forested landscape is being managed? What are the physical boundaries? Who owns the landscape? Who makes policies for conservation, use, and management? What policies are to be fulfilled? Are inventories available?

Location

Nestled on the western slopes of the Craggy Mountains, Buncombe County, NC, and extending north of Craggy Gardens for 8 miles, a forested landscape is viewed and photographed by thousands of people every year. Brochures and maps provided by the Blue Ridge Parkway lead people to Craggy Dome Overlook near mile post 364. Most of the scenic view to the west and north of this overlook is managed by the USDA Forest Service. For purposes of this illustration, this landscape is called the Craggy Mountain Forested Landscape.

The Craggy Mountain Forested Landscape is included in compartments 1 through 24 of the Toecane Ranger District, Pisgah National Forest, USDA Forest Service, Burnsville, NC. This area of about 6289.2 ha is bounded on the north side by Straight Creek. The eastern boundary begins at Flat Springs Knob and follows high elevations of the Craggy Mountains south to Craggy Gardens. The Blue Ridge Parkway forms the southeastern boundary from near mile post 360 to Craggy Gardens. Two distinct areas are separated from the main landscape by Reems Creek Valley on the southern boundary. The western boundary is on private lands.

The Craggy Mountain Forested Landscape is accessible from the Blue Ridge Parkway, near mile post 368, via a road to a picnic area and via Forest Service road 63, which joins county road 2178. The area can be entered from Dillingham, NC, via county road 2173 and via Forest Service road 74. The northern part of the area is accessible on trails from State Route 197. Many trails and unimproved roads provide opportunities for hiking and photography.

Extensive stands of oak, buckeye, beech, yellow poplar, birch, maple, shrubs and herbaceous plants fill the coves and extend up slopes to the top of Craggy Ridge, which features peaks more than 5500 feet above sea level. A few, small stands of spruce and fir trees can be observed on Craggy Ridge. The west slope extends to privately owned farmlands at elevations of about 2100 feet. The presence of fast-flowing streams, waterfalls, steep slopes, and some cliffs makes hiking dangerous in some parts of the area.

Ownership

Compartments 1–24 are public lands managed by the USDA Forest Service, Toecane Ranger District, Pisgah National Forest, North Carolina. The first harvest, by private landowners soon after 1900, removed most merchantable timber, in most places all trees larger than about 28 cm dbh. One residual stand, about 21.4 ha of northern hardwood forest, is more than 300 years old and is named Walker Cove Research Natural Area. Walker Cove is reserved from harvest and is used for research. Since purchase by the federal government, stands are managed with traditional forestry methods. The area is used by hikers, campers, biologists, rock climbers, fishermen, hunters, and photographers.

Riparian Stands

Stands adjacent to streams, lakes, marshes, and other wetlands are called riparian stands. These stands are a primary source of energy for aquatic organisms. Solar energy is trapped in sunlit canopies and in minor amounts in the understory. The energy is stored in leaves, wood, flowers, fruits, and roots. These materials are moved to streams, lakes, and other wetlands as dead or dying materials are shed by the trees. Large woody debris, deposited in streams, is a slow-release source of energy, a barrier to stream flow, and a substrate for many organisms. Streams are a primary channel for the mass export of energy and materials from forested landscapes.

Riparian stands typically contain large, economically valuable trees. Harvest of these trees changes habitats in and near the streams and increases rates of flow of energy and materials out of the forested landscape. Water temperature in the streams may be increased when shading canopies are removed by timber harvest. Studies indicate that harvest of riparian stands shifts flows of energy from sunlit canopies of trees to algae in the streams; material flows are increased due to road construction and disturbance of the forest floor; organic matter is reduced due to low input of leaves and other small terrestrial materials; water temperatures may change; and a pulsed input of large woody material may affect habitats. Over time, trees grow after the harvest of riparian stands, flows of solar energy shift to tree canopies, water is shaded, and habitats on land and in the waters change. Riparian stands are rich in plant and animal species and typically exhibit fast growth of plants due to large amounts of water and nutrients relative to upland stands.

Riparian stands and related streams, lakes, and wetlands are elements in determining states of organization of forested landscapes. The distribution of these elements, in relation to the distribution of stands classified by forest type, age, and area classes, determines productions of goods, services, and effects. A variety of benefits from riparian areas requires that a range of stands be distributed near riparian areas by type, area, and age classes. For riparian stands, a policy is established for each forested landscape to guide managers in scheduling harvests, sizes of openings, and kinds of regeneration to encourage desired benefits. For more information, see the extensive literature (Flebbe and Dolloff 1991; Hornbeck and Swank 1992; Blackmon 1992; Likens et al. 1977; Naiman et al. 1993).

Stand Maps

Stands are located, defined, and mapped by the USDA Forest Service (Fig. 4.1). Many stands are identified by forest type and area from aerial photographs, space imagery, observations, and measurements. Forest type, age class, area class, physical characteristics of soils and geologic features, roads, streams, understory vegetation, and other features are considered in identifying boundaries for stands. The long, narrow stands mapped in the Craggy Mountain Forested Landscape (Fig. 4.1) are riparian stands, which are managed to protect streams and travel lanes for animals and people. Some maps of landscapes may be found in public offices, libraries, and highway department files. Overlays and copies of aerial photographs are often adequate for all uses except for areas of the most intensive development, such as placing a building. Geographic information systems (GIS) produce maps at relatively high costs. Every investment in a map must be recovered from sales, taxes, or donations. Every map is a model that stores information as a diagram. Almost every managerial action requires visits by workers, who perceive and

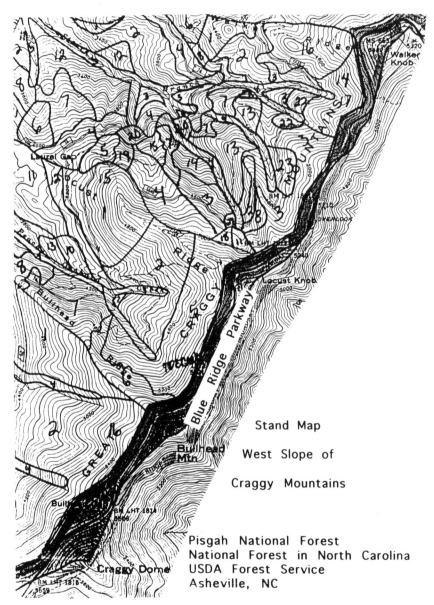

Figure 4.1   Useful, inexpensive stand maps are sketched from aerial photographs; topographic maps; and observations of changes in composition of plant species, ages of stands, areas of stands, and discontinuities between stands. (Published with permission of Forest Supervisor, National Forests in North Carolina USDA Forest Service, Asheville, NC).

mentally store many times more information than can possibly be kept in GIS or other map systems. Typically managers search for the least costly map models to guide decisions and actions of workers.

Relatively inexpensive stand maps can be developed from aerial photographs in combination with topographic maps. An overlay is used to copy the variables of interest. Each stand is outlined on the overlay to make a tentative map of different stands. Such maps are adequate for many analyses. Eventually, a worker must visit the landscape and adjust stand boundaries to fit observations. Few investments are made in identifying permanent boundaries for stands because, over time, changes in managerial actions require changing boundaries. For example, a future decision may change sizes of canopy openings and stand boundaries. Sketch maps of stands (Fig. 4.1) and estimates of stand areas are adequate for most analyses and plans.

Inventory

Stands in the Craggy Mountain Forested Landscape are classified into working groups as upland hardwoods, cove hardwoods, and northern hardwoods. A 'working group' consists of stands classified by forest type and characteristics that suggest similar treatments for planning purposes. In practice, treatments may be adjusted in relation to topography, soils, rock outcrops, and water seepage.

Upland hardwoods are dominated by various combinations of chestnut oak, scarlet oak, white oak, black oak, hickories, and red maple. Yellow poplar, beech, and buckeye may occur as minor components. These stands occupy well-drained soils on dry slopes and ridges below about 4000 feet in elevation.

Cove hardwoods are dominated by various combinations of yellow poplar, northern red oak, white oak, hickories, and red maple. Sugar maple, beech, buckeye, and ash may occur as minor components. These stands occupy moist slopes and coves with soils deeper than those in upland hardwood stands. Most of the cove hardwood stands are below about 4000 feet in elevation.

Northern hardwoods are dominated by various combinations of sugar maple, beech, northern red oak, basswood, buckeye, ash, hickories and red maple. Many other species occur as minor components. These stands are frequent at elevations of 4000 to 5000 feet.

The inventory, by working groups, is graded into 10-year age classes (Table 4.1). An 'age class' consist of a group of stands in which ages of a majority of dominant trees are within a stated range of ages. Age class R (Table 4.1) consist of stands in which a majority of dominant trees are less than 1-year old. Age class A contains stands in which a majority of dominant trees are 1–10 years old while age class O contains stands in which a majority of dominant trees are 151–300 years old. Land areas in each age class are accumulated for each forest type. Codes for each age class are used for reference and for writing equations for simulation models. There is an unequal distribution of forest areas among the age classes. For example, in the upland hardwoods group, relatively small areas occur in the B, BB, and C age classes. A plot of land areas classified by age classes for the initial inventory in the upland hardwoods group reflects irregular distributions of land by age classes (Fig. 4.2).

Inventories are data organized to display states of organization of a forested landscape (Table 4.1). Techniques for collecting and processing inventory data are numerous (Avery and Burkhart 1983). Collecting and analyzing data can be very expensive, confusing, and time consuming. An effective way to limit cost is to collect essential data, invest in analytic procedures that provide a basis for decisions, and update data as uncertain events unfold.

Relationships

Each benefit is related to states of organization of a forested landscape. The livelihood for flickers (a woodpecker species) may be acceptable with 10 percent of the landscape in stands more than 100 years old, 40 percent of the

TABLE 4.1   An Inventory for Three Working Groups by Age Classes for Compartments 1–21 on Toecane Ranger District, Pisgah National Forest, NC

| Code | Age Class | Forest Type (ha) | | |
		Upland Hardwoods	Cove Hardwoods	Northern Hardwoods
R	0–1	16.2	17.8	23.1
A	1–10	146.1	159.4	206.0
AA	11–20	162.3	177.2	229.0
B	21–31	0.0	123.0	192.6
BB	31–40	2.8	0.0	215.3
C	41–50	6.9	208.4	38.4
CC	51–60	137.2	811.4	131.5
D	61–70	230.7	725.2	275.6
DD	71–80	106.4	114.5	90.6
E	81–90	129.5	278.4	264.7
EE	91–100	109.7	113.7	103.6
F	101–110	97.1	110.5	153.4
FF	111–120	14.6	31.0	110.3
G	121–130	20.6	4.9	0.0
H	131–140	8.9	16.9	72.4
I	141–150	0.0	0.0	80.1
O	151–300	0.0	0.0	21.4
	Totals	1188.9	2892.3	2208.0

Note: Numbers do not add to totals because of rounding.

Source: Modified from the *Journal of Forestry* (vol. 92, no. 1) published by the Society of American Foresters, 5400 Grosvenor Lane, Bethesda, MD 20814-2198. The data are originally from the USDA Forest Service.

area in stands 30–50 years old, and 1.5 percent of the area in stands less than 5 years old. A discrete statement of this nature is valuable, but what is needed is knowledge of the relationships, that is, how changes in states of organization affect potential livelihood of flickers. One needs to know how gradual changes in percentages of old, young, and seedling stands affect potential livelihood of the flickers over time. These kinds of relationships are difficult to determine with research because it is too expensive to set up large landscapes with different states to investigate the livelihood of a single species. Research does provide discrete information for existing states of organization. One source for relationships to support management decisions is from trained people who are experienced in integrating observations into relationships that can be expressed on a scale of livelihood from 0 to 1. Such relationships are suppositions subject to adjustment as a course of action is implemented.

Relationships are used to indicate to managers probabilities for acceptable habitats for most, and hopefully all, organisms in a forested landscape. We will never know when a satisfactory livelihood is provided for all organisms because there is no way to know how many or what different kinds of or-

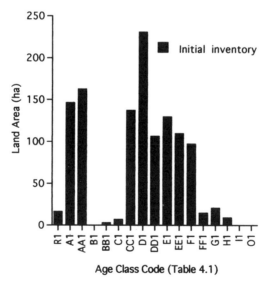

Figure 4.2   The 1992 inventory of stands of Craggy Mountain Forested Landscape reflects past uses by humankind. Small areas of stands in age classes FF1–O1 reflect a massive harvest of old stands before 1915. After harvests, rapid growth of seedlings and sprouts contributed to large land areas in age classes CC1–F1 in 1992. Small areas of forest in age classes B1–C1 reflect low rates of stand regeneration brought about by a policy of selective harvesting of trees between 1930 and 1965. Large land areas in age classes A1 and AA1 reflect harvests scheduled since 1965 to increase proportions of area in young stands and to fill gaps in the distribution of age classes.

ganisms are present in any landscape or in 1 m^2 of a forest (Preston 1960). Stopping all timber harvest may be as discriminatory against some organisms as excessive rates of timber harvest. Until more information is available, the rational approach seems to be to schedule the harvest of stands to bring about states of organization that produce a variety of habitats and that relate the potential livelihood of a variety of animals to these states. As new information becomes available, relationships and courses of action are adjusted. Relatively small adjustments made frequently should not extirpate species or bring major changes in cash flow, aesthetic values, or other benefits.

Some Historic Situations

Forest types in the Craggy Mountain Forested Landscape as we know them today have assembled only in the time interval since the last glacial period, the past 8000–10,000 years. Evidence is available for human beings occupying much of the New World between 12,000 and 15,000 years ago. The presence of Native Americans in the Mississippi Valley and in northern Alabama is relatively well documented for the past 12,000 years. It is likely that prehistoric human activities extended into the Southern Appalachians and intervened over the past 10,000 years in the assembly of forest types, the formation of forest stands, and the distribution of stands by type, age, and area classes. The significance of this information is that forested landscapes as we know them in the New World are the result of responses of plant and animal populations to prehistoric and historic human activities. People used fire, agriculture, and forest clearings for centuries before settlers from Europe appeared, after 1500. European settlers found forested landscapes altered in many ways by Native Americans (Delcourt et al. 1993; Williams 1989; Smathers 1982; Martin et al. 1993a,b; Bass 1978). Over the past 5000-year and possibly longer interval, we can assume all forested landscapes reflect human effects.

Interventions by Native Americans changed states of organization of forested landscapes and changed habitats for plants, animals, and humans. On Craggy Ridge and on lower slopes, aboriginal activities produced a variety of habitats including abandoned cultivated fields, grassy balds, trails, and hunting grounds. Human-caused fires contributed to a variety of habitats. In prehistoric times, deer and other animals increased in numbers in response to interventions by Native Americans. The Early Historic deerskin trade and the export of deer meat from Charleston, SC, probably accounted for the drastic demise of indigenous deer herds. In a good year, tribespeople sold more than 200,000 deerskins to traders from Charleston. Traditional harvesting of deer by rural human populations kept deer populations at low levels until after 1945, when mass migration to urban areas reduced rural populations. Deer populations increased rapidly after 1945 as states put into place various habitat, poaching, and game control programs (Schwarzkopf 1985; Smathers 1982; Bass 1978).

Forested landscapes in the Craggy Mountains are viewed as products of human activity for thousands of years. Humans used the forested landscapes and changed states of organization and the production of benefits. A photograph of the eastern slope of Craggy Pinnacle, when in private ownership in 1915, displays a large open grassy area, called a grassy bald (Fig. 4.3).

In the 1915 photograph, shrubs, mostly purple rhodendron, are on the summit. The presence of small trees suggests that reduced use by humans is permitting trees to invade the grasslands. Native Americans used all forested landscapes in the Southern Appalachians for thousands of years (Wells 1956; Martin et al. 1993a,b). Native Americans kept large numbers of grassy areas open long before European settlers arrived. European settlers built roads, harvested timber, and used the grassy balds for summer grazing of cattle and sheep (Schwarzkopf 1985; Smathers 1982). All grazing ceased after Craggy Pinnacle was purchased by the federal government in the 1930s to construct the Blue Ridge Parkway (Jolley 1969). The area in the photograph is now

Figure 4.3   This 1915 photograph of the eastern slope of Craggy Pinnacle contains grasslands used by Native Americans long before European settlers arrived. After grazing animals were removed and fires prohibited, forests began to return to this and other grassy areas in the Appalachians. All of the world's forests reflect use and change by humankind over many thousands of years. (Photo from Smathers, 1982, published with permission of Supervisor, Blue Ridge Parkway, USDI National Park Service, Asheville, NC. This 1915 photograph was apparently made by William A. Barnhill, Dr. G. A. Smathers made a copy for the Blue Ridge Parkway from a print in Pack Memorial Library, Asheville, NC. The copy used in this book is made from the Blue Ridge Parkway Collection.)

managed by the USDI National Park Service. Smathers (1982) published a 1980 photograph of this area and described the rapid invasion of trees since 1915. A 1993 photograph of the same area shows continued invasion by trees (Fig. 4.4).

Smathers (1982) suggests that natural reforestation, associated with removing sheep and reducing fires, is changing grassy balds and rhododendron shrubs to forest over much of the Southern Appalachians. This transition is changing habitats for many plants and animals, altering scenic views, affecting stream flows, and changing use of the landscape. The explicit and dramatic changes on Craggy Pinnacle and Craggy Dome signal an enormous number of changes taking place in the entire Craggy Mountain Forested Landscape and in forested landscapes in most of the world. Changes in forested landscape come over decades and people rarely make documentary photographs of scenes considered common events.

The Craggy Mountain Forested Landscape is a biological system developed through thousands of years of use by humankind. Fires, hunting trails, camping, horseback riding, felling of trees, and clearcutting for timber before 1930 contribute to the state of organization now found in this forested landscape

Figure 4.4   This 1993 photograph of the eastern slope of Craggy Pinnacle is made from approximately the same position as the 1915 photograph (Fig. 4.3). As described by Smathers (1982), forests are continuing to develop on the pinnacle. Access via the Blue Ridge Parkway, parking lots, and trails are changing human uses from grazing and burning to aesthetics such as walking and observing scenes, plants, and animals.

(Fig. 4.2). Change in the forested areas is as dramatic as on Craggy Pinnacle. A number of documents tell the story (Baker 1923; Frothingham 1931; Spaeth 1928; Cruikshank 1941; Duerr 1949; Jolley 1969; Josephy 1991). From 1955 to 1990, the volume of live trees in the 21 mountain counties of western North Carolina increased in merchantable volume from 129 million m^3 to 254.5 million m^3. During this 35-year period, millions of cubic meters of sawtimber and other products, mostly hardwoods, were removed (Table 4.2).

The relatively rapid increase in volumes occurred in young stands that originated after clearcutting from about 1880 to 1920 (Boyce and McClure 1975; Peterson 1968; Schwarzkopf 1985). Many stands are now more than 50 years old. If volume/hectare is divided by age, the result is a measure of mean annual increments of growth. Typically, mean annual increments indicate faster rates of growth in young than in old stands. Data from Schnur is used in Chapter 3 (Table 3.1, Fig. 3.4) to discover that the maximum mean annual increment for cubic volumes of wood occurs near age 50 for forests that include the Craggy Mountain Forested Landscape.

About 1932, the federal government began to purchase the area now called the Craggy Mountain Forested Landscape. About 95 percent of the forests were in young stands that developed after clearcutting prior to acquisition. Only remnants of old-growth timber remained in inaccessible locations. Some of the remnants are found in the Craggy Mountains Scenic Area, Walker Cove Research Natural Area, and parts of the Linville Gorge Wild Area (Peterson 1968). From about 1932 until about 1965, the forests were protected and only small amounts of timber were harvested because most merchantable timber was removed by private owners before sale to the government. Low rates of timber harvest from 1930 to 1965 reduced areas in today's age classes B, BB, and C (Table 4.1).

After about 1965, average annual rates of harvest and regeneration averaged 15.4 ha/year for the upland hardwoods working group. This estimate is made by adding land areas in age classes R, A, and AA for upland hardwoods and dividing by 21 years (Table 4.1). This rate of harvest is equivalent to a

TABLE 4.2 Merchantable Volumes of Timber in Live Trees for a 35-Year Period in 21 Mountain Counties in Western North Carolina. (Cost, 1975; Craver, 1985; Johnson, 1991)

Year	Softwoods	Hardwoods	Total
	(millions m^3)		
1955	25.8	103.2	129.0
1964	27.8	115.8	143.6
1974	39.8	165.8	205.7
1984	46.6	194.9	241.5
1990	48.1	206.3	254.5

rotation period of 77 years. The rotation period is estimated by dividing total area of upland hardwoods, 1188.9 ha, by the annual harvest rate, 15.4 ha/ year. This rate of harvest is beginning to rebuild the younger age classes, which were lost by about 30 years of harvest by single-tree selection systems (Peterson 1968). The small areas of land in age classes B1, BB1, and C1 are due to harvest with single-tree and small-group selection methods, which did not make canopy openings large enough for seedlings and sprouts to enter the dominant canopies (Fig. 4.2).

Policies for Management

Social, economic, and political forces shape policies far beyond the control of managers. Policies arise within the laws and regulations established by government, the limits of available capital and operating funds, and the economic constraints of national economies and public attitudes. Managers influence policy by informing policy makers of situations and consequences and by participating in public policy debates. Managers of forested landscapes rarely, if ever, are free to devise a policy that is not shaped by external social, economic, and political forces. These forces prevent any forested landscape in the world from being managed to fulfill a policy based purely on a single ideology, such as the Wildlands Project (Mann and Plummer 1993), a biological ideology (Stone 1993), or a social ideology (Goodman 1993). If unlimited capital and operating funds are available, policy makers and managers are not free to follow any single ideological policy. Formation of policy is beyond the scope of this book. This book is about fulfilling policy.

Policies are statements of what is thought to be possible for fulfilling the desires of owners, policy makers, and other interested parties. Policies are statements designed from mental models about future events. As uncertain events unfold, managers adjust courses of action to counter effects of unexpected situations (Fig. 3.1). Whenever social, economic, biological, or legal constraints limit the fulfillment of policy, managers must return to policy makers for a different policy. Sometimes this action requires legal procedures through courts, legislation, or governmental intervention (Egan 1993a,b; Alper 1993). The Craggy Mountain Forested Landscape is managed by the USDA Forest Service under policies established by law and with public involvement. This illustration is not intended to mimic or propose a change in that policy. Rather, the policies used in this illustration are for the purpose of demonstrating how policy determines questions for managers, directs designs for models, and determines objectives for management.

In practice, managers are given a policy. Some managers analyze options with mental models and choose a course of action with minimum documentation. Others may use optimization methods, GIS, or other kinds of physical models. DYNAST includes use of physical models to simulate outcomes for options thought to fulfill a policy. DYNAST outcomes may be inserted into GIS to display relationships as maps. Outcomes from simulation models are not decisions. The simulation models document mental models, and the outcomes are used to inform others, to obtain scrutiny of proposed actions, and to help managers choose a course of action. Managers use their mental models to make decisions. For the Craggy Mountain Landscape, three conflicting policies are illustrated here.

Forest Reserves   A policy of maintaining forest reserves stops all timber harvest. Culture is limited to maintaining primary roads and trails; providing protection from fires, insects, diseases; limiting human uses; and monitoring changes in states of organization. Canopy openings are smaller than ½ ha and are formed by natural events (Runkle 1981, 1982). This policy is similar to policies applied in some parks, wilderness areas, and other kinds of reserves. Suppression of fire, insects, and diseases is based on evaluation of each situation. The general policy is to permit natural events to prevail, subject to maintaining a forested landscape in a near natural state and protecting it from damage by users.

Traditional Forestry   This policy structures stands to maintain a balance of age classes within a range of optimum timber harvests. Stands are scheduled for harvest according to silvicultural systems, which are cutting patterns designed to structure and distribute stands across a landscape for optimal timber or cash flow and to ensure regeneration of harvested areas. Trees are released from competition, thinned, pruned, fertilized, and genetically improved to speed growth of crop trees. Stands are structured and harvested for the production of timber without concern for values that require two or more stands ordered over space and time. Harvest of timber for optimal timber and cash flow incidentally organizes landscapes (D. M. Smith 1977, 1986; Oliver and Larson 1990; Matthews 1991; Davis and Johnson 1987; Buongiorno and Gilless 1987; Spurr 1979; Burns and Honkala 1990; Burns 1983, 1989).

For traditional forestry, canopy openings are about 15 ha. In other landscapes, canopy openings may be larger or smaller. Many landscape benefits are related to canopy openings. However, traditional forestry is a policy for investments to provide sustained flows of timber and cash. This policy is not suitable for public lands that are dedicated to providing multiple goods, services, and effects and is not suitable for areas reserved from timber harvest.

Landscape Forestry   Landscape forestry orders the distribution of stands, step by step, toward a state of organization that produces desired combinations of habitats, aesthetic values, timber, cash flow, and biological diversity. Timber is harvested to organize the forested landscape for jointly produced economic, biological, and social values that cannot be provided with traditional forestry. This is a policy suitable for lands dedicated to providing baskets of multiple goods, services, and effects. This policy provides for positive cash flows and simultaneously the production of habitats, timber, aesthetic values, and biological diversity. Landscape forestry involves mingling traditional forestry and landscape design concepts. It is the art of organizing forested landscapes to produce combinations of benefits that require two or more kinds of stands ordered over space and time.

Sizes of canopy openings can be varied from natural gaps to very large areas, 50 and more ha, for example. For this illustration, canopy openings are simulated at about 15 ha, the same as for traditional forestry. However, canopy openings of about 5–10 ha would reduce differences in tradeoffs among elements in the baskets of benefits.

Choice of a mix of benefits in the basket is made after two to three initial simulations. Initial simulations provide information about what mixes of benefits are possible and how the mixes may change as states of organization change. From this information, an acceptable mix of benefits, not always the most desirable, is selected. The choice of an acceptable mix of benefits identifies a course of action that can be used to move the landscape toward states of organization that best fulfill policy.

STEP 2. IDENTIFY THE QUESTION

The Craggy Mountain Forested Landscape continues to change, as it has for thousands of years, in relation to human policies for conservation and use. There is no way to return to past states of organization. What concerns managers are opportunities to direct the landscape from the current state of organization (Table 4.1) toward future states to fulfill a policy. The question is: What consequences are expected, over the next 50 years, from making the landscape a forest reserve, imposing traditional forestry, or imposing landscape forestry? There are a number of variations within each of these three different policies.

STEP 3. DESIGN THE MODELS

Three simulation models, CRAG-1, CRAG-2, and CRAG-3, have been designed by me and are used to calculate and display expected outcomes. The designs are used to program rules into a computer. The equations are iterated 4 times per simulated year, and the simulations are extended to 50 years. Values are plotted at 5-year intervals for this demonstration. Variations in values between the 5-year intervals are not displayed. The rule-based computations help to organize masses of complex information, such as the data in Table 4.1, and provide us with plots and tables to illustrate consequences. Consequences provide insights into relationships, reveal relationships not previously encountered, and provide a context within which to choose a mix of benefits and a course of action.

Designs for the models, based on use of DYNAMO or STELLA software, are described in Boyce (1977, 1978, 1985, 1986). Design—that is, structure of the models—is essentially the same regardless of the kind of computer programs used. Some elements of design are presented in Chapter 5.

STEP 4. CONSTRUCT PHYSICAL MODELS

Procedures for constructing simulation models with DYNAMO and STELLA are described in Boyce (1977, 1978, 1985). Construction—that is, writing rules for a computer—is dependent on kinds of software employed with computers. Some methods for construction with DYNAMO and STELLA are described in Chapters 6 and 7.

STEP 5. EVALUATE CONSEQUENCES AND ADJUST ACTIONS

For this illustration, only one evaluation will be presented for each policy statement. In practice, controls are changed to examine a number of options for a given policy (Boyce and McNab 1994).

Consequences for Forest Reserves

After 50 years with no timber harvesting, the initial state of organization changes to a state in which most stands are older than 50 years (age class C) (Fig. 4.5).

Stopping all timber harvest stops timber production and limits habitats for plants and animals that depend on seedling stands. For example, litter and hunting spiders are reduced in numbers as stands move beyond 50 years of age. Some animals, such as pileated woodpeckers, benefit as many stands move toward an old-growth state of organization. Cash flow is negative. Taxes, protection, and other costs for ownership must be paid from taxes or other external sources of income. One basket of three benefits is displayed in Fig. 4.6. Each is plotted with normalized indices to provide for comparison of relative consequences over time as the forested landscape changes from the initial state toward an old-growth state.

The policy of forest reserves reduces areas in young age classes and reduces the potential livelihood for spiders dependent on ground webs, trap doors, and hunting. A decline in young age classes reduces the biological diversity of spiders (Fig. 4.6) and possibly some other plants and animals. The normalized index includes habitat potential for spiders found in seedling stands, those found in stands 80 or more years old, and those found in both seedling and old stands. The index is a measure of potential biological diversity for 134 species as affected by management policies (Coyle 1981; Boyce and Cost 1978; Bruce and Boyce 1984; Boyce 1985, 1986).

Habitat quality for the pileated woodpecker is related to the availability of old stands for nesting and shelter and of young hardwood stands for feeding

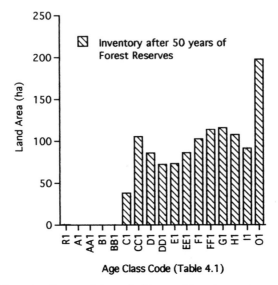

Figure 4.5 When the Craggy Mountain Forested Landscape is converted to forest reserves, no timber is harvested, young age classes decline, and old age classes increase in area.

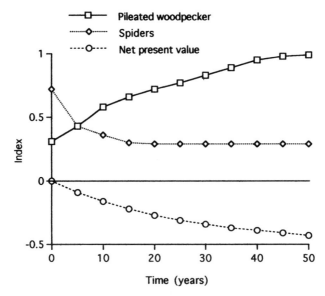

Figure 4.6 When the Craggy Mountain Forested Landscape is converted to forest reserves, changes in states of organization enhance habitats for pileated woodpeckers, produce negative cash flows, and decrease the biological diversity of spiders.

areas. With forest reserves, habitat quality for this bird increases due to increases in nesting habitats. After 50 years, many stands 50–100 years of age provide adequate feeding areas for this bird. Without timber harvesting to increase areas in young age classes, food may become limiting in another 50 years (Martin et al. 1951).

Net present values for the three policies are normalized with the base value of $4 million. The cost for capital, reinvestment rates, and discount rates is 4 percent. The dollar values, such as continuing costs and stumpage prices, are estimates I made from many sources. For forest reserves, no income is received from the forested landscape. The continuing cost produces a negative net present value, which approaches $2 million soon after year 50. The normalized index for net present value approaches −0.5 soon after year 50. The index multiplied by the base value of $4 million is an estimate of the net present value.

The normalized indices provide a way to compare the relative effects of a policy on different kinds of benefits. Comparisons are valid as long as the base values for normalizing the indices are the same for all options.

Consequences for Traditional Forestry

Lengths of rotations are selected to produce sustained flows of desired kinds of sawtimber. Rotation ages are the midpoints of 10-year age classes because, in practice, harvest can come from any stand in an age class. For upland hardwoods stands, the selected rotation period is 85 years; for cove hardwoods, 75 years; and for northern hardwoods, 85 years. The initial inventory provides opportunities to harvest stands older than the rotation ages over the first 10 years at rates that will not depress market prices. After the first 10 years, negative feedback loops in the model adjust rates of harvest to maintain a sustained harvest of timber into the distant future. Size of canopy openings created by timber harvesting is about 15 ha. Natural regeneration is encouraged. No stands are converted from one type to another.

After 50 years, all stands older than the desired rotation ages are harvested and age classes are truncated at rotation ages. A relatively large area is in age classes that are less than 50 years old; old growth is no longer tolerated (Fig. 4.7). Benefits such as habitats, biological diversity, and aesthetic values are incidental to optimal flows of timber and cash (Fig. 4.8).

Habitat quality for the pileated woodpecker is lower for traditional forestry (Fig. 4.8) than for forest reserves (Fig. 4.6). Elimination of stands older than the rotation period reduces nesting habitats for this bird. The index is a straight line because elimination of old-growth stands reduces the potential livelihood to a very low level. The index value remains at about 0.3, because some birds continue to nest in snags in harvested areas and in dead trees in the DD and E age classes (Table 4.1) (Conner et al. 1975).

Under traditional forestry, biological diversity for 134 species of spiders decreases as areas in stands older than rotation periods are harvested (Fig.

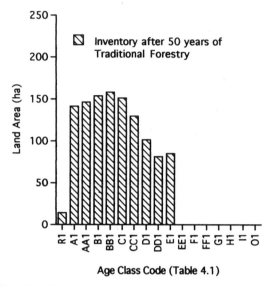

Figure 4.7 When the Craggy Mountain Forested Landscape is directed using traditional forestry, stands older than ages for optimal cash flows are liquidated. Land areas are concentrated in age classes A1–E1.

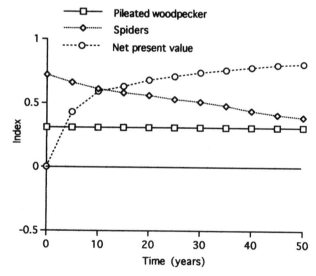

Figure 4.8 When the Craggy Mountain Forested Landscape is directed using traditional forestry, cash flow is optimal, habitats for pileated woodpeckers are very low, and the biological diversity of spiders declines.

4.8). Biological diversity for spiders is reduced by a reduction of young stands under the policy of forest reserves (Figs. 4.5, 4.6) and is reduced under traditional forestry by a reduction of old stands (Figs. 4.7, 4.8).

Under traditional forestry, sales of stands older than the rotation period rapidly increase net present values during the first 10 years (Fig. 4.8). By year 50, net present value approaches the base value of $4 million. The largest cash flows are produced with short rotations (Figs. 3.2, and 4.7). Any retention of stands older than the age for maximum value reduces cash flow.

Consequences for Landscape Forestry

This method is to direct the distribution of stands according to forest type, age, and area classes from regeneration to old growth by using superimposed rotations. This policy illustrates use of landscape forestry procedures. Superimposed rotations are used to organize and maintain stands of all age classes and forest types throughout the forest. For cash flow, some stands are harvested at relatively young ages; other stands are harvested after serving as old-growth habitats for some years or decades. Any stand area can be harvested in a short rotation cycle and in the next cycle be harvested as old growth. In this illustration, 30 percent of the upland hardwoods are harvested at 160 years of age and 70 percent at 85 years of age; 30 percent of cove hardwoods are harvested at 160 years of age and 70 percent at 75 years of age; and 30 percent of northern hardwoods are harvested at 160 years of age and 70 percent at 85 years of age. Sizes of canopy openings created by timber harvesting are about 15 ha because this is the stand area used for traditional forestry. A smaller stand area may be desirable for some benefits. Natural regeneration is encouraged.

After 50 years, the state of organization includes stands in all age classes. The relatively small areas in stands 80–100 years old is due to the initial small areas in age classes 30–50 years old (Table 4.1). This gap will be filled as the model schedules rates of harvest relative to the distribution of stands by forest type, age and area classes (Fig. 4.9). Outcomes include a cluster of benefits at relatively high index values (Fig. 4.10).

Landscape forestry organizes the forest to provide combinations of timber, cash flow, habitats, biological diversity, and aesthetic and economic values. Indices are displayed for only three of the many kinds of goods, services, and effects. Superimposed rotations conserve some old-growth stands and provide habitats in all age classes from 0 years to old age. Benefits are compromised. Cash flow is less than that with single rotations (Fig. 4.8), and the pileated woodpecker index is less than that with no timber harvesting (Fig. 4.6). Young age classes provide habitats for plants and animals that would have very low indices under the policy of forest reserves. For example, young stands enhance the livelihood for the indigo bunting, the Carolina wren, and the common flicker, while old stands enhance the livelihood for the eastern wood pewee, the red-eyed vireo, and the scarlet tanager (Conner and Adkis-

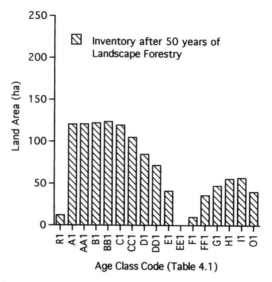

Figure 4.9 When the Craggy Mountain Forested Landscape is directed using landscape forestry, stands are organized to provide habitats from the youngest to the oldest ages for all forest types. Small areas of forests in age classes EE1 and F1 are due to distributions of land in the initial inventory (Fig. 4.2).

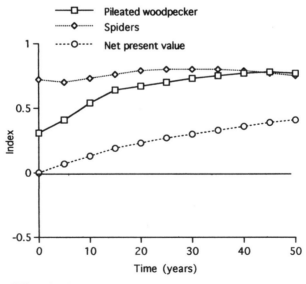

Figure 4.10 When the Craggy Mountain Forested Landscape is directed using landscape forestry, cash flow is less than optimal but is positive. Habitats for pileated woodpeckers and biological diversity of spiders are increased.

son 1975). All the intermediate age classes contribute something to the livelihood of some plant and animal species and to aesthetic values, stream flow relationships, and timber production.

Landscape forestry invariably compromises cash flow for other values. This is true for four reasons. First, conservation of stands older than the age for maximum cash flow increases cost for capital and operating expenses. Second, trees older than ages for maximum cash flow appreciate in value at rates less than discount rates. Stand ages for the fastest rates of appreciation in stumpage values are close to the age for culmination of mean annual increment for a given kind of wood product. Third, limiting sizes of canopy openings to enhance habitats increases costs for harvesting. For example, more haul roads are required to harvest ten 5-ha openings than to harvest two 25-ha openings. Fourth, dependence on natural regeneration of canopy openings reduces control over the dominant species that capture and use the most solar energy. Natural regeneration increases the variety of trees in the sunlit canopy and usually reduces market value of the stand at maturity. Natural regeneration is analogous to permitting naturally regenerated ragweed and crab grass to grow with tomato plants in a vegetable garden.

Landscape forestry can produce positive cash flows as part of a basket of many kinds of benefits. The question for landscape foresters is: How much cash flow is to be traded for baskets of other kinds of benefits? The DYNAST models provide consequences for different tradeoffs. Managers can hold all variables constant except one and simulate outcomes as baskets of benefits, including cash flow. For example, landscape forestry rotates 30 percent of the Craggy Mountain Forested Landscape through 160-year-old stands. Cash flow increases over the 50-year period. A manager can ask: What will be the cash flow and the basket of benefits if 30 percent of the landscape is rotated through 260 years? The effect on age class is to reduce the area in young age classes and increase the area in old-growth stands. The age-class distribution after 50 years, for upland hardwoods, illustrates a new distribution of habitats over time and space (Fig. 4.11). Cash flow is traded for values associated with increased amounts of old-growth forest, such as pileated woodpeckers, aesthetic values, hiking, and photography (Fig. 4.12).

The index for diversity of spiders is changed very little. Potential livelihood for pileated woodpeckers is increased. Net present values are very low but still positive and increasing over time. Policy determines the amount of tradeoffs a manager can accept in the development of plans for producing baskets of benefits. It is social, political, and economic forces that determine options for a given policy. Managers are often the first people to inform policy makers, legislators, and special-interest groups of adverse situations such as negative cash flows and ask for changes in demands and policies (Egan 1993a,b; Alper 1993).

Adjustments

When a course of action is implemented, changes in states of organization of the landscape and changes in productions of benefits are monitored. Moni-

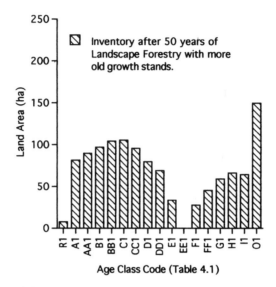

Figure 4.11   Use of landscape forestry to shift harvest ages of old-growth stands from 160 to 260 years increases amounts of forest accumulated in older age classes.

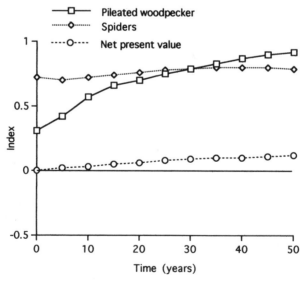

Figure 4.12   An increase in amounts of forest accumulated in older age classes (see Fig. 4.11) enhances habitats for pileated woodpeckers, keeps the biological diversity of spiders, and reduces cash flow.

tored data are compared with desired productions as described by policy (Fig. 3.1). Discrepancies are used to adjust rates of harvest, sizes of canopy openings formed, and kinds of regeneration encouraged. These controls change states of organization and productions of benefits. Continual monitoring and adjustment of controls are necessary to keep productions in agreement with policies.

Managers cannot predict exact outcomes of actions. However, monitoring states of organization in relation to benefits produced provides managers with information to make frequent adjustments in rates of harvest, sizes of canopy openings, and kinds of regeneration (Fig. 3.1). Management is the art of avoiding rapid changes in states of organization, maintaining a diversity of forest types, age classes, and sunlit canopies (Figs. 4.9, 4.11). Stands are sustained in all age classes in combination with positive cash flows with two superimposed rotations. Harvest of a fraction of stands at the youngest rotation age is scheduled to maintain positive cash flow. Harvest of the remaining fraction of stands at an old-growth rotation age provides enough variability in the distribution of stands, over time and space, to provide an acceptable (though not necessarily maximum) livelihood for all endemic plants and animals. Manipulation of the fractions of land rotating through two superimposed rotations is an important way to adjust tradeoffs between livelihoods for specific plants and animals, aesthetic values, biological diversity, and cash flows (Figs. 4.10, 4.12). Frequent adjustments avoid precipitous changes in flows of benefits. A wide variety of forest types, age classes, and areas of canopy openings provide a broad base for adjusting to uncertain future demands of consumers.

A COURSE OF ACTION

Rules programmed into computers rapidly simulate relationships for large numbers of variables changing simultaneously. These outcomes may or may not fulfill a policy. Computer outcomes serve as information to be used in new or revised mental models of managers and other involved people. The learning process that leads to new or revised mental models includes being involved in designing the model, using the model, and evaluating the consequences. These activities give managers and other involved parties an increased understanding of a system's dynamics.

Simulation of mental models with physical models helps participants understand and examine consequences for options thought to resolve differences between involved parties. The procedures presented in this book do not assure resolution of conflicts. Procedures provide a context within which discussions may lead to choice of acceptable courses of action. Methods encourage participants to document their mental models for scrutiny and comment by others and to participate in choosing a course of action before managerial decisions are implemented.

Readers may not agree with any of the consequences displayed in this chapter. There may be disagreements about hidden costs, methods of accounting, government subsidies, and mental models about ecosystem management (Schneider 1993; Alper 1993; Mann and Plummer 1993; Gauch 1993). The significance of these examples is that they illustrate the method of involving all parties in procedures for designing and constructing physical models. Methods are illustrated in the next three chapters.

5

DESIGN OF MANAGEMENT MODELS

Management models are mental or physical models designed to compare expected consequences with policy and adjust courses of action to fulfill policy (Fig. 3.1). Mental models are used to simulate consequences and to choose the most acceptable basket of desirable and undesirable benefits. Since plans are future events, uncertainties are ameliorated with adjustments as future situations unfold (Fig. 3.3). Management models are derived from experimental science, experiences, and observations. Mental models are translated into physical models in order to document mental models, provide for scrutiny by different parties, and reduce complexity.

Complexity results from many variables changing simultaneously and from attempts by managers to match each variable with an action (Ashby 1973; Beer 1966). An important way to reduce complexity is to design or identify a few variables that change feedback loops. Management is the process of changing a few controls to direct feedback loops so that they match responses to a variety of variables. For most complex systems, a few control variables can direct the dynamics of a managed system (Forrester 1961; Beer 1966; Senge 1990). The classic example is the automobile, which is designed to have four controls: steering wheel, accelerator, brake, and gear shift. These four controls are scheduled by many people to direct complex automobiles through uncertain and complex environments of highways and city streets. The analogous situation for forested landscapes is to use three controls: rates of harvest of stands, sizes of canopy opening, and kinds of regeneration. These controls are used to direct forested landscape from an initial state toward a state of organization that produces desired baskets of benefits. This chapter illustrates the design of models that use these three controls to direct forested landscapes.

CORE MODELS

Core models simulate changes in states of organization of forested landscapes over time. Simulated changes are driven by natural events as altered by the three controls. Suppositions are developed about how organisms are expected to respond to removing all human intervention or imposing some combination of the three controls. A core model begins with an initial inventory and changes the inventory in relation to suppositions about how we think forested landscapes respond to rates of timber harvest, sizes of canopy opening, and kinds of regeneration. Core models are the frames on which we hang supplementary models, which are designed to simulate productions of goods, services, and effects.

Design of a Core Model for Forest Reserves

When landscapes are turned into forest reserves, all harvesting of timber stops and natural events transform landscapes. The natural mortality of dominant trees shifts sunlit canopies from high to low, increases germination of seed, stimulates growth of sprouts, and releases space for the growth of roots and crowns of seedlings, saplings, and understory trees. Over time, the natural mortality of sunlit canopies forms openings large enough or in such a sequence as to permit seedlings and sprouts to form new stands and occupy the canopy openings. Without timber harvesting, many canopy openings are relatively small, such as the areas of crowns on two to three adjacent trees. Growth of stands in these small openings is much slower than growth in openings of 1–2 ha (Chapter 2). When openings are equivalent to crown areas of 1 tree, increased growth of branches from surrounding trees often prohibits any understory trees from entering the sunlit canopy. In the Craggy Mountain Forested Landscape, high rates of natural mortality of dominant trees may occur at ages of 150 to 300 or more years. Uncertain events, such as landslides, ice and wind storms, fire, insects, and diseases, may shift sunlit canopies to near the ground over many hectares (Frothingham 1917; Lorimer 1980; Lorimer and Frelich 1994; Sheffield and Thompson 1992).

For forest reserves, a core model is designed around relatively certain events that are associated with time. In a forested landscape these relationships are growth in height and diameter, decline in number of trees that occupy sunlit canopies, suppression and mortality of understory trees in relation to crown closure, natural regeneration, and relatively longer life of dominant trees over suppressed trees. The design is illustrated for upland hardwoods only. The same design is used for cove and northern hardwoods types. The model is designed to simulate consequences of forest reserves and is named CRAG-1. The mental model for changes in forest reserves is documented with a diagram (Fig. 5.1).

On the basis of studies in Walker Cove Research Natural Area (Runkle 1981; Dickison 1980; Lorimer 1980), 300 years is selected as the average age for natural mortality. This is a long delay for canopy openings to form and permit some understory trees to penetrate the sunlit canopy. With this long delay, the average annual rate of formation of canopy openings is about 3.96 ha/year in the upland hardwoods (1189 ha/300 years). Initial openings are as small as the area occupied by a codominant canopy, about 0.016 ha. In these small openings, few species invade and rates of growth of seedlings, shrubs, and herbaceous plants are much slower than in openings of 2 ha (Figs. 2.1–2.4). Many small openings enlarge as surrounding trees die. Eventually some openings become large enough for understory trees to penetrate sunlit canopies. Slow growth and slow replacement of old stands results in more land accumulating in old age classes than in young age classes (Fig. 4.5). The important observation is that rates of formation of young stands are relatively slow without storms, fires, insects, diseases, and other natural events that create openings of more than 2 ha.

   The mental model says that 16.2 ha in age class R1 will be in age class A and about one-tenth of age class A1 will be age class AA1 after 1 year (Fig. 5.1). Transformations of this nature occur in all age classes. The inventory is based on placing stands in 10-year age classes since determination of ages at 1-year intervals, except for stands recently harvested or planted, is very uncertain. Each age class is viewed as the sum of land areas for all stands classified in that age class. Stands remain in the R1 age class for 1

	Code	Age class	Initial inventory
		(years)	(ha)
	R1	0-1	16.2
	A1	1-10	146.1
	AA1	11-20	162.3
	B1	21-30	0.0
	BB1	31-40	2.8
	C1	41-50	6.9
	CC1	51-60	137.2
FLOW	D1	61-70	230.7
	DD1	71-80	106.4
OF	E1	81-90	129.5
	EE1	91-100	109.7
LAND	F1	101-110	97.1
	FF1	111-120	14.6
OVER	G1	121-130	20.6
	H1	131-140	8.9
AGES	I1	141-150	0.0
	O1	151-300	0.0

NATURAL MORTALITY

Figure 5.1   Forested landscapes managed as forest reserves are organized by rates of natural mortality that create canopy openings mostly less than 0.2 ha in area (Figs. 2.1, 2.2). Rates of growth (Fig. 2.3), and net primary production (Fig. 2.4) are less than in larger canopy openings.

year, the delay period; in the A1 age class for 10 years; and in the O1 age class 150 years. The model simulates movement of land from one to another age class as the stands age. This flow of land over ages is the most certain event available for forecasting future relationships. When uncertain events, such as fires, change distributions of land among age classes, models are adjusted with a new inventory. The distributions of land among age classes, by forest type, defines states of organization of forested landscapes.

In forest reserves, flows of land over ages function as positive feedback loops (Fig. 3.2). Rates of flow from a young age class to an older age class are dependent on amounts of land area in the younger age class and not on a goal, purpose, or objective. Growth rates of trees do not change rates of land flow. Natural mortality of dominant trees change flow rates of land by shortening rotation periods. Flow rates are increased whenever canopy openings are formed in young stands. The R1 age class represents time for establishment of seedlings and sprouts. Regeneration begins a new flow of land through older age classes. Whenever advanced regeneration is present, the land area of new stands is simulated to flow into age classes A1 or AA1. Periods of delay for regeneration in age class R1 may be longer than 1 year. Regardless of the details, it is the flow rates of land over age classes that is the basis for simulating changes in states of organization of forested landscapes.

One rule built into the model says $\frac{1}{10}$ of the area in each 10-year age class moves to the next age class each year. Another rule says that when an age class goes to zero or begins at zero, no land moves to the next age class until after 10 years. Another rule says that $\frac{1}{150}$ of the area in age class O1 moves to the regeneration age class R1 each year. A 1-year delay for regeneration and for growth of advanced sprouts and seedlings to begin is the rule used for this illustration. Annual flow rates are dependent on amounts of land in each age class. This relationship reduces flows from age classes with small areas, such as B1, and increases flows from age classes with large areas, such as AA1. Over many years, land in age classes with equal delays is expected to be approximately the same. This state, called steady state, is not likely to occur because storms, fires, and other uncertain events keep age classes in a state of unequal distribution. Rules for the models are changed when adapted to different forested landscapes. Mechanics for structuring computer model CRAG-1 are described in publications (Boyce 1977, 1985; Richardson and Pugh 1981).

Design of a Core Model for Traditional Forestry

Traditional forestry is simulated with a model called CRAG-2. The simulation intervenes in natural events to produce sustained flows of timber and cash. Stands are structured without regard to organizing the landscape for habitats, biological diversity, or aesthetic values. Traditional forestry is used to enhance stand values, such as timber, growth rates, species composition, stand structure, and habitats (D. M. Smith 1986; Matthews 1991; Oliver and Larson 1990; Vardaman 1989; Davis and Johnson 1987). Enhancements may be included in simulation models. However, all productions of benefits are based on organizing stands in a forested landscape by forest type, age, and area classes. This is done by scheduling rates of harvest of stands, sizes of canopy opening, and kinds of regeneration. The inventory for upland hardwood stands (Table 4.1) is used to illustrate simulated consequences for using traditional forestry (Fig. 5.2).

Age for harvest of upland hardwoods stands is 85 years for traditional forestry. This rotation period provides optimal cash flows from hardwood sawtimber and some cash flow from pulpwood. Older age classes have little additional timber value per unit volume because growth rates decline as stands age (Table 3.1). Conserving age classes older than about 85 years increases costs and limits cash flow. Productions of landscape benefits are incident to states of organization brought about by conserving stands from 0 to 85 years of age. When all older stands are liquidated, landscape benefits dependent on old stands are depleted.

The inventory for upland hardwoods (Table 4.1, Fig. 5.2) indicate that annual rates of timber harvest are about 15.5 ha/year [(16.2 ha + 146.1 ha + 162.3 ha)/21 years]. This rate of harvest is equivalent to a rotation period

	Code	Age class	Initial inventory
		(years)	(ha)
	R1	0-1	16.2
	A1	1-10	146.1
	AA1	11-20	162.3
	B1	21-30	0.0
	BB1	31-40	2.8
	C1	41-50	6.9
	CC1	51-60	137.2
FLOW	D1	61-70	230.7
	DD1	71-80	106.4
OF	E1	81-90	129.5
	EE1	91-100	109.7
LAND	F1	101-110	97.1
	FF1	111-120	14.6
OVER	G1	121-130	20.6
	H1	131-140	8.9
AGES	I1	141-150	0.0
	O1	151-300	0.0

SINGLE ROTATION / LIQUIDATE

Figure 5.2   Forested landscapes directed with the traditional forestry policy are organized by harvest of stands near the age for optimal flows of cash and timber. New stands grow faster here than in forest reserves because canopy openings are larger than 2 ha (see Figs. 2.3, 2.4). Combinations of artificial and natural regeneration are scheduled.

of 77 years (1189 ha/15.5 ha/year). This rotation period is made up of 75 years of tree growth plus 2 years for harvest and regeneration. The harvest age for the past 21 years has been about 75 years. The design used for traditional forestry uses a rotation period of 86 years, which is made up of 85 years of tree growth plus 1 year for harvest and regeneration. The annual rate of harvest is reduced from about 15.5 ha/year to about 13.8 ha/year. This rate of harvest, which is the flow rate, is used to project states of the forest from the initial inventory to 50 years into the future (Fig. 4.7).

The model simulates harvest of the oldest age classes until all stands older than 85 years are removed. Rates of harvest are scheduled to maintain sustained flows of timber. The physical model is designed with negative feedback loops that determine rates of harvest as states of organization change. Age classes R–D use the mathematical models designed for forest reserves, which are based on positive feedback loops. For age classes DD–H, algorithms for negative feedback loops are developed. Each algorithm contains two or more sets of rules for decisions in each iteration of the model. The decisions are based on flow rate for the type, which is about 13.8 ha/year.

Design of a Core Model for Landscape Forestry

The purpose for landscape forestry is to provide benefits that cannot be produced with CRAG-1 and CRAG-2. The method is to direct the distribution of stands by forest type, age, and area classes from seedlings to old growth by using superimposed rotations. Instead of bringing the landscape to a steady state with a single rotation age, as in traditional forestry, the forested landscape is moved toward a steady state with two rotation periods. Superimposed rotations provide habitats in all age classes. This procedure provides a way to schedule the harvest of timber at an age that gives relatively large flows of timber and cash and simultaneously schedules a distribution of old-growth stands to provide benefits produced by all age classes from seedling to old growth. A diagram displays the mental model for superimposed rotations (Fig. 5.3).

With superimposed rotations, all age classes are distributed throughout the forest and occur in all forest types. Any stand may be harvested in a short rotation cycle and in the next cycle be harvested as old growth. Stands of all age classes are distributed throughout the landscape.

This illustration is limited to the upland hardwoods type. The same procedure is used for all three forest types. One rotation provides old-growth stands by harvesting 30 percent of the upland hardwoods at 160 years of age. The second rotation provides large sawtimber by harvesting 70 percent of the area at 85 years of age. The 85-year rotation provides cash flow and the 160-year rotation provides habitats for landscape benefits that require old stands.

Superimposed rotations trade cash flow for other benefits. If the percentage of the area harvested at age 85 is reduced from 70 to 0 percent, cash flows become negative (Fig. 4.6). If the fraction harvested at age 85 is increased from 70 to 100 percent, cash flows are maximum (Fig. 4.8). Positive cash flow occurs with a ratio of 30 percent of the landscape harvested at 160 years and 70 percent at 85 years. Adjustments in percentages of areas cycling through two harvest ages change states of organization and combinations of goods, services, and effects. Having two harvest ages in superimposed rotations provides stands of every biologically possible forest type, age, and area class. There is little or no advantage in using three or more superimposed rotations. The consequences for three or more superimposed rotations are easily simulated, but the complexity of implementation makes this approach impractical.

Every choice is a compromise in the mix of benefits. The chore for most managers is to choose a course of action that provides consumers with acceptable, not ideal, baskets of benefits. Mixes in the baskets will change over time as consumer demands change. Managers can adjust to these changes by adjusting fractions of landscapes cycled through two superimposed rotations. Many different states of organization and consequences are simulated by simultaneously adjusting fractions of land rotating and the rotation ages. Almost any biologically possible basket of goods, services, and effects is simulated.

The physical model for superimposed rotations is a modification of CRAG-2. Age classes E1 through O1 are modified to calculate harvest rates relative

Code	Age class	Initial inventory
	(years)	(ha)
R1	0-1	16.2
A1	1-10	146.1
AA1	11-20	162.3
B1	21-30	0.0
BB1	31-40	2.8
C1	41-50	6.9
CC1	51-60	137.2
D1	61-70	230.7
DD1	71-80	106.4
E1	81-90	129.5
EE1	91-100	109.7
F1	101-110	97.1
FF1	111-120	14.6
G1	121-130	20.6
H1	131-140	8.9
I1	141-150	0.0
O1	151-300	0.0

FLOW OF LAND OVER AGES

SUPERIMPOSED ROTATIONS

Figure 5.3 Forested landscapes directed with the landscape forestry policy are organized by harvest from a fraction of stands near the age for optimal flows of cash and timber and from the remaining fraction of stands at old-growth ages. Canopy openings are about 2–4 ha, and natural regeneration is encouraged with cultural practices.

to fractions rotating through age classes E and O. For this example, mathematical rules are included in age class E1 to calculate rates of succession to older age classes in order to fulfill the requirement that 30 percent of the area cycle through age class O1. Constants selected for fractions cycling determine amounts of land allocated to one of the rotation periods. For example, the area of land allocated to cycle through age class O1 is 356.7 ha (1189 * 0.3). The remainder of the land, 832.3 ha, which is 70 percent of the total, cycles through age class E1.

At steady state, the flow rate for age class E1 is 832.3 ha/86 years = 9.7 ha/year; the flow rate for age class O1 is 356.7 ha/161 years = 2.2 ha/year. Total annual harvest is 9.7 + 2.2 = 11.9 ha/year, which is 3.6 ha less than the annual harvest rate under traditional forestry. Superimposed rotations trade timber and cash flow for benefits that require old stands. An example is the tradeoff of timber for more nesting habitats for the pileated woodpecker (Figs. 4.6, 4.8, 4.10, 4.12). Landscape forestry is used to produce baskets of benefits that cannot be produced by structuring stands for optimal flows of cash and timber (Fig. 4.7).

SUPPLEMENTARY MODELS

Supplementary models use information from core models to simulate consequences of changing states of organization of a forested landscape. As states of organization change (Figs. 4.5, 4.7, 4.9), the availability of goods, services, and effects changes (Figs. 4.6, 4.8, 4.10). Supplementary models use information about states of organization to calculate relative values for amounts and kinds of benefits available at each iteration of the core model. Managers choose a course of action based on combinations of consequences that are relatively more desirable than the consequences of other courses of action. Supplementary models are derived by translating insights from research conclusions, documented information, and personal experiences. Supplementary models are used to compare relative differences in benefits with different management schemes (Figs. 4.5, 4.7, 4.9, 4.11). The indices help managers choose courses of action in the same way that km/h, simulated with an odometer, are useful to automobile drivers for directing an automobile.

Indices are viewed as units of measurement of potential livelihood for specified species and guilds. Livelihood is the opportunity for a species or guild of species to obtain food and shelter and to reproduce. Biological diversity is the potential livelihood of multiple species or multiple guilds of species. Potential livelihood implies that habitats are available for specified organisms to acquire food and shelter and to reproduce. The larger the index values, the greater the opportunities. The index values neither measure nor predict the presence or numbers of organisms.

As a course of action is imposed on a forested landscape, consequences are observed, measured, and used to adjust relationships that underlie supplementary models. For example, a timber yield table relates volumes of timber to age of stands and other variables (Table 3.1). As results unfold, values in yield tables are adjusted to fit a particular forested landscape. This procedure is straightforward for benefits with monetary values. An important question is how to evaluate benefits that have no monetary equivalents. One method is to normalize indices for all benefits, including monetary values, from 0 to 1 or from -1 to $+1$ (Figs. 4.6, 4.8, 4.10).

There is still a question of what standard to use for measuring different kinds of habitats that may be required to support the livelihood of pileated woodpeckers and many other kinds of benefits. This question is arbitrarily resolved by developing standards that apply to specific forested landscapes. Different landscapes require different sets of standards for two reasons. First, forested landscapes vary from place to place. Second, individual organisms self-organize in relation to different environments. Because of self-organization, organisms respond differently in different landscapes to the same managerial action (Martin et al. 1951). For example, forests in northeastern Oregon are expected to require a different standard for pileated woodpecker habitat (Bull and Holthausen 1993) than are forests in the Appalachian Mountains (Conner 1979a,b, 1980). For both landscapes, standards of measurement, each with different specified conditions, are developed to define the magnitude of potential livelihood for pileated woodpeckers, and the measures are normalized from 0 to 1 for purposes of evaluating management options. The standards of measurements are called *white boxes;* the units of measurement are called *indices.*

White Box

A white box is a two-dimensional graph conveying information about the way one variable is thought to change in relation to another. A white box is a model which, for a specified forested landscape, serves to relate, define, or record the magnitude of a benefit in relation to elements in the core model. Except for being specific to a forested landscape, the development of white boxes is analogous to the development of world standards of measurements. In 1960, the 11th General Conference on Weights and Measures defined 1 meter as equal to 1,650,763.73 wavelengths of the orange-red radiation from krypton-86. Kilogram is defined by a standard mass of platinum-iridium kept at Sevres, France, by the International Bureau of Weights and Measures. These operational definitions are standards for different people to consistently arrive at approximately the same answer for a measurement. From research reports and experience, white boxes are developed as operational standards for measuring relative differences in consequences for different courses of action. The units of measure are normalized from 0 to 1 or from -1 to $+1$.

White boxes are used to document, quantify, and explicitly display mental models about future events.

White boxes help managers exchange perceptions of mental models with others. For example, delays of years and decades between implementing an action and changing baskets of benefits exert pressures on managers to take action for short-term gains to the detriment of sustained yields of benefits. A fundamental theorem of traditional forestry, expressed more than 100 years ago, is to resist temptations to liquidate sunlit canopies that have high market values because they are the fastest producers of timber for future sales (Schenck 1897, 1974; Fernow 1891, 1893). Intensive culture of trees in plantations, genetic increases in growth rates, and other cultural practices are used to reduce delays for growing maximum volumes of timber and reducing discounting times for investments. Yet temptations are high to harvest stands for immediate cash flows to the detriment of future cash flows. Temptations are much greater for liquidating sunlit canopies for cash flows in preference to conserving stands for benefits that have no present or future market values. Regardless of policies for conservation and use of a forested landscape, an important concern of many consumers is for supplementary models to be explicit and subject to scrutiny and adjustment by all interested parties.

Managers want white boxes to display relationships derived from the most reliable research and experiences available. However, research conclusions and experiences from forested landscapes are past events not likely to ever be repeated. Approximations based on conclusions must be used since there is no way to research the future before making choices. Information about past events is incomplete. Managers can never expect to have a complete database of past events to insert in mental models or white boxes. Mental models are used to interpret information from the past in order to design white boxes to simulate, not predict, future events. Missing information is synthesized by translating insights from research conclusions, documented information, and personal experiences. White boxes explicitly display suppositions for scrutiny and adjustment by all interested parties. White boxes are not confirmed predictions of future events. Supplementary models for pileated woodpecker habitats and for the biological diversity of spiders are used to illustrate the method (Halls 1978; Verner et al. 1986; Wood 1990).

Design of a Supplementary Model for Pileated Woodpeckers

A number of publications provide information about pileated woodpeckers in the Appalachian Mountains (Conner 1979a,b, 1980; Conner et al. 1975, 1979; Conner and Adkisson 1975; Martin et al. 1951; Hoyt 1957). A synthesis of the literature suggests that the potential livelihood of pileated woodpecker is enhanced by stands of large hardwoods for nesting and some feeding; by young stands of suppressed oaks for wood-boring grubs and carpenter ants; and by young stands that support fruiting grape vines, Virginia creeper, sassafras, viburnum, and black gum. Although this bird is observed feeding on ants in large canopy openings, this habitat is not considered essential. A distribution of old and young stands seems to be important. White boxes are designed around this mental model (Fig. 5.4).

The two-dimensional graph shown in Fig. 5.4 is an arbitrary standard for simulating relative differences between proposed management actions. The graph is called a white box because relationships are explicitly displayed for scrutiny and adjustment. This method provides participants and members of teams opportunities to contribute to the development of a set of standard white boxes for a particular landscape. White boxes are developed in many ways. This example normalizes an index from 0 to 1 for nesting habitat and another for food habitat. Waveforms of the relationships are the same as those for food and nesting; thus, one plot is displayed. The index for nesting habitat is a function of the ratio of the actual amount of habitat simulated for a management option to the desired proportion of nesting habitat in the Craggy Mountain Forested Landscape. Nesting habitat is defined as the area of stands in age classes E–O for all forest types (Table 4.1). For this illustration, the desired proportion of stands in these age classes, 81–300 years, is 40 percent. Food is defined as the area of stands in age classes C–E for all forest types (Fig. 4.2). For food, the desired proportion of stands in these age classes, 41–90 years, is 30 percent. The two index values, one for nesting and one for

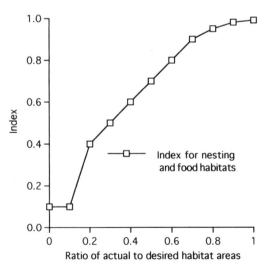

Figure 5.4   This white box displays and documents a mental model that relates nesting habitat for pileated woodpecker to an increasing proportion of stands in old-growth ages and an increase in food habitats to an increasing proportion of stands in age classes 41–90 years.

food, are averaged exponentially. The result is a normalized index for the potential livelihood of pileated woodpeckers for this particular forested landscape.

The waveform of the curve begins with two points (Fig. 5.4). First, when the ratio of actual habitat to desired habitat is equal to or exceeds 1, the habitat index is maximum and has a value of 1. A second point is established by a 0 value for the ratio of actual to desired habitat. When the ratio is 0 for either old-growth or young stands, there is still some habitat potential available. The lowest point on the curve begins at an index of 0.1. Between these two points, the waveform of the curve is subject to differences of opinion. As drawn, the mental model says a small increase in an essential habitat from a small base, from a ratio of 0.1 to 0.3, makes a greater contribution to potential livelihood than an increase from a large base, from a ratio of 0.7 to 1. An argument could be made for a straight line. However, most biological relationships are curved. This method provides for fitting relationships to observed waveforms.

Interested parties change coefficients in this model in three ways. First, the desired fraction of stands for nesting and the desired fraction for food are changed from 30 and 40 percent to some other amounts. Second, the waveform of the relationship is changed as new information becomes available and the waveform is made different for nest and food habitats. Third, the age classes allocated to nesting and food habitats are changed as observations indicate use by the birds. These changes provide considerable flexibility in fitting a standard measure to a particular forested landscape, such as northeastern Oregon. Construction of the model is illustrated in later chapters.

Design of a Supplementary Model for Spiders

Coyle (1981) identified 134 kinds of spiders in four stands on the Nantahala National Forest near Highlands, NC (Table 3.2). Twenty species are listed as occurring only in a stand more than 80 years old and with canopies more than 80 feet above the ground. Spiders limited to old stands are labeled "old stand." Seventy-two species are listed as being found only in stands less than 5 years old. Spiders limited to young stands are labeled "young stand." Forty-two species are listed as being found in both ages of stands. These indifferent spiders are labeled "both stands."

No spiders are listed for stands 5–80 years of age. As stands develop, I assume species composition of spiders shifts from species found in young habitats toward species found in old habitats. In the original form, Coyle's data are not very useful to managers. I translated the data into relationships that could be used to design supplementary models.

Increased numbers and areas of seedling habitats, formed by natural disturbances and timber harvesting, increase the potential livelihood for 72 species that apparently find improved livelihood in this kind of habitat (Table 3.2). If all of a landscape consists of recently harvested land, that is, less than

5 years ago, the expectation is for most of the spiders present to consist of the 42 species that are indifferent to stand age plus 72 species limited to young age classes. If there is no timber harvest and no disturbances to form canopy openings larger than the crown areas of one or two trees, the expectation is for most of the spiders present to consist of the 42 species that are indifferent to stand age plus 20 species limited to old-age habitats.

These mental models are translated into graphs, which serve as arbitrary standards for simulating relative differences between proposed management actions (Fig. 5.5). An index of 0 to 1 is plotted against the percentage of area in stands older than 80 years. When there are no 80-year-old stands, I assume the livelihood is very low for the 20 spider species limited to old habitats. As the proportion of stands older than 80 years increases to 50 percent or more of the area, the potential livelihood is assumed to increase to an index of 1, the maximum. The index is plotted as an exponential growth curve. There are no experimental data to support the waveform for this curve. However, explicitly displaying the waveform is a way to involve others in research and observation in order to refute, change or accept the curve as a basis for managerial decisions. The curve is not accepted as events discovered by scientific evidence. An important consideration is that managers have no better information to use for decisions that cannot wait for years of research and debate. The DYNAST method is to design supplementary models with existing information, monitor the consequences of a selected course of action, and adjust both models and the actions as uncertain events unfold.

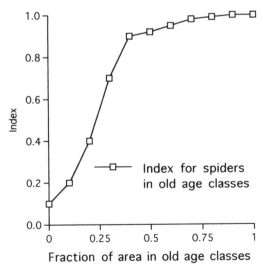

Figure 5.5   This white box displays and documents a mental model for increased biological diversity of spiders that benefit from stands more than 80 years old.

Managers are always faced with inadequate and inappropriate information for designing models to fulfill policies. Translations of research results, observations, and recorded information are essential for providing goods, services, and effects to meet consumer demands and to fulfill policies for managing forested landscapes. Another example of translation is a graph for the mental model about livelihood for spiders limited to young age classes (Fig. 5.6).

My translation for seedling spiders is based on the proportion of seedling habitats 0–5 years of age. Actually, some of the 72 spiders found in habitats of these ages likely occur in habitats of 6, 8, 10, or older ages. I will ignore this possibility until more information is available. The maximum amount of habitat that can be made available to these spiders under any one of the three policies (see Chapter 3) is limited by the shortest rotation period permitted. The policies do not set a minimum rotation period. I choose a limit of 50 years for the standard. At steady state the proportion of area in ages 0–5 years for a 50-year rotation is about 10 percent [($\frac{1}{50}$ years) $*$ 5 years]. It is unlikely that any managers will use rotations shorter than 50 years because maximum economic gain occurs at age 65 and older (Schnur 1937; McClure and Knight 1984). About 1.7 percent of the area will be in age classes 0–5 years for forest reserves [($\frac{1}{300}$ years) $*$ 5 years], which provides an upper limit for the index with an assumed natural rotation period of 300 years. I assume an exponential curve for increases in potential livelihood for spiders limited to young habitats.

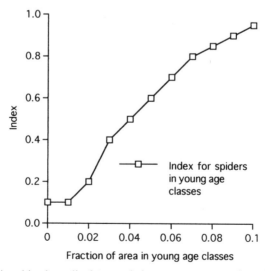

Figure 5.6   This white box displays and documents a mental model for increased biological diversity of spiders that benefit from stands less than 5 years old.

The supplementary model for spider livelihood is a function of the two translations, which are considered suppositions based on existing information. Since the indices are fractions from 0 to 1, an exponential average or weighted average can give relative values that help managers choose courses of action (Figs. 4.6, 4.8, 4.10). Construction of the models is described by Boyce (1977, 1985).

6

CONSTRUCTION OF CORE MODELS

Core models simulate changes of land in age classes. The amount of land distributed among forest types by age classes is a measure of states of organization. Core models are constructed by linking models of age classes to simulate changes in states as stands are harvested and permitted to change naturally (Figs. 5.1, 5.2, 5.3). Each model is a reusable set of equations that can be copied, modified, and linked to construct new models or to modify existing models (Boyce 1977, 1985, 1986; Richardson and Pugh 1981).

Two pieces of software are used. DYNAMO version 3.1 is software for DOS-based computers. STELLA II version 2.2 is software for Macintosh computers. Manuals come with the software and contain instructions for use. A few hours with the manuals and software will start most readers on their way to constructing models. This book does not teach use of the software (Richardson and Pugh 1981). A few equations are illustrated here in the DYNAMO format, and some diagrams are made with STELLA II. Other kinds of software may be used.

KINDS OF EQUATIONS

Construction of a model begins with a small part of the design, such as age class A1 (Fig. 5.1), and proceeds step by step to build a model. Models of all 48 age classes (Table 4.1) are linked to simulate changes in a landscape as different policies are imposed. Every age class has similarities, such as inflows, outflows, and accumulations of land. For example, age class A1 is an accumulation of land area for upland hardwood stands 1–10 years of age (Fig. 5.1). Regenerated land flows from R1 into A1. When stands in age class

107

A1 age to 11 years, the land supporting these stands flows into age class AA1. These relationships are illustrated with a diagram made with STELLA II (Fig. 6.1).

Level Equations

For the purposes of this book, accumulations are represented by rectangles called *levels.* Equations for these symbols are called *level equations,* as used in DYNAMO. Age classes R1, A1, and AA1 (Fig. 5.1) are represented with rectangles (Fig. 6.1). Level equations represent physical amounts of forested landscapes that can be measured, photographed, and recorded in an inventory (Table 4.1). In STELLA, level equations are called *stocks.* For any specified interval of time, the amounts of land in each level represent the initial amounts of land plus amounts of land moved into the age class during a time interval minus amounts of land moved out during the same time interval. The time interval is called the *differential time* DT and may be 1 second, hour, day, month, year, or some other stated interval of time.

Rates

As stands age, land flows from one to another age class. This flow is diagrammed with pipes tipped with arrow points (Fig. 6.1). Arrow points indicate directions of flow of lands into and out of age classes. Attached to each pipe is a symbol that represents rate equations. The symbol, called *flow* in STELLA, implies regulation of flows of materials through the pipes. In DYNAMO and in this book, this symbol is called *rate.* In the diagram, one rate is labeled REG1 and another is labeled SUAA1. REG1 is a mnemonic for regeneration of forest type 1, upland hardwoods. In the models, REG1 is

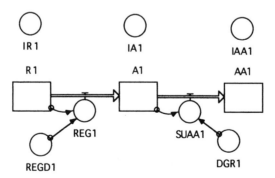

Figure 6.1   A diagram to represent changes in age class A1 (Figs. 5.1–5.3) illustrates a way to begin construction of core models. This diagram is made with STELLA II software.

a measure for "rates of flow of land from age class R1 to age class A1." SUAA1 is a mnemonic for succession into age class AA1. In the models SUAA1 is a measure for "rates of flow of land from age class A1 to AA1."

Connectors

Connectors are lines with a pointer on one end and a "button" on the other end (Fig. 6.1). Connectors are used to display flows of information. For example, calculations of amounts of land in A1 require flows of information from level R1 to rate REG1 and from level A1 to rate SUAA1.

Constants and Auxiliaries

Rates are ultimately controlled by sets of constants put into models by designers and users. Constants are used to calculate rates of flow and identify initial values. Constants affect rates of change in levels over time. The congruence of levels with real situations is traced to values assigned to constants and to kinds of auxiliary equations that modify the way constants affect rates. In STELLA, auxiliary equations are called *converters.* Much of the logic in mental models is expressed mathematically in auxiliary and converter equations. Constants and auxiliaries are represented by circles. Constants have connectors leaving the circles and none entering. Auxiliary equations have connectors entering and leaving the circles. Two constants, labeled REGD1 and DGR1, are displayed in Fig. 6.1. REGD1 is a mnemonic for "regeneration delay period for type 1," upland hardwoods. The constant value is 1 year. DGR1 is a mnemonic for "delay period for growth of stands through specified age classes for type 1," upland hardwoods. The constant for DGR1 is 10 years.

Initial Values

Every level equation must be given an initial value. For this illustration, initial values, IA1 and IAA1, are the initial inventory for each age class. Initial values have no connectors.

CONSTRUCTION OF CRAG-1

Equations for Levels

Equations are illustrated for age class A1 in Fig. 6.1. Level equations, in DYNAMO format, are identified with an "L" in column 1 (Eqs. 6.1 and 6.2):

```
L  A1.K=A1.J+DT*(REG1.JK-SUAA1.JK)
   Amounts of land in A1 simulated over time (ha)   Eq. 6.1
```

```
N  A1=146.1    Initial land in A1 (ha)                    Eq. 6.2
```

Level equations are followed by initial equations, N, which specify the initial amount of land found in the inventory (Fig. 5.1). One to six spaces separate L and N from their mathematical equations. Each equation is documented with short statements. As time progresses from one DT interval to another, all values are calculated and related to simulated time. Outcomes are examined at intervals of DT, typically less than 1 year. Subscript K, attached to A1 on the left side of Eq. 6.1, signifies that a value for A1 is calculated for the present DT interval of time. The subscript J, attached to A1 on the right side of Eq. 6.1, signifies that a value for A1 is from the preceding DT interval. At time 0, A1.J is equal to the initial value. The subscript JK, attached to the rates, signifies that values are for DT interval J to K. The level equation for A1 says: The value of A1 at time K equals the value of A1 at time J, plus the amount of land added by rate REG1 over time J to K, minus the amount of land removed by rate SUAA1 over time J to K.

All level equations are of the form illustrated by Eq. 6.1. In both DYNAMO and STELLA, the Euler method of integration is used. Runge-Kutta methods of integration are available. For simulations of most situations in landscape forestry, the Euler method is adequate. DT is chosen to give acceptable accuracy for the shortest simulation time. Typically, the shortest delay period for most landscape forestry models is 1 year. A DT interval of 0.25 year is usually a good compromise between simulation time and accuracy.

Equations for Rates

Rates of flow of land from A1 is the amount of land in A1 divided by the delay period DGR1. Rate equations are calculated at time .K for the next DT interval. The following rate equation is written in DYNAMO:

```
R  SUAA1.KL=A1.K/DGR1  Succession from A1 to AA1 (ha/year)
                                                      Eq. 6.3
```

In DYNAMO format, an R in column 1 followed by spaces identifies a rate equation. The amount of land removed from A1 and put into AA1 in the next DT interval, KL, is the amount of land in A1 at the present time K divided by the delay for flow of land through A1. Rates are calculated over time KL. Since DGR1 equals 10, removals for each DT interval is $\frac{1}{10}$ of the amount of land in A1 adjusted for width of the DT interval, which is 0.25 years. Adjustments are made by multiplying differences between inflow and outflow rates by DT (Eq. 6.1).

Auxiliary Equations

Auxiliary equations modify rates according to logic expressed in mental models. There are as many different formulations for auxiliary equations as there are forms of mental models.

Simulation models use equations to correct for an initial inventory of 0 in an age class and for times when a simulated inventory becomes 0. The mental model is to develop a set of mathematical switches that change rates of land removals from A1 over the delay period when triggered by the event of 0 land in A1. The original diagram (Fig. 6.1) is modified to display mathematical switches, which are auxiliary equations based on rules designed by mental models (Boyce 1985).

Positive Feedback in CRAG-1

When landscapes are managed as forest reserves, all age classes change as positive feedback loops (Fig. 3.2). Positive feedback loops contain no actions to direct distributions of stands by forest type, age, and area classes. As land area in A1 increases, rate SUAA1 increases. Flows of land decrease exponentially as amounts of land in A1 decrease. There is no decision-making mechanism to direct rates of flow of land or amounts of land in A1. There is no goal and no decision-making mechanism. Rates of flow for land from levels are area-dependent when rules are for positive feedback. Unequal rates of natural mortality from age class O1 is calculated as land area in O1 divided by a delay of 150 years. The model CRAG-1 is a system of positive feedback loops.

Positive feedback loops are driven by mass flows of solar energy and materials and result in aimless states of organization. There are no decision-making mechanisms and no goals, such as providing habitats for one or more organisms and moving the forested landscape toward a desired state. Positive feedback drives stands toward the oldest biologically possible ages. Numbers and species of trees in sunlit canopies die from mass flows of energy and attacks of insects, birds, fungi and other organisms. There are no scheduled rates of mortality to bring about a particular distribution of age classes. Potential livelihood for many plants and animals, and thus biological diversity, is dependent on unpredictable changes in mass flows that are related to events such as storms, landslides, floods, diseases, insects, and fires. Mass flows of energy kill trees in sunlit canopies, create canopy openings, form new stands, and provide habitats for species that do not thrive under old stands (Franklin 1993a,b).

Outcomes from CRAG-1

CRAG-1 calculates land areas in age classes every 0.25 years for 50 years. No trees are harvested. Natural mortality from age class O1 creates canopy openings of less than 0.016 ha. An example of outcomes is illustrated here with plots of three selected age classes: A1, E1, and O1. Age class A1 has stands aged 1–10 years. Age class E1 has stands aged 81–90 years. Age class O1 has stands aged 151–300 years. Land areas in each age class are plotted at 5-year intervals in Fig. 6.2.

Land areas in age class A1 approach 0 in about 15 years because few canopy openings are formed and most openings are too small to stimulate establishment and growth of seedlings. With no timber harvest, rates of formation of canopy openings are very low. No seedling stands with sunlit canopies are formed in age class A1 for the next 10 years. The initial land in A1 succeeds to older age classes, and A1 contains 0 ha after year 15 (Fig. 6.2). After 50 years, age classes A1 through BB1 contain 0 ha of land (Fig. 4.5). These events affect the livelihood of organisms dependent on young age classes (Fig. 4.6).

Land areas in age class E1 rise for 15 years and then decline as lack of regeneration reduces land areas in younger age classes. This age class provides hard mast and habitats for escape and reproduction for many kinds of animals. This age class provides habitats for understory herbaceous and shrubby plants that benefit from some shade (Holbrook 1974; Adams and Barrett 1976; Nixon et al. 1980). Outcomes for this age class suggest how initial inventories may influence production of benefits for many decades.

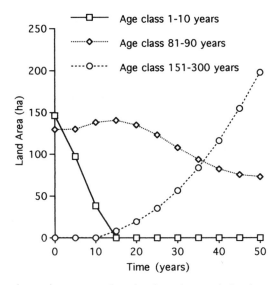

Figure 6.2   Level equations are used to simulate changes in land areas by age classes. This graph illustrates simulated changes in land areas for three age classes when the Craggy Mountain Forested Landscape is converted to forest reserves.

Land areas in age class O1 begin to rise rapidly after 15 years. This rise in old growth is due to movement of land from young age classes. Natural mortality is assumed to increase after sunlit canopies exceed 150 years of age. This model does not include equations for massive tree mortality related to storms, fires, insects, diseases, and other unpredictable events. When these events occur, new inventories are used to update the models.

Age class O1 is of interest because a few animals, such as pileated wood-peckers and black bears, use old-growth stands for reproduction, feeding, and hibernation. Age class O1 contains no land area until after year 10 because 10 years are required for land to age through age class I1 (Fig. 5.1). Delay for age class O1 is 150 years, from age 151 to 300 years. Natural mortality is assumed to occur at the rate of $\frac{1}{150}$ of the land area in age class O1, and sizes of canopy openings are assumed to be less than 0.016 ha. Over 50 years, larger canopy openings may be formed as a result of storms, fire, landslides, and other unpredictable events. Without the harvest of timber, most land in the Craggy Mountain Forested Landscape will accumulate in age class O1 between 151 and 300 years of age. Benefits will be those produced in old stands. Most benefits that require combinations of old and young stands will be limited. The landscape is being directed toward producing benefits from a single kind of stand, old growth.

Many different kinds of plots and tables are produced with simulation techniques. Typically, managers are interested in a few selected outcomes, such as changes in relative values for potential livelihood of selected plants and animals (Figs. 4.6, 4.8, 4.12).

SIMULATION

Simulation is an iterative process in which all equations in a mathematical model are calculated at every interval of differential time, DT. The DT intervals for all CRAG models are set at $\frac{1}{4}$ of a year (0.25). At time 0, all level equations for age classes have values equal to the initial inventory (Fig. 5.1). When operated with a computer, rates are calculated from current values for levels and from constants. Then rates are used to calculate levels. The effect is to step values in the model into the future at DT intervals. For example, when DT is set at 0.25 years, amounts of land in each age class change at years 0.25, 0.5, 0.75 and succeeding 0.25-year intervals. Iterations continue to the end of a desired simulation time, possibly 50 years. Over this period, amounts of land in age classes increase and decrease relative to how we use our mental models to construct physical models.

Simulations with physical models change many variables simultaneously and display consequences not discovered by our mental models. Our mental models can rarely manipulate more than three or four variables simultaneously. Mentally, we ignore variables not thought to be important. This is one way to reduce complexity in our mental models. A better way is to use physical models to simulate changes in many variables simultaneously and display combinations of consequences too complicated to be calculated and displayed by mental models alone. Displays from physical models may reveal to our mental models relationships previously undiscovered. Computer programs add no new information to the analyses. Advantages of computers are speed of interrelating many variables and displaying consequences in explicit forms.

Usefulness of outcomes from physical models depends on rules derived from mental models. Mental models rely on past experience and research to derive suppositions about future events. For example, trees 1.5 cm dbh this year are expected to have larger diameters next year (Table 3.1). Each succeeding state is dependent on immediately preceding states of organization. Mental models provide rules to simulate future states from requirements that every organism must pass through a known sequence of states as time progresses. No state in the sequence can be bypassed. Some mental models are based on requirements that every organism must capture energy by photosynthesis or consume bodies of other organisms. Other mental models are based on findings, for example, that volumes of wood in tree stems are related to dbh^2 multiplied by tree height (Table 3.1).

An inventory of stands classified by forest type, age, and area classes describes an existing state of organization of a forested landscape. Such an inventory is the basis from which states of organization are simulated, step by step, into the future. As simulations proceed, outcomes tend to deviate more and more from real situations. It is important to make new inventories at relatively short intervals, possibly 5–10 years. Each new combination of inventory, experiences, and research information is used to adjust the model. Outcomes provide information about future states of organization and future productions of baskets of benefits. Models are not intended to mimic the real world. Models provide insights and information about expected changes as a basis for managerial decisions.

CONSTRUCTION OF CRAG-2

When landscapes are managed as forest reserves, age classes change as positive feedback loops (Fig. 3.2). Under traditional forestry, landscapes become directed systems. Managers are the decision-making agents. Inventories are a part of information networks and policies establish goals for organizing forested landscapes (Fig. 3.1). Models for CRAG-2 use rules for simulating negative feedback loops. Harvest rates are scheduled for optimal flows of timber and cash into the distant future.

The mental model for CRAG-2 uses single rotations to schedule harvest of lands from a given age class, such as E1, at rates that maintain an equal area of land in every 1-year age class younger than the rotation age (Fig.

5.2). Older age classes are liquidated. This method schedules harvest rates around the flow rate for a single rotation. For E1, the flow rate is 13.8 ha/year for a single rotation of 85 years (Chapter 5). Rules are included in the model to dampen oscillations in land areas that result from unequal initial inventories (Fig. 5.2). Rather than an aimless system of positive feedback loops, such as CRAG-1, the forested landscape becomes a system managed to achieve a goal. The goal is to direct the forested landscape toward a steady state in an orderly way. CRAG-2 schedules the harvest of timber to sustain annual harvesting into the distant future.

A NEGATIVE FEEDBACK MODULE

Situation

Growth rates, biochemistry, mortality, and reproduction are examples of age-related events. These events are continuous. That is, no existing state can occur except by organisms passing through preceding states. Thus, a tree 10 cm dbh achieves this state by passing through all smaller dbh classes. Changes in states are irreversible. Thus, a tree 10 cm dbh does not grow into a tree 5 cm dbh. Functions related to age provide a basis for simulating future events. However, continuous and irreversible events limit managers to regulating rates of mortality as the most practical way to change states of organization of landscapes. For example, rates of regeneration are dependent on rates of mortality of dominant trees when the landscape is not increasing in area. The way to dampen oscillations in land areas is to regulate harvest rates.

Simulation of age class E1 in CRAG-2 requires a negative feedback module that schedules rates of harvest in relation to the liquidation of older age classes and as succession occurs across younger age classes. Sales of stands are adjusted around flow rates, which are calculated as the total area divided by the rotation period. For upland hardwoods in the Craggy Mountain Forested Landscape, the flow rate is about 13.8 ha/year for a rotation period of 85 years (Chapter 5). The mental model is to liquidate stands older than 85 years over the course of 10 years. If areas harvested from older stands are equal to or greater than 13.8 ha, then no stands are harvested from E1. If areas harvested from older stands are less than 13.8 ha, then differences are made up by harvesting stands from E1 provided that land areas in E1 are larger than the equilibrium area required for steady state. Steady state is measured as a sustained harvest of 13.8 ha/year for a single rotation period of 85 years.

Question

Construct a model to schedule rates of harvest from age class E1 to fulfill policies for traditional forestry. Harvests are scheduled so as to direct the forested landscape toward a steady state for a rotation period of 85 years, dampen oscillations in land areas among age classes, and liquidate surplus stands in E1 and older age classes according to a sales policy.

Design

The basic design for negative feedback is illustrated and described in Chapter 3 (Fig. 3.1). The design for CRAG-2 includes a negative feedback loop (Fig. 6.3). Thick lines represent flows of land; thin lines show flows of information. As stands age, land flows from age class DD1 to E1. Harvest rates remove stands from E1. A simulated inventory of E1 provides information to the decision equations CVE1 and SELF. These equations compare inventories of land in E1 with the goal, EQE1, which is the equilibrium area for E1 at steady state. When there is a surplus of land in E1, the equation SELF signals to the sell equation, SLE1, to increase sales. When land areas in E1 are less than EQE1, SLE1 reduces rates of sales. The simulation seeks a steady-state situation for the forested landscape. However, steady states are rare because over periods of 50–100 years, noise, such as unexpected storms, fires, insects, and diseases, changes the rates of natural mortality. Nevertheless, negative feedback loops dampen oscillations in land areas in age classes, moderate the effects of noise on productions of baskets of benefits, and direct the forested landscape toward sustained productions of timber and cash flow.

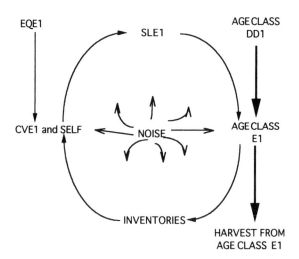

Figure 6.3   Construction of the models for CRAG-2 and CRAG-3 include negative feedback loops in which rules for sell rates are included in equations CVE1 and SELF. Feedback loops in which rules can be written for preconceived decisions may be viewed as computer robots.

Construction

The diagram for CRAG-2 (Fig. 6.3) is redrawn to illustrate linkages among equations in the model (Fig. 6.4). Rectangles represent level equations, which include land areas in age classes DD1, E1, and EE1. A rectangle labeled ASE1 keeps account of accumulated sales of stands. When these stands are harvested, land is transferred to R1 for regeneration. Valve-shaped symbols represent rate equations SUE1, SUEE1, and SLE1. Elliptical symbols represent auxiliary equations and constants. Thick lines are flows of land, and thin lines are flows of information. Equations of special interest are those in the negative feedback loop, CVE1, SELF, PSEL, FLE1, and EQE1 (Fig. 6.4). Rules written into these equations schedule rates of sales, SLE1, from age class E1.

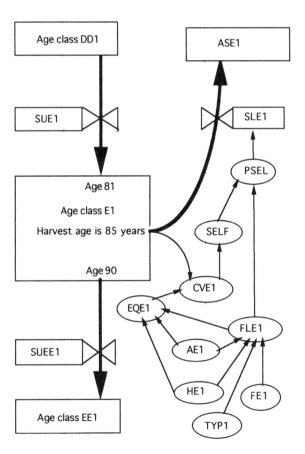

Figure 6.4   Linkages between equations for a negative feedback loop are illustrated with symbols typical of flow diagrams for models.

From age class DD1, stands older than 80 years are transferred to age class E1. At steady state, few stands in E1 exceed 85 years of age because stands are harvested at about this age. Land area in stands aged 81–85 years at steady state is labeled EQE1 and is named the equilibrium area. EQE1 is calculated by multiplying the flow rate FLE1 by the number of years that land remains in age class E1 before harvest. For this illustration, that period is 5 years, from age 81 through 85 inclusive. The EQE1 value is 69 ha (13.8 * 5). The goal for the negative feedback loop is to bring land area in E1 to approximately 69 ha. In practice, noise introduces oscillations into the values of land areas among age classes, and these oscillations increase and decrease the land area in E1 to something above and below the equilibrium area EQE1. Rules included in the auxiliary equations adjust rates of sale, SLE1, to dampen oscillations in flows of land through E1.

Rates of sale are calculated in equation PSEL, called the policy for steady-state sales. Values for PSEL are calculated by multiplying the flow rate FLE1 by a sell fraction SELF. The flow rate for age class E1 is the total area of upland hardwoods, TYP1, divided by the harvest age HE1. The harvest age is 85 years, the rotation period. The flow rate for this example is 13.8 ha/ year at steady state (Chapter 5). The sell fraction SELF increases and decreases FLE1 in relation to the amount of land in E1 divided by the equilibrium area EQE1. This ratio, called coverage, CVE1, has a value of 1 when land area in E1 equals EQE1. As land area in E1 oscillates due to noise, values for CVE1 oscillate around the value of 1. CVE1 is the basis for a table function that inserts into the module a policy for scheduling rates of sales in relation to noise and initial unequal age classes (Fig. 6.5).

The sell fraction SELF is calculated with an equation in which values are a function of CVE1. When CVE1 equals 1, sales are at the steady-state rate of 13.8 ha/year. When CVE1 exceeds 1, sales are increased according to the policy curve SELF. When CVE1 is less than 1, sales are decreased relative to the policy curve (Fig. 6.5).

The policy curve is another example of a white box (Chapter 5). The graph displays explicitly a manager's rules for changing rates of sales in relation to amounts of land in age class E1. The sell fraction defines magnitudes of a harvest schedule. Ways to define and change policy curves are easy and quick for both DYNAMO and STELLA. In DYNAMO, equations are illustrated for SELF:

```
A  SELF.K=TABHL(TSLF,CVE1.K,0,2,0.1)  Sell Fraction (Decimal)
                                              Eq. 6.4
T  TSLF=0,0.1,0.2,0.3,0.4,0.5,0.6,0.7,0.8,0.9,1,∧
       1.1,1.2,1.3,1.4,1.5,1.6,1.7,1.8,1.9,2
    Table for SELF (Decimal)                  Eq. 6.5
```

The auxiliary equation for SELF informs the computer to use a built-in table function TABHL. Values for the *x*-axis are defined by CVE1, and the values vary from 0 to 2 in units of 0.1. The table equation TSLF informs the computer of values at the 0.1 intervals for CVE1. The computer interpolates values within the 0.1 intervals. The subscript .K informs the computer of a variable, and calculation is for present time. The policy curve is rotated, and the waveform is changed, by changing numbers in the table equation TSLF.

The policy curve expresses a manager's mental model about markets, conserving timber for future sales and other variables external to the managed system. When the policy curve is a straight line extending from the value of 1 for SELF through the steady-state point (Fig. 6.5), sales are never greater than the flow rate FLE1. Managers change the policy by rotating the curve about the steady-state point and changing the waveform. The illustration rotates the curve counterclockwise and changes the waveform to establish a policy that sells excessive areas of stands in E1 and older age classes at rates faster than FLE1. For example, when E1 contains 2 times as much land as required at steady state, the sell rate is about 42.8 ha in the next year (13.8 * 3.1). After this sale, coverage CVE1 is reduced and sales are reduced but are still greater than 13.8 ha. This process moves the sell fraction SELF down the policy curve to approach the steady-state point. When the steady-state point is achieved—that is, when CVE1 equals 1—the sell fraction oscillates around the equilibrium point relative to noise in the forested landscape. When

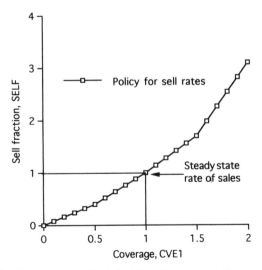

Figure 6.5   Rules for a preconceived decision about scheduling rates of timber sales can be inserted into models with a white box. The policy for timber sales is changed by rotating the curve about the point for the steady-state rate of sales and by changing the waveform of the curve.

CVE1 is less than 1, the sell fraction is less than 1. The sell fraction remains below the flow rate until land area in E1 increases to equal the equilibrium amount EQE1 (Figs. 6.3, 6.4).

Stands older than 85 years are considered surplus under traditional forestry. These stands are arbitrarily scheduled for liquidation during the first decade. The rate equations for selling stands from age classes older than 85 years include a switch function that sells equal areas over the liquidation period. The rate equation SLE1 is written with a switch to limit sales from age class E1 when sales of older stands are equal to or greater than the flow rate for E1. After all older stands are liquidated, sales shift to age class E1 and sales are scheduled with the negative feedback loop. The negative feedback loop operates to achieve the goal of maintaining land area in E1 at approximately the equilibrium amount. Over 50–100 years, with minimum noise, the forested landscape is brought to an approximate steady state. During this period, yields of timber are sustained within limits of the initial inventory.

Outcomes from CRAG-2

Land areas in age class O1 are zero under traditional forestry. All stands older than the rotation age, 85 years, are harvested during the first 10 years. Habitats are eliminated for plants and animals that require these older age classes (Figs. 4.7, 5.2).

About 140 ha are kept in age class A1, stands less than 10 years old. This area is about equal to the equilibrium area for 10-year age classes (10 years * 13.8 ha, the flow rate). Land area in all age classes from A1 through DD1 oscillate around the equilibrium area, 138 ha, after 50 or more years of following traditional forestry (Fig. 4.7). Browse is increased for many ruminants, insects, and other animals. Habitats are enhanced for plants and animals that benefit from sunlit canopies close to the ground. The important consequence of this policy is to produce timber and cash flow. Habitats, aesthetics, and biological diversity are incident to states of organization that favor young age classes and produce large volumes of sawtimber.

Harvest rates for age classes older than E1 are scheduled to provide timber sales for 10 years. During this time, land areas accumulate in E1 and provide a backlog of stands that are sold in future decades. These events maintain land areas in E1 well above the equilibrium amount, 42.8 ha. Between years 10 and 50, the policy curve for calculating sell fractions (Fig. 6.5) rapidly reduces surplus land area in E1 to about 43 ha, the equilibrium area. Some consequences of this policy include limiting biological diversity for spiders, pileated woodpeckers, and possibly other organisms. Manipulation of the policy curve by managers is based on mental models of how markets and other situations are perceived. The physical model CRAG-2 fulfills the intent of traditional forestry, which is to produce timber and cash flow and incidentally contribute to benefits that have little or no market value.

CONSTRUCTION OF CRAG-3

CRAG-3 is constructed with modules designed for CRAG-1 and CRAG-2. Modules with positive feedback loops are used for age classes R1–CC1. Modules with negative feedback loops are adjusted and used for age classes D1–O1. The primary difference between CRAG-2 and CRAG-3 is the use of superimposed rotations to distribute stands across all age classes (Fig. 5.3). This is achieved by adding negative feedback loops and switches to age classes D1–O1. This method provides opportunities to examine the consequences of using different combinations of age classes to superimpose rotations.

The goal is to schedule rates of harvest from two or more age classes to maintain a distribution of stands by type, age, and area class at an approximate steady state for the superimposed rotations. From simulations made for different forested landscapes, two superimposed rotations are found to provide many possible combinations of habitats, possibly all biologically possible combinations. The largest number of benefits are produced by setting one rotation at the youngest age for producing old-growth habitats and one rotation at the age for producing large cash flows. For this illustration, policies are to produce most of the timber and cash flow by cycling 70 percent of the landscape through an 85-year rotation and to provide old-growth habitats by cycling 30 percent of the landscape through a 160-year rotation (Fig. 5.3). No age classes are liquidated.

Outcomes from CRAG-3

Land area in age class A1 is maintained at about 119 ha, which is the equilibrium state for this age class (Fig. 4.9). The flow rate is composed of 11.9 ha/year for the 85-year rotation and 2.2 ha/year for the 160-year rotation. All age classes including A1–DD1 are moved toward the equilibrium state of 119 ha. Age class E1 is moved toward the steady-state area of about 48.5 ha (9.7 ha/year * 5 years). Age class O1 is moved toward the steady-state area of 22 ha (2.2 ha/year * 10 years). Age classes EE1–I1 are moved toward the steady-state area of 22 ha. Every age class from regeneration to old growth is represented in habitats that contribute to the livelihood of many kinds of organisms (Figs. 4.9, 4.11).

Outcomes for the landscape are simulated with different combinations of habitats, all changing to an older age class until harvested. Diversity of habitats is much greater if one considers differences in forest types and variations in size of canopy openings within forest types and annual changes in transition areas between age classes. The mental model is to have many different kinds of stands changing at different rates in relation to time, space, and preceding states. The result is an enormous diversity of habitats, each changing toward an older age class until stands are harvested. Diversity of habitats is driven by rates of harvest that form young stands and thus keep a continuum of age classes shifting across the forested landscape and contributing to the livelihood of most, not all, endemic species (Figs. 4.10, 4.12, 5.3).

Different combinations of habitats are available to plants and animals that require a variety of food, solar radiation, cover, and protection to survive and complete their life cycles. Fast and slow rates of change in habitats permit migration, selection, and evolution to structure varieties of viable populations. As states of organization of the landscape change, different combinations of benefits are produced. No two baskets of benefits are ever repeated.

Harvesting of stands is used to organize the landscape as a dynamic system that provides habitats for a great variety of organisms of unknown kinds and numbers. Productions of marketable products, such as timber, are incident to ordering the landscape. However, if policies require positive cash flows, superimposed rotations provide opportunities to change mixes of benefits to bring about positive cash flows (Figs. 4.10, 4.12). Options for tradeoffs are simulated by changing the fractions rotating through superimposed rotations and by changing rotation ages as social, economic, and political situations change demands for baskets of benefits.

From experiences over more than 200 years, a course of action rarely last longer than 10 years (Schenck 1897, 1974; USDA Forest Service 1991b, 1992a). Plans are changed every 10 years or less with feed-forward loops (Fig. 3.3). When interest rates, stumpage prices, and consumer demands are volatile, plans may change frequently. DYNAST models are designed to be easily, quickly, and inexpensively adjusted as situations change. Simulation of states of forested landscapes for more than 10 years provides managers with relative relationships, not predictions, of future events as a basis for choosing a course of action known to last for only 5–10 years. Adjustments in a course of action every 5–10 years and simulations for long periods help managers keep actions congruent with the landscape. Feed-forward procedures are a way to choose actions for sustained yields of baskets of benefits (Fig. 3.3).

7

CONSTRUCTION OF SUPPLEMENTARY MODELS

Supplementary models simulate consequences of changes in states of organization of a forested landscape. Managers use this information to adjust rates of harvest, sizes of canopy openings, and kinds of regeneration. Outcomes from supplementary models provide a basis for making tradeoffs among benefits. More management decisions are based on outcomes from supplementary models than from core models. Yet management of forested landscapes involves directing core models to bring about states of organization that produce acceptable benefits. This chapter illustrates construction of supplementary models.

A MODEL FOR PILEATED WOODPECKERS

A white box displays a mental model about nesting and feeding opportunities for pileated woodpeckers in the Craggy Mountain Forested Landscape. Since food and nesting relationships are assumed to have equal waveforms and slopes, a single white box is used (Fig. 5.4). A normalized index from 0 to 1 says that nesting indices for pileated woodpeckers increase as the proportion of stands older than 120 years increases from 0 to 40 perent of the total area in the forested landscape. In each model, land areas in age classes G, H, I, and O (Figs. 51.–5.3) are summed and divided by the total area of the Craggy Mountain Forested Landscape to produce a percentage of total area older than 120 years. This simulated percentage is divided by 40 percent to produce a ratio of actual habitat to desired habitat, the *x*-axis for the white box (Fig. 5.4).

A second supposition that says opportunities for this bird to find grapes, carpenter ants, grubs, and other food increase as the proportion of stands between ages 40 and 90 years increases from 0 to 30 perent of the landscape (Fig. 5.4). In each model, land areas in age classes C, CC, D, DD, and E are summed and divided by the total area of the Craggy Mountain Forested Landscape to produce a percentage of total area between ages 40 and 90 years of age. This fraction is divided by an amount of habitat assumed to be the maximum for feeding, which, for this example, is assumed to be 30 percent. This ratio is the x-axis for a white box that calculates an index for food habitats as states of organization in the forested landscape change for different options (Figs. 4.5, 4.7, 4.9, 4.11).

Two points are established in the white box for nesting and feeding habitat (Fig. 5.4). When the ratio of simulated habitat area from the core model is equal to the desired habitat area, the coverage ratio—that is, the ratio of actual habitat to desired habitat—for the x-axis is equal to 1 and the habitat index is 1. The second point is at the opposite end of the curve. When ratios of actual habitats to desired habitats approach 0, habitat index is given a value of 0.1 because the absence of old growth or of intermediate-aged stands does not prohibit use of the forested landscape by some pileated woodpeckers (Conner 1980). However, the potential livelihood for these birds is very low when old growth is absent (Fig. 4.8).

The next step is to choose a waveform for the curve. One possibility is to draw a straight line between the maximum and minimum points. However, biological systems rarely transform from state to state as functions defined by straight lines. The more likely situation is a curved relationship. The mental model perceives little change in the potential livelihood of pileated woodpeckers as feeding and nesting habitats increase from 0 to small amounts, such as a ratio of actual to desired habitat of 0.1 (Fig. 5.4). From this point, the mental model perceives a relatively rapid increase in potential livelihood as food and nesting habitats increase to coverage values of 0.2. From this point, the model assumes a straight line increase to a coverage ratio of about 0.7. As coverage ratios increase beyond 0.7, increases in potential livelihood increase slowly to approach the maximum value of 1. The result is a sigmoid waveform, which is characteristic of many biological relationships.

Since indices are decimals and are given equal weight, for nesting and feeding, exponential averaging is used to calculate an index for the potential livelihood of pileated woodpeckers (Figs. 4.6, 4.8, 4.10, 4.12). The square root of the product is used to combine two decimal values. Logarithms are used to calculate the nth root of the product for a number of decimal values, n. With this method, a 0 value for one index makes the habitat index 0. This is effective if one variable is essential for the livelihood of an organism. However, the white box for pileated woodpeckers says that an absence of either old growth or of stands 40–90 years old produes a low index, about 0.1, but does not eliminate the livelihood for this bird (Fig. 5.4). This supposition is based on personal observations and those of Conner (1980). This method illustrates one of many ways to relate indices for livelihood, biological diversity, and other values of interest.

If no timber is harvested for the next 50 years, habitat indices for pileated woodpeckers increase (Fig. 4.6) because the initial limiting variable, nesting habitat, increases (Fig. 4.5). If the model is simulated for more than 100 years, habitat indices for this bird decline because feeding habitat declines as young stands move into old growth. A relatively high index is maintained over long periods of time by regulating rates of harvest to conserve a combination of nesting and feeding habitats (Figs. 4.10, 4.12).

Use and Misuse of White Boxes

People with different mental models, based on different experiences, may disagree on the original waveform used in the white box (Fig. 5.4). Sensitivity analyses are used to examine the effects of differences of opinion on simulated outcomes and on managerial decisions. With both DYNAMO and STELLA programs, alternative shapes for curves in a white box are made and different outcomes are quickly examined. Two opinions, different from the original model, are used here to illustrate sensitivity analyses (Fig. 7.1).

An opinion, called change 1, may be preferred by one party; change 2 may be preferred by another party. Differences may be based on the same research

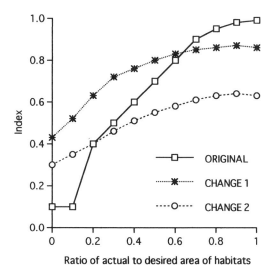

Figure 7.1 White boxes are used to make sensitivity analyses. This example examines the consequences for changing the suppositions about habitat indices for pileated woodpeckers. Similar analyses can be used to examine the effects of cost of capital, changes in sales prices, tradeoffs between elements in a basket of benefits, and many other variables that may be included in simulation models.

reports but on different interpretations by mental models (Fig. 7.1). One question is whether differences are within bounds suggested by research conclusions and accepted by interested parties. For this illustration, the three curves are considered to be within the range of experiences and published results (Conner 1980). A second question is how much different mental models affect original outcomes (Figs 4.6, 4.8, 4.10, 4.12). This latter question is examined by comparing simulated outcomes for changes 1 and 2 with the original white box (Fig. 7.2).

Differences in potential livelihood for pileated woodpeckers for changes 1 and 2 are plotted with the index values simulated for landscape forestry (Fig. 4.10). Change 1 results in smaller indices, and change 2 produces larger indices, than the original.

Simulated outcomes provide insights for recognizing one mental model as clearly superior to the other two. Yet criteria for acceptability of a waveform in a white box are subjective. A compromise between different opinions is essential for management decisions, which are based on mental models and not on rule-based equations and computer programs. Attempts to mimic research findings with managerial decisions increase uncertainty because research results are constrained to limit noise (Gauch 1993).

Uncertainty about the validity of any of the three mental models (Fig. 7.1) may argue for arbitrarily choosing any one of the curves to initiate an action. Regardless of the decision, white boxes are easily changed as new information

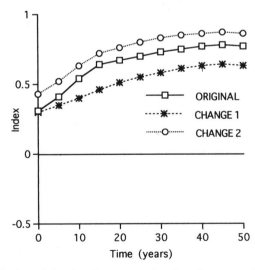

Figure 7.2   A display of simulated outcomes for changing suppositions about habitat indices for pileated woodpeckers (Fig. 7.1).

is received from monitoring results and from new observations and research. White boxes are most useful when continually adapted to unfolding events.

White boxes provide managers and interested parties with increased understanding of relationships in managed landscapes. Insights previously not discovered in mental models become apparent with sensitivity analyses of white boxes. For this reason alone, it is important that managers and others be involved in designing white boxes and in questioning the assumed waveforms. White boxes are viewed as rules developed by mental models and used to design physical models.

White boxes can be misused. Waveforms can be used to produce an outcome to support a preconceived argument. Managers and other interested parties should see white boxes, be permitted to scrutinize relationships, and question the logic for waveforms. Explicitly displayed white boxes provide a focus for differences in mental models and a basis for consensus. A consensus is not proof for a future event. Consensus is a step toward implementing a course of action, monitoring consequences, and making adjustments so plans will be congruent with outcomes. White boxes can be used to delay or prohibit decisions. There is no way to experimentally prove or disprove a white box. Yet white boxes are the most explicit physical models available to managers.

There is no way to scientifically, experimentally prove a waveform for white boxes. Experimental statistics and other techniques, such as multiple regressions, can derive equations based on past events. Conclusions from research are constrained to reduce noise. When applied to managerial decisions, experimental results become suppositions. It is the mental model that interrelates research results, experiences, and insights to develop white boxes (Fig. 7.2), which are used to guide managerial decisions.

White boxes are linked in different ways to form a single value. The purpose is to reduce complexity when many variables are changing simultaneously. Linkages can confound relationships, produce misleading indices, and be illogical. Every linkage should be based on logic and insights about the managed system. For example, coefficients and operation signs in a multiple regression are derived from logic and insights used to collect, summarize, and transform data before a regression equation is formulated. It is the constraints placed on a collection of data that determine the outcomes of multiple regressions. An important concern in linking white boxes is to keep mathematical operations congruent with what is known about biologial relationships in forested landscapes.

Future events cannot be experimentally confirmed. Research results and experiences are sources of information about past events. This information is used in mental models to form relationships. Relationships may be displayed as white boxes and used as rules in the construction of physical models, such as CRAG-1 for the Craggy Mountain Forested Landscape. White boxes provide interested parties an opportunity to express perceptions of their mental models. Sensitivity analyses for waveforms in white boxes inform interested parties of how much change in a white box is required to change a managerial decision. It is relative differences in simulated amounts of benefits that help managers choose a course of action.

Outcomes are relative differences between consequences and not exact values (Figs. 4.6, 4.8, 4.10). Relative relationships provide a basis for simulating differences among options without predicting precise outcomes. Precision in outcomes is, by definition, a past event. Immediate past events are used to adjust the slopes and waveforms of white boxes in hopes of bringing the white boxes within an acceptable range of real-world outcomes. Noise maintains discrepancies between white-box suppositions and real outcomes (Fig. 3.1). Yet white boxes remain a practical, and possibly the only, way to devise physical models for simulating future consequences to aid managerial decisions. White boxes are a way to reduce noise, and thus complexity, for comparing managerial options (Gauch 1993).

BIOLOGICAL DIVERSITY OF SPIDERS

The biological diversity of species of spiders is thought to increase as a function of three variables (Table 3.2). One guild of spiders seems to exhibit a better livelihood in stands older than 80 years of age than in younger stands. A mental model for this guild of spiders, called an old-stand guild, is based on the percentage of total area in stands older than 80 years. Equations are written to sum areas in age classes E, EE, F, FF, G, H, I, and O. This total is divided by the total area in the Craggy Mountain Forested Landscape to produce the x-axis for a white box (Fig. 5.5). The y-axis expresses a supposition about how the potential livelihood for these spiders increases as proportions of old stands increase in a forested landscape (Coyle 1981; Bruce and Boyce 1984; Boyce 1985, 1986).

The livelihood for a second guild of spiders, called the young-stand guild, is related to the percentage of area in stands younger than 5 years of age. Equations are written to calculate sums of areas in R age classes plus ½ sums of areas in A age classes. This total is divided by the total area in the Craggy Mountain Forested Landscape to produce values for the x-axis of a white box (Fig. 5.6).

The potential livelihood for a third guild of spiders, called the indifferent guild, seems relatively high for all age classes of hardwood forests. For these spiders, the habitat index in the Craggy Mountain Forested Landscape is set at a constant of 1 because hardwood forests occupy almost all of the landscape. The constant value of 1 can be converted to a white box if investigations discover some different relationships.

The mental model, based on Coyle's studies (1981), is for the biological diversity of spiders to be relatively high when stands are distributed across all age classes (Figs. 4.10, 4.12). Reduction of stands in young age classes

(Fig. 4.6) reduces the biological diversity of spiders because habitat is limited for spiders in the seedling guild. Reduction of areas in stands older than 80 years (Figs. 4.7, 4.8) reduces biological diversity because habitat is reduced for spiders in the old-age guild. These mental models are built into the white-box relationships (Figs. 5.5, 5.6).

Waveforms of the relationships are curved to display perceptions of the mental model. For example, inventories of hardwood forests in the eastern United States indicate that maximum proportions of forested landscapes in stands older than 80 years rarely exceed 50 percent. Because of this relationship, the potential livelihood for spiders in the old-age guild is assumed to rise rapidly as the percentge of stands older than 80 years rises from about 10 to 50 percent (Fig. 5.5).

For most hardwood forests in the eastern United States, proportions of forested landscapes in stands less than 5 years old are between 1.5 and 5 percent. Maximum potential livelihood for these spiders is assumed to occur when 10 percent of the stands are less than 5 years old. From this point, the relationships extend to a low index for potential livelihood when less than 1 percent of the landscape is less than 5 years old (Fig. 5.6).

Logarithms are used to calculate an exponential average for values taken from the white boxes (Figs. 5.5, 5.6) and the value of 1 for the indifferent spiders. For guilds such as the spider guilds, the index for potential livelihood is perceived to be a measure of biological diversity. When the index is low, one or more kinds of habitats to support one or more guilds are limited by an imposed policy (Figs. 4.6, 4.8). A high index requires a distribution of habitats that favors all guilds (Figs. 4.10, 4.12). This index, the exponentially averaged values for habitat relationships for guilds of species, provides managers with a basis for adjusting cultural actions to enhance biological diversity (Boyce and Cost 1978).

Management to Enhance Biological Diversity

For decades, biologists and ecologists have searched for functional relationships to explain distributions of species by numbers of individuals (Pielou 1977; Odum 1983; Peet 1974; Wilson and Shure 1993; Ludwig and Reynolds 1988; Martin et al. 1993a,b). Many kinds of indices have been developed and used to search for relationships that may help to explain and predict distributions of plants and animals. However, these functional indices are of little or no value to managers (Boyce and Cost 1978; Preston 1960).

Pielou (1977) noted that many biological diversity indices confound species and numbers of individuals per species. This confounding results in one value for an index derived from differences in numbers of species and numbers of individuals per species. Confounding prohibits any meaningful relationships for managers. Attempts to find meaningful expressions of biologial diversity led Boyce and Cost (1978) to propose operational definitions and procedures for managers. They defined biological diversity as the meaningful differences in elements of biological communities. Meaningful differences are specified by elements, measurements, and significance.

Elements   Elements are physical items, such as plants and animals, that can be measured with conventional methods, counted, and related to states of organization of forested landscapes. One may choose stands of trees classified by forest type, age, and area class; spiders classified by habitat guilds; herbaceous plants classified by elevation and species; genetic features of a species; depth of litter; kinds of soils; and classes of streams.

Measurements   Measurements are specified by procedures that distinguish an element from all other elements in the landscape. Measurements may be ways to identify elevations and contour lines, diameters of trees and tons of biomass, definitions and keys to species in a given manual, and procedures for measuring temperature and rainfall.

Significance   Significance describes how differences between measures of elements are meaningful for managerial decisions, for example, how the biological diversity of spiders (Figs. 4.6, 4.8, and 4.10) provides managers with information for fulfilling a policy.

Populations of hundreds of species of plants and animals in the Craggy Mountain Forested Landscape are thought to vary in relation to distributions of stands by forest type, age classes, and area classes. Each change in one or more of these elements, that is, in the state of organization of the landscape, enhances habitats for some animals and reduces habitats for other animals. There is no way of knowing a state of organization that provides an optimum combination of habitats for all organisms because we know not the number and kinds of organisms present. Because of this uncertainty, the mental model is to maintain a distribution of stands in all possible forest types, age classes, and area classes. This is accomplished by scheduling the harvesting of stands with superimposed rotations (Fig. 5.3), choosing sizes of canopy openings, and encouraging natural regeneration.

Management can enhance biological diversity for any selected species or guild of species that can be related to combinations of habitats to complete their life cycles. An example is the seedling guild of spiders. Managers can enhance the livelihood of a large number of seedling spiders by scheduling rates of timber harvest and sizes of canopy openings formed. As young stands grow older, new kinds of spiders enter stands and some kinds of spiders leave. These changes are apparently related to changes in species of plants, which change prey for spiders and change structure of stands to favor different guilds of spiders (Fig. 3.6). These kinds of changes in plant and animal populations together constitute *succession*. What is important is that a landscape organized with a variety of stands distributed across time and space by forest type, age, and area classes enhances biological diversity more than converting landscapes to forest reserves.

An argument for forest reserves says that organisms have evolved to survive in forested landscapes that are organized by natural events rather than in those systematically organized by humankind. This supposition may be found to be true for some number of organisms, yet inventories of ordered landscapes suggest that many kinds of organisms survive at very low population levels in forest reserves (Roughgarden et al. 1989; Pickett and White 1985). Organized changes in ages of stands provide benefits other than biological diversity for spiders. For example, timber is produced; habitats are provided for browsing animals, insects, birds, and rodents; and areas are available for hiking, bird watching, and hunting. The standard of living for humans, as well as for many plants and animals, would be greatly reduced by conversion of millions of hectares of forested landscapes to forest reserves in hopes that natural events would create dispersions of stands by type, age, and area classes to produce desired aesthetics, habitats, biological diversity, fuelwood, and timber (Sheffield and Thompson 1992; Lorimer and Frelich 1994).

SOURCES FOR MODELS

The argument in this book says that every management action is an option simulated with a mental model. We inherently design many mental models every day, and for each model we simulate options, choose a course of action, adjust the model as events unfold, and eventually discard the model. If we pause to analyze our actions, we find that most decisions are to control flows of energy and materials, which are core models, such as flows of land across age classes in a forested landscape (Figs. 5.1–5.3). From the time of our birth, we have been designing and using mental models.

The single most important source of information for mental models is memory of personal experiences. Personal experiences include reading a scientific paper, attending an athletic event, visiting forested landscapes, and exchanging ideas with colleagues. Information for designing and constructing managerial models is everywhere. The problem is to sort and select those bits of information that can contribute to the kinds of models we need in order to help us make decisions congruent with the real world.

Journals, textbooks, and reports are primary sources of information from which white boxes are constructed. Rarely do we find a complete data set for a core model or a white box. Yield tables (Schnur 1937; McClure and Knight 1984) and regression equations (Clutter et al. 1983; Buongiorno and Gilless 1987; Buford 1991) are sources that often have to be extended or modified to fit a specific landscape. There are gaps and deficiencies in every data set. These gaps are filled by synthesis and integration of many bits of information from many sources. White boxes are examples of synthesizing mental models to fill gaps in information (Figs. 5.4–5.6). Mental models synthesize bits of information into a coherent perception of future events as affected by different courses of action (Armstrong 1985; Norman 1981).

Norse (1990, page 109) displays a white box for the effects of logging on salmon and trout biomass. I use Norse's white box to add an index for the biomass of fish and to extend the time since logging from 120 to 200 years (Fig. 7.3).

The version displayed by Norse (1990) begins as an ancient forest in the Pacific Northwest. His mental model assumes the forest is harvested at time 0. Trees shading streams are removed. For the next 15 years, the biomass of fish in the exposed streams increases because increased solar energy and nutrients in the water increase the growth of algae, which is food for animals eaten by fish. After about 15 years, the growth of new trees and shrubs shades the streams. Flows of nutrients and organic matter into streams declines. Food production decreases and the biomass of fish declines. The period for rapid growth of young stands closes canopies and keeps penetration of solar energy to the water at very low values (Fig. 7.3). Norse assumes this period of closed canopies lasts for 120 years after the harvest of an ancient forest.

I have extended Norse's white box to 200 years and assumed that increased rates of natural mortality after 135 years open the canopies and increase radiation to the streams. My mental model says that the biomass of fish increases to approach that of the ancient forest about 200 years after timber is harvested (Fig. 7.3).

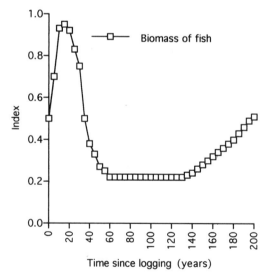

Figure 7.3   An example of a white box derived from suppositions expressed by others. This supposition is derived from a presentation by Sedell and Swanson (1984) as presented by Norse (1990). (Granted with permission from *Ancient Forests of the Pacific Northwest*, by E. A. Norse. Copyright 1990 by the Center for Resource Economics/Island Press. Published by Island Press, Washington, D.C. and Covelo, California.)

Norse (1990) suggests that salmon production can be increased by the manipulation of habitats in conjunction with timber operations. An insight obtained from the white box for fish biomass (Fig. 7.2) relates to changing the harvest of ancient forests from single to superimposed rotations. If a model, such as CRAG-3, is designed to direct the forest toward a state of organization that provides for all age classes to be represented in the landscape, then harvest rates for superimposed rotations should maintain a sustained yield of fish biomass at an index level well above that found in the ancient forests. The tradeoff for fish biomass is to delay the harvest of some amount of ancient forest until a desired state of organization is obtained.

Superimposed rotations could be used in the riparian zones to maintain a constantly changing sequence of deep shade and bright light on the streams. Stream temperatures and the growth of algae and other foods could be directed. Canopy openings would be kept relatively small along the streams. Superimposed rotations would perpetuate a continuum of age classes in the riparian zone from one year to the oldest ages (Fig.5.3). Fish biomass, biological diversity, and timber production would be kept well above minimum amounts by directing rates of timber harvest, sizes of canopy opening, and kinds of regeneration as given by the CRAG-3 model (Figs. 4.10, 4.12).

8

FUELWOOD, TIMBER, AND CASH FLOW

More than half of all wood harvested in the world is used for fuel (FAO 1993). As populations increase, more and more wood is demanded for fuel, paper, construction, furniture, and many other products (Ulrich 1990). This chapter describes relationships for constructing supplementary models to simulate flows of fuelwood and timber.

TRADEOFFS BETWEEN WOOD AND OTHER VALUES

Forest reserves trade fuelwood and timber for values produced when natural mortality organizes forested landscapes. Traditional forestry produces the largest sustained volumes of fuelwood and timber. Aesthetics, habitats, and biological diversity are traded for harvested wood. Landscape forestry provides an opportunity to adjust tradeoffs between harvested wood and other values. Timber harvests are limited in landscape forestry by requirements for conserving habitats in age classes older than stand ages that produce optimal flows of fuelwood, timber, and cash. Superimposed rotations help to maintain positive cash flows while providing old habitats for some kinds of plants and animals (Figs 4.10, 4.12). Since timber is the primary source of income for forest operations, including those to conserve aesthetic values and biological diversity, supplementary models for growth and yield of wood are important for managerial decisions.

WHITE BOXES FOR GROWTH AND YIELD

Estimates of future growth and yields of all forest benefits, including fuel-wood and timber, are uncertain because variables such as weather, stand density, browsing animals, diseases, soil nutrients, and fire effects are difficult to predict (Armstrong 1985; Buongiorno and Gilless 1987; Avery and Burkhart 1983; Clutter et al. 1983). Standards for measuring standing timber and timber products are variable (Wenger 1984), and processing methods determine yields (Koch 1984).

Accumulations of wood in boles of trees are estimated from measurements of dbh and height (Avery and Burkhart 1983). Growths are estimates of differences between measured accumulations for a specified interval of time. Each increment of growth moves trees through a sequence of size classes that cannot be bypassed or reversed. This irreversible direction of change is a basis for simulating future volumes and weights (Boyce 1975b). Many different units of measure are used (Munns et al. 1949; Everard 1971). Measures for this illustration are limited to thousands of board feet per hectare and biomass of merchantable wood per hectare.

Mental models say multiple regressions of data from different stands, distributed over a range of ages, indicate future growth and yield of single stands that have characteristics similar to the measured stands. This mental model is considered acceptable because data from a few single stands, measured periodically for a few decades, support the model (Beck 1978; Della-Bianca 1983). Confidence in this mental model is strengthened by findings that curves derived 50–60 years apart by different methods and people have similar waveforms and acceptable values (Lohrey 1987; Schnur 1937; McClure and Knight 1984). Acceptance of this mental model results in growth and yield tables being constructed from the measurements of many stands that are classified by a set of suppositions as similar. Results are white boxes in which gaps in data are filled in using a set of mathematical rules called multiple regression.

For the Craggy Mountain Forested Landscape, white boxes are designed from empirical yield tables published by McClure and Knight (1984) and Schnur (1937). Published data do not extend beyond 100 years. Unpublished information for a 300-year-old stand and from personal measurements of a few stands older than 100 years contributes to my mental model for extending white boxes to 300 years (Table 8.1). Numbers in column 1 are ages at 10-year intervals. Numbers in column 2 are suppositions about yields in thousands of board feet per hectare (MBF/ha). Board feet are defined by the International ¼-inch log rule. Board feet are estimates for trees larger than about 28 cm dbh. Estimates include sawlog portions of boles from a stump about 30 cm high to a top diameter of about 23 cm outside of bark.

Column 3 gives yields divided by ages to estimate mean annual increments (MAI) in MBF/ha/year. MAI is used to indicate a harvest age thought to produce maximum yields over successive rotations. Age for culmination of

TABLE 8.1   Data for White Boxes to Estimate Yields and Mean Annual Increments (MAI) in Board Feet/ha (International Scale) and Mg/ha for Upland Hardwood Stands in the Craggy Mountain Forested Landscape. (Data Extended from Schnur 1937 and McClure and Knight 1984)

Age (years)	Board feet (MBF/ha)		Biomass (Mg/ha)	
	Yield	MAI	Yield	MAI
0	0.00	0.00	0.0	0.0
10	0.00	0.00	6.9	0.7
20	7.41	0.37	62.8	3.1
30	11.12	0.37	190.8	6.4
40	15.32	0.38	236.0	5.9
50	19.77	0.39	272.1	5.4
60	22.98	0.38	310.5	5.2
70	25.95	0.37	328.9	4.7
80	28.66	0.36	341.4	4.3
90	31.13	0.35	350.7	3.9
100	33.36	0.33	360.0	3.6
110	35.83	0.33	366.9	3.3
120	38.55	0.32	371.6	3.1
130	41.76	0.32	376.2	2.9
140	44.97	0.32	380.9	2.7
150	48.18	0.32	385.5	2.6
160	51.40	0.32	390.2	2.4
170	54.61	0.32	394.8	2.3
180	57.82	0.32	399.5	2.2
190	59.30	0.31	404.1	2.1
200	60.54	0.30	408.7	2.0
210	61.78	0.29	411.1	2.0
220	59.94	0.27	410.5	1.9
230	57.97	0.25	409.2	1.8
240	54.89	0.23	408.2	1.7
250	53.37	0.21	406.7	1.6
260	51.85	0.20	405.7	1.6
270	48.36	0.18	404.2	1.5
280	47.53	0.17	402.2	1.4
290	46.17	0.16	400.2	1.4
300	45.71	0.15	395.4	1.3

MAI varies with units of measure. Data from McClure and Knight (1984) indicate that the age for the culmination of MAI for board feet to be 50 years (Table 8.1), which is the age reported by Schnur (1937) about 50 years earlier. Maximum yields for successive rotations would occur with rotations of 50 years. However, trees 50 years old have smaller diameters and less value than trees 70–90 years of age.

Numbers in column 4 are suppositions about yields of biomass, which are estimated as green Mg/ha (metric tons per hectare) for all live trees larger than 12.7 cm dbh. Measurements include the bole to a 10-cm top outside of bark, excluding leaves, needles, buds, twigs, and lateral limbs that cannot be converted into merchantable products. Column 5 gives biomass yields divided by age to estimate MAI values for biomass. Age for culmination of MAI for biomass is 30 years. If managers are concerned with producing only biomass for fuelwood and fiber, rotations of 30 years would produce maximum yields for successive rotations.

Stumpage prices per thousand board feet (MBF) are estimated by me from many sources for the Craggy Mountain area in 1992. The estimates are intended to reflect relative increases in prices as stands increase in age (Table 8.2).

SUPPLEMENTARY MODELS FOR TIMBER

Since no timber is harvested from forest reserves, CRAG-1 does not include supplementary models to estimate flows of timber and receipts. CRAG-2 and CRAG-3 contain supplementary models designed to use information from core models to estimate yields of timber in board feet and receipts from sales

TABLE 8.2   Estimated Prices for Hardwood Sawtimber in the Craggy Mountain Area by Age Classes of Stands in 1992.

Age (years)	Price ($/MBF)	Age (years)	Price ($/MBF)	Age (years)	Price ($/MBF)
0	0	100	95	200	120
10	0	110	97	210	126
20	0	120	98	220	132
30	6	130	101	230	138
40	8	140	102	240	144
50	9	150	103	250	151
60	43	160	107	260	158
70	66	170	110	270	166
80	92	180	113	280	174
90	94	190	117	290	182

of these volumes. Volumes in board feet per hectare (Table 8.1) are multiplied by stumpage prices (Table 8.2) and by acres scheduled for harvest each year to simulate receipts from timber sales.

Regeneration costs for harvested areas are set at $74.13/ha for upland hardwoods and at $98.84/ha for cove and northern hardwoods. A continuing cost of $12.35/ha is estimated for all other management activities. Discount and reinvestment rates are set at 4 percent. These variables are used to simulate economic indices such as net present values (Figs. 4.6–4.12).

Rotations longer than about 90 years for hardwood forests in the Craggy Mountains do not increase tree values fast enough to compensate for declining growth rates. Board foot volumes decline after age 50 and biomass volumes decline after age 30 (Table 8.1). When values for MBF/ha and price/MBF are normalized and plotted, interactions between growth and price are observed to affect choice of rotation periods to maintain positive cash flows. For this illustration, plots are limited to 160 years since few changes occur after that age. The base for normalizing MBF/ha is 51.4 and for price/MBF is $107, both at age 160 (Fig. 8.1).

Values for timber are relatively low for the first 20 years of naturally regenerated upland hardwood stands. From 20 to 50 years of age, diameters of trees are small and the trees are more suitable for fuel and fiber than for furniture and other high-value products. Between 50 and 80 years of age, an increasing number of trees exceed 30 cm dbh (Schnur 1937; McClure and

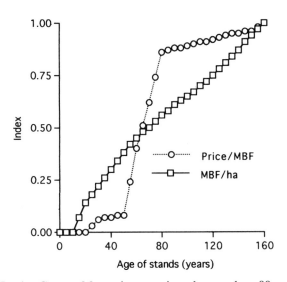

Figure 8.1 In the Craggy Mountains, rotations longer than 90 years for upland hardwood stands do not increase tree values fast enough to compensate for losses from discounting at rates larger than 2 percent.

Knight 1984). As dbh approaches 50 cm, wood quality increases rapidly in the outer layers of boles and prices increase rapidly (Carmean and Boyce 1973). After age 90, trees continue to increase in diameter, but stumpage prices rise slowly as long as trees in the 80- to 100-year age classes are available. Increases in prices for older trees do not offset increasingly large costs for capital invested in old-growth stands. This situation is a deterrent for managers to keep stands beyond ages for maximum monetary value.

Harvest ages that return maximum monetary values can be found with a model that examines the sensitivity of net present values to the cost of capital across a range of age classes. For this illustration, continuing costs per hectare and regeneration costs are assumed to be the same for traditional and landscape forestry. A supplementary model is designed to simulate present values of receipts for timber sales for an average hectare of forest (Fig. 8.2).

For every differential time interval, 4 times per simulated year, stumpage prices/MBF are multiplied by MBF/ha (Fig. 8.1) to calculate gross receipts. The gross receipts are calculated for every ¼ of a year for ages 0–160 years. Gross receipts are discounted at interest rates thought to represent an average cost of capital over the 160-year period. The discount divisor is the base *e* of natural logarithms raised to the product of the discount rate and time. This is continual discounting (Fleischer 1984). The discount is a constant that can be changed to examine the sensitivity of present values to different costs of capital (Fig. 8.3).

As the cost of capital increases, discounted present values peak at younger ages and at smaller amounts because of interactions between discount rates, stumpage prices, and volumes per hectare. For example, when the cost of capital is 8 percent, present values peak at stand age 60 for a peak value of $8.13/ha. When the cost of capital is 2 percent, discounted present values peak at 80 years of stand age for a peak value of $532.42/ha. Since peak

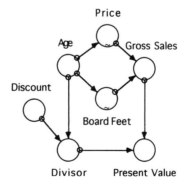

Figure 8.2   One structure of a number of supplementary models that can be attached to core models to simulate present values of receipts for timber sales for an average hectare of forest. The diagram is produced with STELLA II software.

values are different for different costs of capital, peak values are used to normalize present values and plot results in order to examine waveforms for different costs of capital (Fig. 8.3).

Plots provide insights about interactions between stumpage prices, growth rates, and costs of capital on rotation periods for traditional and landscape forestry. Curves displayed for this illustration (Fig. 8.3) reflect suppositions about prices and growth rates (Tables 8.1 and 8.2). However, waveforms are not as sensitive to changes in yields and prices as to costs of capital, which are the single most important factor guiding choice of rotation periods for economic values. The mental model says that a low cost for capital favors longer rotations, a higher quality of wood products, old-age habitats, enhanced aesthetic values, and conserved stream flows. This model is illustrated with the curve for a 2 percent cost of capital (Fig. 8.3). The mental model says that a high cost for capital, the curve for 8 percent discount, favors short rotations, a low quality of wood products, few old-age habitats, reduced aesthetic values, and increased peaking of stream flows.

The curve for the 8 percent discount rate contains two peaks. The first peak is at 30 years of stand age with a discounted peak value of $6.05/ha. This peak is based on growing pulpwood on a 30-year rotation. At age 60, prices for sawtimber begin to exceed pulpwood prices at a rate that moves discounted receipts to a peak of $8.13/ha at 60 years of age (Fig. 8.3). If the cost of capital is 2 percent, the economic advantage is to harvest all stands

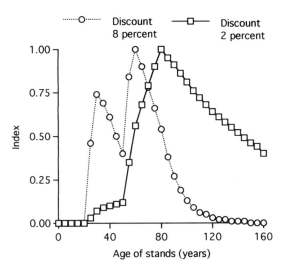

Figure 8.3   Discount rates of 8 percent in the Craggy Mountains encourage sales of pulpwood at 30 years of age rather than between ages 30 and 60. More profits are expected from sales between ages 60 and 80 years for sawlogs. Discount rates of 2 percent encourage sales of all products at longer rotations.

in the Craggy Mountain Forested Landscape at 80 years of age for sawtimber. As the cost of capital approaches 8 percent, the economic advantage is to harvest all stands between 60 and 80 years of age. If the cost of capital exceeds 8 percent, the economic advantage is to harvest all stands for fuel and fiber at 30 years of age.

COST OF LANDSCAPE FORESTRY

Landscape forestry is concerned with producing benefits that require two or more kinds of stands distributed over space and time. Aesthetic values, biological diversity, conserved stream flows, and habitats for some plants and animals are enhanced by organizing landscapes such that stands range from 0 years to old ages. These objectives cannot be accomplished without capital and cash flows to fulfill plans (Figs. 4.10, 4.12). If capital and cash flow must be generated from forested landscapes, landscape forestry is at a distinct disadvantage compared with traditional forestry. Cost of capital and long periods for discounting cash flows make conservation of old stands very expensive. Since markets rarely exist for aesthetics, habitats, or biological diversity, increased production of these benefits reduces cash flows.

When stands are conserved beyond ages for peak cash flows (Fig. 8.3), receipts from timber are not large enough to pay the costs of conserving biological diversity, aesthetic values, stream flows, and scenic views. Single rotations at ages to conserve old growth produce negative cash flows. However, superimposed rotations provide opportunities to maintain positive cash flows and simultaneously enhance biological diversity, habitats, and scenic values (Figs. 4.10, 4.12). An important consequence is tradeoffs in some fuelwood, timber, and cash for aesthetics, habitats, and biological diversity.

For forested landscapes held in public trust, such as the Craggy Mountains, costs for conserving old stands are paid from public taxes (Raines 1993; Egan 1993a; Ellefson 1993; Payne et al. 1992; Baumol and Oates 1989). For private landowners, costs for conserving old stands must be paid from revenues forgone (Fig. 8.3), public subsidies, foundations, trust, or other outside sources. However, there are many opportunities for investors to enhance biological diversity, habitats, and aesthetic values while making profits less than optimal (Fig. 4.10). Simulation models, such as CRAG-3, give managers insights and a basis for choosing a course of action when policies are to enhance aesthetics, habitats, and biological diversity and to maintain positive, not optimal, cash flows (Figs. 4.10, 4.12).

Capital for Landscape Forestry

Mental models using government subsidies to enhance forest benefits for public welfare have been known for more than 100 years (Conrad 1889; Fernow

1893; Baumol and Oates 1989). Subsidies to private landowners from many levels of government are known to make important contributions to reforestation of retired farmlands, production of timber and wildlife habitats, enhanced biological diversity, improved quality of water, and scenic values (USDA 1983, 1993; Douglas 1983). Accountability for receiving subsidies is directed toward measurable achievements, such as areas of land planted to trees and areas of stands treated with sets of specifications. Biological diversity, old-growth stands, and aesthetic landscapes are enhanced incident to reforestation and cultural activities. If desired, public subsidization of landscape forestry practices can be implemented with the use of superimposed rotations.

Reduced Cost of Capital as a Subsidy

The single most important subsidy for stimulating conservation of old stands, biological diversity, and aesthetic values is to provide capital at rates of 1–2 percent for private investments in superimposed rotations (Fig. 8.3). The intent is to increase the production of benefits that require two or more stands distributed over time and space. Without low-cost capital, private landowners are forced to sell stands near the age for optimum cash flow. As costs for capital decline below market values, landowners have an economic incentive to shift from traditional to landscape forestry. The cost of capital to landowners could be made available in proportion to the ratio of forestlands harvested at the age for maximum cash flow to the lands harvested at old ages. The public would be paying landowners to use landscape forestry. Superimposed rotations would conserve stands to older ages and enhance biological diversity, habitats, scenic values, high-quality logs, and cash flow (Fig. 8.3).

Low-cost capital is a way to compensate private landowners for cash flows foregone (Fig. 4.10) and to maintain portions of their landscape in stands beyond ages for optimal cash flow. Management plans would contain two superimposed rotations (Fig. 5.3). A portion of the landscape would be harvested at ages for optimal cash flows; another portion with longer rotations. Amounts of low-cost capital made available to a landowner would be related to amounts of biomass retained in stands older than a specified age and distributed over time and space. Biomass estimates would be based on measures of trees 12 cm dbh and larger. Benefits to landowners would be higher net present values that would result from paying market prices for capital. Differences in discount divisors and present values for interest rates of 2 and 8 percent applied to stand values per hectare for an average stand in the Craggy Mountains emphasize advantages to landowners when the market price for capital is 8 percent and the subsidized price is 2 percent (Table 8.3).

Costs of capital as large as 8 percent produce discount divisors many times larger than discount rates of 2 percent. Present values for gross receipts for a rotation of 160 years are about \$224 for a 2 percent cost of capital and only $0.02 for 8 percent. Without low-cost capital, private landowners are forced to market their timber at short rotations with many adverse consequences for biological diversity, habitats, and aesthetic values (Figs. 4.8, 8.3).

If 70 percent of a typical forest ownership in the Southern Appalachians is rotated through 80 years, and 30 percent is rotated through 160 years, positive cash flows and enhanced landscape values are expected (Fig. 4.10). Cash flows would not be optimal (Fig. 8.3), but for landowners, present values would be considerably higher, about $439.65/ha [(0.7 * $532.42) + (0.3 * 223.18)] compared with $8.13/ha at a capital cost of 8 percent for all the forest in 60-year rotations (Table 8.3).

There are many pressures on landowners to ignore a program that provides low-cost capital to the landowner in return for the landowner providing society with values not readily produced at market values for capital. The biggest deterrent is the long time, 100 years and more, required for organizing forested landscapes to produce desired combinations of aesthetics, habitats, and biological diversity. The size of ownerships could be relatively small, 20 ha and more, as long as adjacent ownerships participated in the program. A variety of stands dispersed over a landscape by type, age, and area classes would result. Expected benefits could include large trees harvested at old ages for high-value wood products; enhanced biological diversity; diversity of light, shadows, and colors in scenic views; a variety of habitats for many kinds of plants and animals; low-cost capital loans repaid to governments; and increased cash flows and jobs in forested areas.

CASH FLOW

Cash flow refers to outflows and inflows of money for management. Flows of cash are important because money is used by managers to change states

TABLE 8.3   Relation of Gross Receipts, Discount Divisors, and Present Values for an Average Stand Discounted to Age 0 at Cost-of-Capital Rates of 2 and 8 Percent. Values are for Selected Stand Ages.

Stand age (years)	Gross receipts (dollars)	Discount Divisors (dimensionless)		Present Values (dollars)	
		2 percent	8 percent	2 percent	8 percent
30	66.72	1.82	11.02	36.62	6.05
60	988.18	3.32	121.51	297.63	8.13
80	2,637.09	4.95	601.85	532.42	4.38
100	3,169.11	7.39	2,980.96	428.89	1.06
120	3,777.70	11.02	14,764.78	342.71	0.26
140	4,587.25	16.44	73,130.44	278.95	0.06
160	5,499.59	24.53	362,217.45	224.18	0.02

of organization of forested landscapes and thereby change productions of benefits. Outflows are payments for labor, services, materials, taxes, and other services and goods. Outflows must be replenished by inflows from sales of benefits, gifts, appropriations from taxes, or other sources. Positive cash flows are desired.

Investments in forested landscapes are different from investments in many businesses, such as a grocery store. In a grocery store, the costs and sales of each item are entities accounted for independently of the costs and sales of other items; a change in prices for milk does not change prices for apples. A change in the state of organization of shelves in a grocery does not change the availability of benefits or the cost of the benefits; grocery items can be arrayed in terms of their profitability, and the inventory can be distributed to optimize profits and present values in a specific market. The cost of a basket of goods in a grocery is the sum of the cost for each item; removal of any one item from the basket reduces the cost by the value of that item. Production of a basket of benefits in a grocery is discrete; a basket of goods is filled item by item. Management of a grocery does not involve changing states of organization of the store to produce baskets of benefits in the aggregate.

In contrast to a grocery, forested landscapes produce baskets of benefits in the aggregate and not in discrete units. Baskets of benefits from a forested landscape are produced by changing states of organization of the landscape and cannot be produced discretely. Any change in states of organization of stands in a forested landscape changes the availability of benefits and cost of the benefits in the aggregate. There is no way to allocate any costs for management to individual benefits, such as a habitat, a scenic value, or a volume of timber. Productions, costs, and sales of the baskets of benefits are all in the aggregate. There is no way to develop a matrix of production functions because items change in the aggregate as any cultural practice is implemented to change one item. For example, the cost for construction of a road may be allocated to the cost of harvesting timber, but long-term returns on the road may come from leases for hunting rights, camping, hiking, fishing, fire protection, and other values. The road increases travel lanes for animals, increases food along the roadside for animals, and causes other consequences, some desirable and some undesirable. Investments in landscape forestry are evaluated in the aggregate rather than in separate parts.

The analytic procedures in this book evaluate aggregate costs in relation to aggregate consequences. Simulations use the math of finance equations to simulate economic indicators over time and produce curved outcomes in relation to a course of action (Figs. 4.6–4.12). Conventional finance equations are described by Fleischer (1984), Gunter and Haney (1984), Clark et al. (1979), and Baumol and Oates (1989). Simulations of cash flow, in terms of net present values, profitability index, realizable rates of return, internal rates of return, and equivalent annual rents are elements in aggregated baskets of benefits. A change in states of organization of forested landscapes changes the cash flows, aesthetic values, biological diversity, timber, and other benefits as an aggregated basket. Evaluation of the benefits from a forested landscape is as an aggregated basket produced by changing states of organization and not as discrete items added to a grocery cart.

Model NPV

The assumption for the net-present-value model (NPV) is that intermediate cash inflows are reinvested at interest rates different from the cost of capital. Investments of intermediate cash flows are usually at rates less than the cost of capital. The simulation method is to accumulate the intermediate inflows of cash at assumed reinvestment rates and discount the accumulated inflows at the interest rate equal to the cost of capital. The difference between accumulated, discounted inflows, and outflows at each differential time (DT) interval provides a curve of net present values over time (Figs. 4.6–4.10). In addition to net present values, other economic indicators, such as the benefit/cost ratio, the equivalent annual rent, and internal rates of return, can be simulated over time. In this book, only net present value is used.

Calculations of net present values are normalized and plotted on a scale of 0 to 1. Changes in net present values are comparable with other items that are plotted as normalized values. An alternative is to plot cash flows in monetary values and other benefits in normalized scale. Either way, the significance of the method is to give managers a basis for choosing a course of action that produces the most acceptable basket of consequences (Figs. 4.6–4.12).

9

PRINCIPLES AND THEOREMS

PRINCIPLES

Principles state observations as procedures that others can repeat in order to experience the observation. Principles are accepted as valid relationships after many people repeat procedures and make the same observations. Principles are used to structure mental models and to frame theorems that give us confidence in decisions. Three principles and four theorems help us design mental models to direct forested landscapes for many different baskets of benefits.

Principle of Continuity

The principle of continuity says that biological systems cannot pass from one state to another without passing through all intermediate states that are subject to the same processes of change. A chicken egg develops step by step. There is no way people can restore a broken egg, a harvested tree, a strip-mined area, or a harvested cornfield to its original state. Each state of organization develops step by step in relation to past environments that are never repeated. The presence of one or more organisms makes a system dynamic. An oak tree grows, step by step, from an acorn into a large tree. As oak trees age, physical variables and habitats near the trees change. As these changes occur, different organisms find a livelihood near, on, or in oak trees of different ages. Communities of ogranisms around a 100-year-old tree are brought about by continual change from the past. There is no way to direct a community around a 2-year-old oak to become a community around a 100-year-old oak without passing through all the intermediate stages. A forested landscape develops, step by step, from one to another state of organization.

Forested landscapes do not randomly jump from state to state. Each succeeding state is dependent on preceding states. A stand of old trees must pass through seedling, sapling, small tree, large tree, and other intermediate states. Simulation models are based on the principle of continuity. On the basis of this principle, stands in a forested landscape are expected to change, state by state, through a sequence of events that can be simulated over time. These kinds of changes are sometimes called ecological succession, growth, or transformations. For managers of forested landscapes, the principle of continuity is important for developing suppositions about future events.

Principle of Irreversibility

The principle of irreversibility says that forested landscapes pass through irreversible states of organization, step by step, never to be repeated. Stated another way, this principle says that all future states of biological systems are different from all past states, although some future states may superficially appear to be like past states.

Fragmented chicken eggs represent an irreversible state of organization. Chicken eggs cannot be preserved in the state of organization found at the time the egg is laid by a hen. Being placed on a shelf, freeze-dried, or kept in a refrigerator does not keep eggs in the original state. The new states are irreversible. A rotten egg cannot be restored to a fresh egg. Strip-mined lands cannot be restored to an assumed original state.

Change from one to another state of organization is irreversible for eggs, trees, and forested landscapes. Extinct forms of life are not known to reappear on earth. People do not change from adults to children. Respiration is not the reverse of photosynthesis. Regeneration of a forest is not the reverse of harvesting.

Natural changes in forested landscapes change biological systems state by state into states that never before occurred on earth. Natural mortality and harvest of trees form canopy openings that irreversibly change forested landscapes to states of organization that never before occurred. Consumption of plants and animals by predators and humans irreversibly changes states of organization.

The principles of continuity and irreversibility explain why ecological succession is irreversible and never exactly repeated; why strip-mined lands are changed to desired states, not restored to original states; why wilderness cannot be preserved as first observed; why forested landscapes cannot be kept in one constant state of organization; and why an observed state of biological diversity cannot be preserved. Procedures for the conservation and preservation of biological systems must function within the principles of continuity and irreversibility. Natural events and management direct the replacement of individuals and populations with combinations of genotypes derived from, but different from, preceding individuals and populations.

Principle of Structure

The principle of structure says that configurations and linkages of parts of a system form structures that determine flows of information, energy, and materials and thus the dynamics of systems.

Structure is the way parts are linked. Structure determines flows of information, energy, and materials through biological systems. Flows of energy and materials determine the dynamics and behavior of biological systems. The structure of organisms determines whether essential variables are kept within the limits of life (Ashby 1973).

Structure is the configuration of elements, parts, and constituents to create form in a system. The structure of buildings such as homes, schools, barns, and manufacturing plants is related to how those buildings are used. Structure determines the values people place on works of art, pieces of furniture, and clothing. Structure determines the performance of an athlete, a musician, or a surgeon.

Natural mortality and the harvest of trees change the structure of stands and thus the dynamics of a stand. Death of a sunlit tree changes reception of radiation and flows of organic compounds to soil, animals, and forest floor. Natural events and the harvest of trees shift the formation of organic compounds from a few individuals and species with high canopies to many species and individuals of seedlings and herbaceous plants on the forest floor (Figs. 2.1–2.4). These changes in structure alter the flows of carbon compounds to soils, the transfer of water and nutrients from one group of species to another, the flows of droppings from worms feeding on high-canopy leaves to worms feeding on low-canopy leaves. Predator and prey relationships are changed. These are some of the ways natural events and scheduled harvests of trees change states of organization of forested landscapes.

Structure in a forested landscape determines aesthetics, habitats, biological diversity, and the availability of timber and fuelwood. States of organization of forested landscapes are determined by dynamic structures, called stands, distributed in time and space.

Validity of the Principles

Personal experiences and observations provide evidence for recognizing these three principles as beliefs each of us use in our day-to-day activities. We may not state the relationships as principles or carry the statements with us for reference, yet the relationships are deeply embedded in our mental models of how the world works. Our actions confirm our acceptance of the validity of the principles.

These three principles are the basis for culturing animals for food, skins, and pets; for weeding and organizing vegetable and flower gardens; for culturing a potted plant in a kitchen window; and for directing states of organization of forested landscapes. Continuity, irreversibility, and structure are used to formulate four theorems.

THEOREMS

Theorems are statements of beliefs we have formulated by interrelating a number of principles. A theorem may never be observed directly since each is constructed mentally from principles. Theorems help us limit confusion when designing mental models and when many variables are changing simultaneously. Theorems may be viewed as foundations on which we construct mental models, simulate consequences, and choose courses of action. Four theorems provide the foundation for models in landscape forestry.

Theorem 1. Individualistic Systems

The statement for Theorem 1 is:

> Each living organism and its environment form an individualistic system with the goal of survival and the dynamics of systems with negative feedback loops.

Negative feedback loops act to maintain the structure of an organism within the limits of life. A system of negative feedback loops directs changes in structure, and thus in dynamics, as uncertain events unfold. Each loop responds to an immediate state of the system (Fig. 3.1). Change in structure of one or more loops adapts organisms to immediate events just like a tinkerer, who does not know exactly the consequences of an action (Jacob 1977). Continuity, from organisms that survived some period of time, carries loops and structures for survival into succeeding generations. Failure of one or more loops to maintain one or more essential variables within the limits of life brings death to biological systems (Ashby 1973, Jacob 1977).

The highest level of organization that can control the destiny of itself in uncertain environments is the individualistic system. Every organism is a self-organizing system, which can direct flows of energy and materials that are captured from mass flows in the environment. Self-organization is directed by decision-making mechanisms in each negative feedback loop (Fig. 3.1) that is linked through an information network to sensors and a goal. Negative feedback loops alter states of organization of the organism in response to immediate information about the state of the system. A mouse self-organizes itself as negative feedback loops in the central nervous system and in the muscle system change states of organization in attempts to escape the claws of a predator. Since the mouse does not know exactly the consequences of an action, response to signals about states of organization of mouse and predator may bring survival or death to the mouse.

Individualistic systems change from state to state by the dynamics of negative feedback loops and are not simply molded by external forces of the environment. Individualistic systems react to uncertain environmental changes in attempts to survive or to achieve other goals. The goal of survival is described by Slobodkin (1975) as "permitting the organism to continue in the game." The analogy is to the gambler's "ruin game" in which the payoff is to continue in the game as long as possible. Each player self-organizes in relation to the states of organization of other players. Expulsion from the game occurs when individuals fail to keep essential variables within the rules of the game. In forested landscapes, "expulsion" (death) occurs when individuals fail to maintain some essential variable within the limits of life. Theorem 1 is a very much condensed restatement of the model of organisms developed by biologists over many years (Becht 1974; Gleason 1939; Machin 1964; Tansley 1935; Jacob 1977; Murdy 1975).

Forested landscapes, stands, and communities are composed of individualistic systems, each functioning in relation to its own negative feedback systems and its own uncertain environment. Each individualistic system self-organizes in relation to environmental changes and within limits set by past events and genetic codes. Individuals self-organize in response to information about solar energy, water, nutrients, food, shelter, and other kinds of energy and materials. Self-organization by individuals that capture the most solar radiation, water, space, or nutrients may keep organisms from maintaining essential variables within the limits of life. Mortality changes states of organization of stands and changes the distribution of stands by forest type, age, and area classes. For example, many small trees, seedlings and other plants die in the understory of sunlit canopies (Figs. 3.4, 3.6). There is no evidence that sunlit canopies are directed to expand or contract by a central decision-making mechanism to eliminate or favor understory species (Fig. 3.6). Without human intervention, formations of canopy openings are related to aimless, unpredictable mass flows of energy and materials across landscapes (Scheffield and Thompson 1992; Lorimer and Frelich 1994). These aimless biological systems are changed to directed systems for productions of desired benefits through the use of negative feedback loops (Fig. 3.1).

The theorem of individualistic systems is falsified by discovery that any individualistic system's existence is for the exclusive achievement of a community goal; that a stand or community has a central negative feedback loop (Fig. 3.1) that directs behavior of individuals toward a goal for natural forested landscapes. Proof of the null hypothesis requires evidence for a centralized decision-making mechanism, for sensing mechanisms, and for communication channels to control the behavior of each individual as uncertain events unfold.

Theorem 2. Community Organization

The statement for Theorem 2 is:

> The irreversibility of biological processes results in the mortality of individualistic systems and organizes survivors into aimless communities.

Communities, forested landscapes, and stands are not known to have decision-making mechanisms linked to sensors and an information network to control or direct flows of resources to benefit or suppress species (Engelberg and Boyarsky 1979). Mass flows of energy and materials may elicit similar responses from many individualistic systems, but these responses result from the dynamics of individualistic systems and not from centralized controls of the community.

Forested landscapes, communities, and stands consist of individualistic systems joined without central decision-making mechanisms, sensors, and information networks. Communities and stands are aimless and unstable because biological processes are irreversible. In the absence of a reversible procedure, negative feedback loops cannot bring life to a dead tree. The capture of limited resources, such as water and prey, by some individuals may bring death to others. Those who fail to capture enough resources to maintain essential variables within the limits of life perish. Mortality of individualistic systems for whatever reason releases resources such as space, light, water, and nutrients for use by other individuals and changes states of organization of the system.

Forested landscapes, stands, and communities cannot self-organize to achieve a goal of survival, structure, species composition, or kinds of regeneration. Populations that maintain essential variables within the limits of life grow exponentially until some force external to the population slows growth or eliminates the population. The dynamics are those of positive feedback systems (Fig. 3.2). There is no way communities can direct members to reduce rates of consumption relative to regeneration and the availability of resources. Forested landscapes, stands, and communities expand to consume resources, such as space, solar radiation, water, and nutrients, to the limits without any inherent systems to evaluate consequences. Natural, unmanaged communities, stands, and forested landscapes are aimless.

Theorem 2 is the basis for management to convert aimless forested landscapes to directed systems: systems ordered to enhance the potential livelihood of one or more endangered species; to reduce the populations of undesirable species; and to increase wildlife habitats, stream flows, recreation opportunities, and timber production.

Theorem 2 is falsified by discovery of an information network that links a centralized decision-making mechanism in natural communities. Such a network is required to sense states of community organization, make decisions, and direct behavior and mortality of individuals to achieve community goals.

Theorem 3. Flows of Energy and Materials

The statement for Theorem 3 is:

> Flows of energy and materials are unidirectional and have the dynamics of systems with positive feedback loops.

Forested landscapes are dependent on mass flows of solar energy, water, nutrients, carbon dioxide, oxygen, and other materials. Kinds, amounts, and sizes of organisms in a forested landscape are dependent on kinds and amounts of mass flows and the ability of organisms to capture energy and materials from mass flows. Organisms capture relatively small fractions, possibly less than 2 percent, of mass flows and delay these small fractions for relatively short periods of 1–50 years. Longer delays may occur for very small fractions of mass flows in some trees, soil, organic matter, charcoal, peat, coal, and petroleum. But eventually, all of the energy and materials are released. Energy is dissipated to the universe and materials are released to the biosphere.

Solar energy passes through forested landscapes and escapes to the universe as heat, never to return. Every day, hundreds of kilograms of material enter the earth's atmosphere and fall to the surface as tiny grains and fine dust. Nutrients in this material add to mass flows through forested landscapes. Escape of materials, other than energy, to the universe is not recorded (Gaffey 1993). Accumulations of organic matter, in various forms, provide measures of organic production in units such as biomass, timber volumes, pulpwood volumes, and heights of trees (Mengel and Tew 1991).

Natural mortality and harvest of trees increase mass flow rates of energy and materials, such as water, nutrients, and clay particles. Decay of dead organic matter and increased rates of mortality or removals of organic matter increase mass flows of energy and materials. Various forms of disturbance such as storms, insects, diseases, fire, and harvest increase mortality rates. The result is to speed natural aimless change in states of organization of forested landscapes. There are no negative feedback loops in forested landscapes to conserve or direct mass flows to achieve certain states of organization. All forested landscapes are in nonequilibrium states. New states never repeat past states because the dynamics of nonequilibrium states are those of positive feedback loops and not that of negative feedback (D. M. Smith 1977, 1986; Boyce 1985; Vitousek and Reiners 1975).

Theorem 3 is falsified by discovery of negative feedback systems, sensors, and decision-making mechanisms that regulate flows of energy and materials through communities relative to a community goal.

Theorem 4. Baskets of Benefits

The statement for Theorem 4 is:

States of organization of forested landscapes determine productions of goods, services, and effects.

States of organization change over time as individualistic systems strive to keep essential variables within the limits of life and as mortality changes flows of captured energy and materials. An increase in the variety and quality of benefits results only from increasing the variety of stands classified by forest type, age, and area class. By directing the distribution of stands by forest type, age, and area classes, managers enhance aesthetics, habitats, timber, fuelwood, cash flows, and biological diversity.

Between the one extreme state of a single kind of stand and the other extreme of many kinds of stands, managers choose states of organization to provide acceptable baskets of goods, services, and effects. Because of the principle of continuity, states of organization of forests are moved toward desired states, step by step, over time and space. The principle of irreversibility requires constant management to keep the state of organization oscillating around the desired state.

Theorem 4 is falsified by discovery that all potential benefits are simultaneously available from a landscape composed of stands of the same forest type, age, and area classes.

CONTROLS

The purpose for organizing forested landscapes is to bring about states of organization that provide human populations with opportunities to use desired forms of goods, services, and effects. As benefits are consumed, energy and materials are discarded. For example, heat is discarded and dissipated to the universe when wood is burned to cook a meal. New meals require more solar energy from wood. Continual diversions of solar energy to satisfy consumer demands is achieved by directing forested landscapes with managerial controls.

Complex systems, such as forested landscapes, cannot be effectively directed if managers must simultaneously adjust large numbers of variables, such as habitats for each kind of plant and animal. Effective management depends on using a few primary controls to alter large numbers of variables in the managed system. For an automobile, the primary controls are the steering wheel, brakes, gear shift, and accelerator. Drivers learn to change two or three of these controls simultaneously to direct the complex systems that are designed into automobiles.

Fortunately, the principles and theorems described here reduce the management of forested landscapes to three primary controls. The single most important control is to schedule rates of harvesting stands of trees. The second control is to schedule sizes of canopy openings formed by harvesting trees. The third control is to encourage kinds and numbers of desired plants in canopy openings. All other cultural practices, such as maintaining certain distances between canopy openings, adding fertilizer, introducing genetically altered organisms, weeding, controlling stand density, controlling insects and diseases, harvesting game animals, and pruning trees and shrubs are enhancements to primary controls.

Rates of Harvest of Stands

From principles and theorems, desired baskets of goods, services, and effects are produced in relation to the way stands, classified by forest type, age, and area class, are distributed over time and space in a forested landscape. Since any desired state of organization is in a nonequilibrium condition and is irreversibly changing from state to state, harvest schedules must continually pressure the system toward a desired state. Harvests must distribute stands across the landscape by type, age, and area classes to support the livelihood of organisms that provide desired baskets of benefits. Baskets of benefits may include wilderness effects, aesthetic values, timber production, biological diversity, water quality, habitats of endangered species, and many other values.

Rowe (1991) makes the point that there is no substitute for any patch of the earth's surface. This observation makes replication of experimental areas difficult and limits our ability to transfer experimental results from one place to another. In forested landscapes, there is no way to locate experimental plots to include a number of large, sunlit trees without making the plots so large as to include considerable variability in soils, solar radiation, rainfall, water flow, temperature, understory plants, animals, and other variables. As plot size increases, variability increases for species and physical elements. Results from one experimental area may not apply to any other area. This situation means that the consequences of experimental observations must be considerably greater than natural variability in order to be important to managers. White boxes provide managers with a tool for interrelating results from many experimental studies and developing a generalized model to guide decisions (Figs. 5.4–5.6, 7.1–7.3).

Sizes of Canopy Openings

Sizes of canopy openings in forested landscapes influence mass flows of energy and materials and the responses of organisms to these flows. If a canopy opening is minimum—that is, equal to the area of the crown of a single sunlit tree—mass flows of solar radiation through the opening will be different than if canopy openings are several hectares in size. The area of canopy openings formed by mortality and harvest of stands is a second important control for managers (Figs. 2.1–2.4).

Traditional forestry is concerned with the area of canopy openings in relation to kinds and quality of trees regenerated (Burns and Honkala 1990) and the economics of harvesting trees. In addition to these interests, landscape forestry is concerned with areas of canopy openings in relation to the establishment of all kinds of plants, habitats for plants and animals, mass flows of energy and materials, and the availability of many kinds of benefits.

Regeneration of Canopy Openings

Kinds and numbers of plants occupying canopy openings determine the kinds of trees that will dominate future stands. Managers have limited ways to influence natural regeneration of plants in canopy openings. Artificial regeneration may be expensive and may require killing and suppressing existing plants. Landscape forestry encourages natural regeneration in canopy openings unless artificial regeneration is required to fulfill policy (Figs. 3.4, 3.6).

10

LANDSCAPE FORESTRY AND CARBON

Carbon and solar energy are stored in tree boles primarily as cellulose, a family of compounds consisting of carbon, hydrogen, and oxygen. These compounds are made from water and carbon dioxide in the green tissues of sunlit canopies. The significance of this situation is that boles of wood in forested landscapes are packages of carbon removed from the atmosphere and are one of the most accessible sources of stored solar energy (Fig. 2.6). Trees are readily harvested, transported, burned as fuel, and manufactured into a variety of chemical and physical products to support human society. More than half of all wood harvested in the world is used as fuel (FAO 1993).

States of organization of forested landscapes determine rates of collection of carbon and solar energy. This chapter examines the effects of three policies—forest reserves, traditional forestry, and landscape forestry (Chapter 3)—on accumulations of carbon for fuel and for other products. Direct measurements are not made of solar energy. However, amounts of carbon, calculated from weights and volumes of wood, provide an indirect measure of solar energy.

FLOWS OF CARBON

Large amounts of carbon are trapped by photosynthesis in sunlit canopies of forested landscapes. Small amounts are trapped in understory plants (Fig. 2.6). Solar energy is trapped as photosynthesis combines water and carbon dioxide to form carbon compounds that contribute to food, habitats, aesthetic values, biological diversity, and shelter for humans and many kinds of plants and animals. Carbon is transported from sunlit canopies to form parts of trees,

157

such as limbs, boles, and roots. Some carbon is oxidized in respiration and some is used by animals, fungi, bacteris, and humans. Some carbon accumulates on forest floors as herbaceous plants, shrubs, dead leaves, fruits, flowers, bark, animal droppings, and fallen trees. Average amounts of carbon stored in forests in the continental United States is about 177 Mg/ha. Soils retain more than half of all carbon stored in forested landscapes (Table 10.1).

Boles of living trees, which contain about 15.5 percent of all carbon in a landscape, are harvested and used by humans in many ways. In managed forests, tree harvests serve a dual purpose. First, harvested boles are raw materials for fuel and many products. Second, canopy openings formed by harvest of trees are the most important way to organize forested landscapes for aesthetics, habitats, timber, fuelwood, and biological diversity. The managerial issue is to order forested landscapes for capture and use of desired forms of carbon and solar energy.

Net accumulations of carbon in forests of the continental United States in live and dead trees is about 461 million Mg/year, while removals to clear land and produce fuel and timber are about 355 million Mg/year. Forests in the continental United States, in 1990, accumulated carbon at the net rate of about 106 million Mg/year. For the continental United States, carbon in boles are estimated to contain about 8.16 billion Mg of carbon. (Birdsey 1992; Post et al. 1990; Harmon et al. 1990; Schobert 1990).

Changes in the storage of carbon and solar energy are difficult to estimate for the world. Thousands of acres of forests are cleared every year for agriculture, highways, airports, lakes, and urban developments. Thousands of acres of land in agriculture and in urban areas are planted to trees every year. Millions of acres of forests are harvested every year and naturally and artificially regenerated. Millions of acres of trees are killed by fires, storms, insects, and diseases. On a world scale, there are no good estimates of how

TABLE 10.1   Percent of Carbon by Weight Stored in an Average Hectare of Forested Landscape and In Parts of Trees in the Continental United States. (Adapted from Birdsey, 1992)

	(Percent of Total Weight)	
Component	Stand	Trees
Soil	58.7	
Trees	30.6	
Boles		15.5
Roots		5.1
Foliage		0.7
Other parts		9.3
Forest floor	9.2	
Understory	1.5	
Totals	100.0	30.6

much carbon flows through trees, is stored in trees, and is consumed by humans.

Possibly the most reliable world figures are those published by the Food and Agriculture Organization (FAO) for cubic volumes of wood harvested and consumed for major uses (FAO 1993). Volumes of wood harvested and used for the years 1969 through 1991 provide relative estimates of amounts of carbon harvested from the world's forest and amounts used for major purposes. The harvest of carbon from the world's forested landscapes now exceeds 1 billion Mg/year (Table 10.2).

The data in the "Total Harvested Carbon" column are from the table for roundwood in thousands of cubic meters without bark (FAO 1993); an average cubic meter of roundwood is assumed to contain 0.2941 Mg of carbon. Percentages for fuelwood include all species and the roundwood equivalent of charcoal. Percentages for sawlogs and veneer logs are from the table that includes all species. The "Pulpwood/Particles" data are from the table that includes pulpwood, chips, particles, and wood residues. Data for other industrial roundwood are from the table that includes wood of all species used for many kinds of items such as poles, posts, blocks, tanning, piling, and pit props.

More than half of all carbon harvested from the world's forest is returned to the atmosphere within 1–2 years by domestic cooking, heating, and burning in industrial plants. This cycle of water, carbon dioxide, solar energy, and fuelwood is millions of years old and represents an important way humankind traps and stores solar energy for future use. Data for fuel do not include incineration of waste paper and wood products or excavation of landfills as sources of energy from buried paper and paperboard. These data suggest that solar energy, collected and stored in forested landscapes, is an essential part of the world's energy supply and consumption.

Sawlogs and veneer logs are made into wood products, such as industrial buildings, houses, and furniture. These products have average delay periods

TABLE 10.2   World's Annual Harvest of Carbon, and Percentages Used for Fuel and Wood Products for Selected Years. (Data Calculated from FAO 1993)

Year	Total Carbon Harvested (million Mg)	Percentages of Total Used for:			
		Fuel Wood	Sawlogs/ Veneer	Pulpwood/ Particles	Other Products
1991	1009	53.3	27.3	12.5	6.8
1990	1031	52.6	29.8	12.3	6.7
1985	935	52.1	29.0	11.9	7.0
1980	861	50.4	30.0	12.7	6.9
1975	811	53.5	27.3	11.9	6.3
1970	771	51.4	28.9	12.0	6.4
1969	754	51.9	28.7	9.0	6.6

of about 20 years, although some items may be kept in use for more than 100 years. Most kinds of wood included in Table 10.2's "Other Products" category, such as poles and post, have turnover times of about 20 years.

Paper is used for short periods of time. About 2 years after harvest, carbon in newsprint, writing papers, and many other products is oxidized. Small amounts of paper may remain in landfills for decades. Recycling extends periods of use for paper and board to possibly 4 years (Diaz et al. 1982).

These data (Tables 10.1, 10.2) are not very useful to managers concerned with a few thousand hectares, or even smaller units, of forested landscapes. The Craggy Mountain Forested Landscape is used here to illustrate analytic procedures for evaluating carbon and energy flows for forested landscapes.

Carbon in the Craggy Mountain Forested Landscape

Evaluation of carbon flows through the Craggy Mountain Forested Landscape are limited to trees with boles 12 cm dbh from a 30-cm stump to a 12-cm top diameter. Harvested areas are naturally regenerated from advanced regeneration, sprouts, and natural seedlings. Harvesting is conducted to reduce soil compacting and conserve carbon in the soil.

A volume table gives yields of wood in ft^3/acre (McClure and Knight 1984). Values are converted to carbon in metric tons per hectare. A cubic foot of hardwood contains about 19.82 lb of carbon (Birdsey 1992). Pounds of carbon per acre multiplied by 0.00112085 gives the metric tons per hectare (Everard 1971). Mean annual increment for carbon (MAIC) is the rotation age for maximum removal of carbon dioxide from the atmosphere by growing and harvesting trees. MAIC is calculated by dividing yields of carbon by age. Age for MAIC in the Craggy Mountains is 30 years (Table 10.3).

Yields and MAIC are conservative estimates that include stands with different rates of growth. The significance of the analyses lies not in exact predictions of values but in relative differences in carbon storage and other benefits for the three policies of forest reserves, traditional forestry, and landscape forestry.

Maximum Harvest of Carbon—A Basis for Comparison

If the Craggy Mountain Forested Landscape is dedicated to maximum harvest of carbon, the maximum sustainable area of harvest for a 30-year rotation is 209.6 ha/year (6289.2 ha/30 years), and the average annual harvest of carbon is 6751 Mg/year (32.21 Mg/ha * 209.6 ha).

Under a maximum carbon scenario, harvested carbon, all removed from the atmosphere, is a little more than 2,025,000 Mg for a period of 300 years (6751 Mg/year * 300 years). Trees harvested are about 30 years old, and products are mostly fuel and paper with 1–4 years of use. Emissions to the atmosphere are about 1951 million Mg of carbon over the 300 years. Stored carbon, the sum of carbon in use and in standing trees, is only 74,000 Mg in year 300.

The maximum rate of carbon harvest sets upper sustainable limits for harvesting carbon for energy and paper products. If energy becomes more important than aesthetics, habitats, and biological diversity, this scenario would provide society with an important source of solar energy. Repeated removal of 6751 Mg of carbon per year is known to be feasible because of long histories, more than 200 years, of repeated harvest of forests for firewood (Schenck 1897; James 1897; Fernow 1891, 1893; Conrad 1889; Spaeth 1928; Frothingham 1931; Steenberg 1972; FAO 1993).

The maximum carbon scenario is not socially acceptable in the 1990s because the Craggy Mountain Forested Landscape is a scenic area viewed from the Blue Ridge Parkway each year by millions of people. Organization of this landscape with stands no older than 30 years limits opportunities to distribute stands by type, age, and area classes over time and space and thus limits opportunities to enhance biological diversity, scenic values, production of certain kinds of wood products, and potential livelihood for many kinds of plants and animals. Alternatives to maximum harvest of solar energy include managing the landscape with policies for forest reserves, traditional forestry, and landscape forestry.

TABLE 10.3   Yield Table for Wood and Carbon for the Craggy Mountain Forested Landscape. Yields Are for Boles Larger than 12 cm dbh from a 30-cm Stump to a 12-cm Top Diameter Inside Bark. (Modified from McClure and Knight 1984; Johnson 1991; Birdsey 1992)

Age (years)	Wood Yield (ft³/acre)	Carbon	
		Yield (Mg/ha)	MAIC (Mg/ha/yr)
0	0	0	0
10	57	1.27	0.13
20	600	13.33	0.67
30	1450	32.21	1.07
40	1838	40.83	1.02
50	2000	44.43	0.89
60	2222	49.36	0.82
70	2450	54.43	0.78
80	2510	55.76	0.70
90	2590	57.54	0.64
100	2668	59.27	0.59
...	...	...	...
150	3004	66.73	0.44
200	3319	73.73	0.37
250	3555	78.98	0.32
300	3718	82.60	0.28

FLOWS OF CARBON UNDER THREE POLICIES

Three policies, called forest reserves, traditional forestry and landscape forestry (Chapter 3), are used to simulate amounts of carbon stored in living
boles, amounts of carbon harvested, and amounts of carbon stored over periods of 300 years.

CRAG models (Chapter 5) are modified to simulate the number of metric
tons of carbon in standing boles 12 cm dbh and larger, of carbon removed
by harvest, and of carbon in use. For forest reserves, stored carbon is amounts
of carbon in standing boles per hectare (Table 10.3). For traditional and landscape forestry, stored carbon includes amounts in standing boles plus carbon
in use. Models are iterated 4 times per year for 300 years. Iteration at 10
times per year gives no increase in accuracy of outcomes. No provisons are
made for random disturbances, such as large areas of increased mortality from
ice storms, fires, insects, and diseases. Average amounts of carbon stored
(Mg/ha) in the Craggy Mountain Forested Landscape are plotted at 5-year
intervals for the three policies (Fig. 10.1).

After 300 simulated years, effects of initial inventories (Table 4.1) are
dampened. More carbon is stored in boles when the Craggy Mountain Forested Landscape is turned into a forest reserve than when it is managed with
traditional or landscape forestry (Chapter 3). As a forest reserve, steady-state
storage of carbon is about 56.3 Mg/ha. Storage of carbon in boles and in use

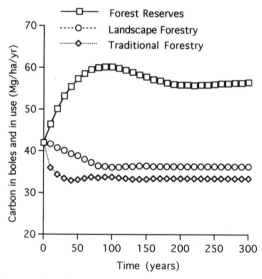

Figure 10.1   More carbon is stored in boles of standing trees when the Craggy
Mountain Forested Landscape is converted to forest reserves than when trees are harvested for fuel and timber.

is about 33.4 Mg/ha for traditional forestry and 36.3 Mg/ha for landscape forestry. There seems little doubt that forest reserves consisting of undisturbed stands more than 200 years old store more carbon in standing boles than do forested landscapes managed under traditional forestry or landscape forestry (Harmon et al. 1990; Kershaw et al. 1993).

These simulations exclude massive disturbance by storms, fires, and other natural events. When uncertain, massive disturbances aimlessly change forested landscapes, amounts of carbon trapped and stored vary over time (Sheffield and Thompson 1992; Lorimer 1980; Lorimer and Frelich 1994). Uncertain, natural events do not produce predictable combinations of benefits that depend on the consistent availability of habitats from age classes of 1 year to very old ages and of canopy openings of about 0.2–10 ha (Figs. 4.10, 4.12).

Delay for harvesting, processing, marketing, and putting wood into use is set at 2 years. Processing loss, including incineration of bark and waste, is 10 percent of the harvested wood. Shavings, chips, and other processing waste go to pulp mills. At pulp mills, some waste is burned for energy. Fractions of wood placed into short-term use include paper and paperboard products. This short-term fraction is 36 percent of harvested wood (Ulrich 1990) less 10 percent lost. The average time for short-period use is set at 2 years for material not recycled. During any given year, ½ of all paper and board products in use is discarded or lost during processing, transportation, and marketing. The recovery rate for discarded paper and board products is 30 percent (Ulrich 1990). All of this recovered material is assumed to be recycled or marketed to extend time in use from 2 to 4 years. Annually ¼ of recycled material is discarded or lost.

Fractions of wood placed into long-term use include solid wood products, such as furniture and houses. The long-term fraction is 64 percent of harvested wood (Ulrich 1990) less 10 percent lost. Average time in long-term use is set at 20 years. Each year 1/20 of all material in long-term use is assumed to be discarded. All discarded materials are assumed to oxidize and return to the atmosphere within 1 year. Paper and wood known to remain in landfills for 4–5 decades represents a relatively small fraction of total production. Some governments, such as Schnectedy, NY, may mine landfills for fuel and shorten delays for carbon in use.

The fastest net accumulation of carbon occurs when trees in sunlit canopies are close to the age for cumulation of MAIC (Table 10.3). As stands age beyond the age for culmination of MAIC, rates of mortality increase and emissions of carbon may exceed accumulations in live boles. In old-growth stands, net carbon accumulations tend to oscillate near a maximum limit for the species and geographic location. When old-growth stands are harvested, amounts of standing carbon are reduced because boles in young stands contain less carbon per hectare than boles in old stands (Table 10.3). Other reservoirs of carbon, such as soils and forest floors, are altered when soils are disturbed by the construction of roads, skid trails, and log storage areas. These effects are small relative to total amounts of carbon stored and occur once in a rotation of 85 or more years for the Craggy Mountain Forested Landscape. Carbon losses from these effects are assumed to be restored within 10–20 years after a harvest of trees.

Both traditional and landscape forestry organize landscapes with more young stands and larger canopy openings than occur in forest reserves (Runkle 1981, 1982). Under management, a larger number of stands are retained near the age for MAIC (Table 10.3) than when the landscape is converted to forest reserves (Figs. 4.5, 4.7, 4.9). More carbon is removed from the atmosphere annually with traditional and landscape forestry than for forest reserves (Table 10.4).

These numbers are calculated from yield tables (Table 10.3), simulations of growth and harvest rates (Chapter 4), and estimates of natural mortality (Runkle 1981, 1982, Lorimer 1980). Estimates are for boles larger than 12 cm dbh from a 30-cm stump to a 12-cm top diameter. Numbers are given when forest stands are at approximately steady-state rates of change for each of the three policies. Values are considered to reflect relative relationships for this landscape and are not predictions for every kind of forest.

Carbon removed from air is the net annual metric tons of carbon added to standing boles plus metric tons of carbon harvested from the landscape. Removal values are low for forest reserves because no timber is harvested and MAIC for most stands is about 0.2–0.3 Mg/ha/year. Natural mortality reduces net removals of carbon from the atmosphere to low and sometimes negative values. Removal values are relatively high for traditional and landscape forestry because young stands have MAIC values of 0.7–1 MG/ha/year (Table 10.3).

Carbon emitted to air is the average annual oxidation of carbon in use plus the average natural mortality of standing boles. Oxidation of carbon in use includes fuelwood and discarded products that may be burned or permitted to decay. Carbon emissions to the air are high for traditional and landscape forestry because humans consume large amounts of wood (Table 10.2). Con-

TABLE 10.4   Annual Flows of Carbon through Merchantable Boles in the Craggy Mountain Forested Landscape and Amounts Temporarily Stored when Forest Stands are at Steady-State Rates of Change for Three Policies

	(Mg/ha/yr)		
Policy	Carbon Removed from Air	Carbon Emitted to Air	Temporary Storage of Carbon from Air
Forest reserves	0.049	0.041	0.008
Traditional forestry	0.687	0.576	0.111
Landscape forestry	0.622	0.506	0.121

sumption of wood results in relatively rapid rates of oxidation of carbon. Forest reserves emit small average amounts of carbon from boles to the atmosphere because removals are small. Hiking, camping, and other uses of forest reserves increase the oxidation of carbon by unknown but apparently small amounts.

Temporary storage of carbon removed from air is the annual amount of carbon stored in standing boles plus the carbon in use. Values are differences between carbon removed and emitted. The assumption is that these values represent average annual periods of storage. Small amounts of carbon in use may be stored for decades in houses, landfills, and other places. There is little evidence that large amounts of carbon removed from the atmosphere by harvest of tree boles is stored for hundreds and thousands of years. Traditional and landscape forestry increase temporary rates of storage well above rates for forest reserves. Temporary storage may be important for keeping some carbon out of the atmosphere (Post et al. 1990; Harmon et al. 1990; Schobert 1990).

Data are not available to estimate rates of carbon flows through roots, foliage, and other parts of trees as management policies are changed. An important question is whether increased flows of carbon through boles change accumulations of carbon in soils, on forest floors, and in understory plants. Data to answer these kinds of questions are not available for the Craggy Mountain Forested Landscape.

Sustained flows of carbon, in combination with other benefits, are assured by organizing forested landscapes with landscape forestry methods (Chapters 3–9).

MENTAL MODEL FOR CARBON AND SOLAR ENERGY

The mental model says landscape forestry is a way to direct flows of carbon and solar energy through a forested landscape. All forest benefits are related to amounts of carbon captured by sunlit canopies. The availability of carbon compounds to humankind and other organisms is determined by states of organization of stands in the forested landscape (Tables 10.3, 10.4). Landscape forestry provides managers ways to allocate solar energy and carbon compounds to aesthetics, habitats, fuelwood, timber, cash flow, and biological diversity. Although forest reserves store large amounts of carbon from the air, the tradeoff for stored carbon is loss of forested landscapes organized for aesthetics, habitats, fuels, timber, cash flow, and biological diversity.

The carbon model is important to resource managers and consumers for a number of reasons. First, consumers in different societies demand different tradeoffs among forest reserves, fuels, and wood products (Gomez-Pompa and Kaus 1992). Second, although more than half of all harvested carbon is returned to the atmosphere within 3–4 years, organized forested landscapes provide a way to increase the capture of carbon from the atmosphere and increase temporary storage (Table 10.4). Third, any long-term storage of used forest products, such as paper and construction wood, may be excavated by future generations and used for energy. Fourth, landscape forestry is a way to divert solar energy and carbon compounds to sustained production of an enormous variety of forest-based goods, services, and effects (Figs. 10.1, 4.10, 4.12).

11

AN ENDANGERED SPECIES

Survival of a population is related to the ability of individuals to keep essential variables within the limits of life (Chapter 8, Theorem 1). As states of organization of forested landscapes change over time, rates of mortality and potential livelihood of individuals change (Theorem 2). No course of action by managers can assure survival of individuals or a population. However, simulations of potential livelihood, based on observations, research, and experience, provide insights about opportunities for populations to survive in relation to different states of organization (Theorem 4). Landscape forestry helps managers choose a course of action to trade some benefits for the livelihood of an endangered species. This chapter illustrates one situation.

The situation is the potential livelihood for an endangered species, the red-cockaded woodpecker, as an item in a basket of benefits. The basket of benefits is kept simple by illustrating the potential livelihood for flicker woodpeckers and net present values. Simulation models provide opportunities to include in the basket a number of benefits, such as livelihood for red-cockaded woodpeckers, flicker woodpeckers, and cash flow.

THE SITUATION

The red-cockaded woodpecker (hereafter RCW), is classified as an endangered species under the Endangered Species Act of 1973 (USDA Forest Service 1983; Tear et al. 1993). Many dollars are spent on research, recovery plans, debate, and activities to conserve habitats for this bird. Many dollars in cash flows are foregone by managers in attempts to comply with laws and regulations based on mental models of states of organization that favor the potential livelihood of this bird. Mental models shift as new observations and research findings enter debates. However, there is agreement among many concerned individuals about some states of organization that favor the potential livelihood for RCWs.

Models for RCW

Potential livelihood of RCWs is enhanced by hundreds of hectares of pine forest, especially longleaf and loblolly pines in the southeastern United States. Most observers agree that RCWs prefer to nest in pine stands old enough to contain some trees with decayed wood in the stem at about 30 feet above the ground. Cavities, constructed by RCWs, provide for nesting, protection, sleeping, and escape. It is believed trees adjacent to cavity trees should have heights well below those of the cavity holes. Desirable ages for cavity trees are considered to be more than 95 years for longleaf pines and more than 75 years for loblolly and other pines. Feeding is enhanced by the presence of pine and hardwood stands more than 30 years old. Disturbance, such as harvesting trees more than 180 feet from cavity trees, seem not to disturb nesting activities. Prescribed burning of stands to reduce fuels for wildfires and to reduce amounts of understory trees seems a desirable practice. Nest cavities are known to occur near busy highways and subdivisions and on military bases. RCWs are known to use bird feeders close to houses (Roise et al. 1990; Wood et al. 1985; Wood 1983; McFarlane 1992; Kelly et al. 1993).

The CRAG models are modified to construct a model called RED1. The model is designed to examine tradeoffs for organizing forested landscapes that contain colonies of RCW.

The Inventory

An inventory is available from the USDA Forest Service, which provides management for some forests on the Savannah River Plant area in Aiken, SC (Table 11.1). Hardwood forests are not included in the simulations. Pine forests are classified into three types: longleaf, slash, and loblolly. Longleaf stands are mostly longleaf pine with many oaks and hickories characteristic of the sandy soils of this area (Martin et al. 1993a,b). Most of the slash pine stands and many of the loblolly pine stands are planted on areas formerly occupied by longleaf pines (Boyce et al. 1986).

Lands on the Savannah River Plant area are owned by the federal government. Pine forests in the inventory are managed by the USDA Forest Service. There is no intent to simulate current management plans or to recommend any specific plan. Rather, this illustration simulates baskets of benefits produced by the three policies of forest reserves, traditional forestry, and landscape forestry (Chapter 3). Maximum net present values are calculated as a basis for comparison.

A Basket of Benefits

The primary concern may be for RCWs, yet cash flow, timber production, habitats for other species, and biological diversity are also important values to be considered. Outcomes of a given course of action are expected to include habitats for many plants and animals, recreation opportunities, and other values. Surrogates for other benefits are potential livelihood for flicker woodpeckers and net present values for timber sales. Nesting requirements for RCWs and flicker woodpeckers overlap. Flickers nest in dead trees and in cavities found in stands suitable for RCW cavities. Feeding requirements are different for these species. RCWs are tree- and shrub-feeding birds and benefit from feeding in stands 30 years and older. Flicker woodpeckers feed on ants on the ground and on grubs in dead material on the ground. Canopy openings larger than 0.5 ha provide habitats for flicker woodpeckers to use for feeding.

The mental model says that if the potential livelihoods for these two birds are relatively high, then biological diversity for many species should be relatively high. That is, stand age classes must extend from 0 to about 90 years to favor both birds. This range of age classes favors many kinds of plants and animals. Canopy openings of about 0.5 ha favors many plants and animals. Relatively high habitat indices for both flicker and pileated woodpeckers should favor enhanced biological diversity.

Net present values are consequences of rates of harvest required to change the inventory from the initial state (Table 11.1) toward a state that favors both birds. Consequences for recreation, hunting, aesthetics, and other values are

TABLE 11.1 Initial Inventory of Pine Forests on the Savannah River Plant Area Around 1988. (USDA Forest Service, 1991a).

Code	Age Class (years)	Longleaf Type	Slash Type	Loblolly Type	Total
		(ha)			
A	0–9	428.2	19.8	7,219.6	7,667.6
B	10–19	577.9	230.7	1,992.7	2,801.2
C	20–29	5,876.9	6,659.9	1,613.9	14,150.7
D	30–39	4,852.2	5,441.0	8,802.3	19,095.5
E	40–49	1,996.3	285.3	2,464.9	4,746.6
F	50–59	1,038.0	0.0	1,128.3	2,166.3
G	60–69	648.3	24.7	339.9	1,012.9
H	70–79	347.2	0.0	30.4	377.6
I	80–89	70.4	0.0	12.1	82.6
O	>90	0.0	0.0	0.0	0.0
	Totals	15,835.4	12,661.4	23,604.1	51,200.9

not displayed. Indices for these values can be attached to the model (Chapter 5).

THE QUESTION

The question is: What are the consequences of imposing the three policies of forest reserves, traditional forestry, and landscape forestry (Chapter 3) on pine forests of the Savannah River Plant landscape? Potential livelihood for the RCW, an endangered species, is a primary concern. Equally important is the biological diversity of habitats for thousands of other species, positive cash flow, and wood for consumers.

SIMULATED CONSEQUENCES

RED1 is a program of the same design as CRAG-3 (Chapter 5). Constants and delays are changed to simulate different courses of action for the Savannah River pine forests. Supplementary models are for RCWs and flicker woodpeckers.

Maximum Cash Flow—A Basis for Comparison

This course of action ignores habitat and other values to achieve maximum cash flow over the next 100 years. Discount and reinvestment rates are set at 0.07. I estimate stumpage prices and cost from many sources. This is an acceptable approach since simulations provide relative differences for different policies and do not estimate exact values. Older stands are liquidated over the next 10 years. Outcomes from this simulation provide a basis for comparison with other options.

Net cash flow at time 100 is $25 million. This number is used to normalize all net present values for the policies called forest reserves, traditional forestry, and landscape forestry.

Forest Reserves

No timber is harvested. The initial state of organization (Table 11.1) is permitted to change without any intervention. The initial unequal distribution of age classes affects the potential livelihood for RCWs and flickers (Fig. 11.1).

By year 10, seedling age classes have declined and reduced the potential livelihood for flickers. As stands accumulate in the older age classes, natural mortality increases numbers and sizes of canopy openings. Increased feeding areas increase the potential livelihood for flickers.

By year 40, potential livelihood for RCWs is maximum. The RCW index declines after year 60 because of small reductions in feeding areas. These reductions are related to the initial inventory (Table 11.1). At 100 years, the index is relatively stable, with a value of about 0.8.

Net present values decline because there are no sales. Values are normalized by dividing by $25 million, which is the net present value at age 100 for the maximum cash-flow scenario. By year 100, the index for net present value is a negative 0.43 (Fig. 11.1).

Traditional Forestry

This policy is to constrain net present values only to the extent required to conserve existing habitats for RCWs and flickers. There is no intent of maximizing cash flow at the expense of habitats and biological diversity. After several changes in harvest schedules, the following controls were selected. Longleaf pine is harvested at 75 years of age to produce high-quality lumber and to provide some habitat for RCWs. All lands initially in longleaf pine are kept in longleaf pine.

A 35-year rotation is imposed on slash pine, and 80 percent of the harvested slash pine areas are converted to loblolly pine. Twenty percent of the

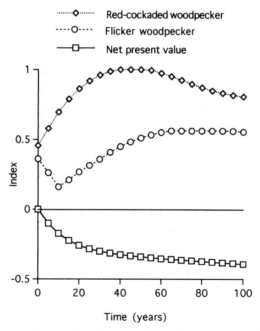

Figure 11.1   Conversion of the Savannah River Landscape to forest reserves increases the potential livelihood of RCWs to 0.8–0.9 and produces negative cash flows. The index for net present value is a negative 0.43 in year 100. Indices for flickers decline for the first 15 years then increase to 0.54 by year 100.

initial slash pine area is kept in slash pine. Loblolly pine is harvested with superimposed rotations to produce pulpwood and lumber. Seventy percent of the loblolly areas is harvested at age 35, and 30 percent is harvested at age 45. The total area in loblolly pine increases over time until slash pine is reduced to 20 percent of the original area. Consequences are plotted in Fig. 11.2.

The potential livelihood for RCWs and flickers are kept near initial values of about 0.35–0.45 for 100 years. Indices for net present values rise to a positive 0.66 in year 100 (Fig. 11.2).

Landscape Forestry

The policy for landscape forestry is to organize the landscape for a basket of benefits. Emphasis is on improving habitats for RCWs and flickers and on maintaining positive cash flows. After several changes in rates of harvest, the following controls were selected. Eighty percent of the longleaf pine is harvested at 100 years of age, and 20 percent is harvested at 35 years. This combination of rotations contributes to nesting and feeding habitats for RCWs and flickers. Initial areas in longleaf pine are kept in longleaf pine.

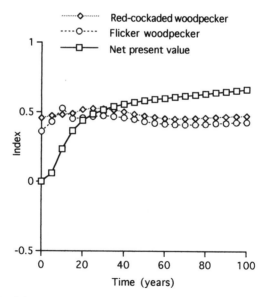

Figure 11.2 Traditional forestry, constrained to conserve RCW nesting habitats, keeps indices for RCWs and flicker woodpecker near initial values of about 0.35–0.45. Indices for net present values rise to a positive 0.66 in year 100.

Slash pine is harvested at age 35. Twenty percent of the harvested slash pine area is converted to longleaf pine, and 80 percent is converted to loblolly pine. By year 50, all slash pine stands are liquidated.

Forty percent of loblolly pine stands are harvested at age 90, and 60 percent are harvested at age 35. All areas initially in loblolly pine are kept in loblolly pine. Simulated consequences are plotted in Fig. 11.3. By year 20, the habitat index for RCWs rises to about 0.7 and then declines to about 0.64 by year 100. The habitat index for flickers rises to 0.5 and 0.56 for the 100-year period. In year 100, the simulated index for net present value is a positive 0.32.

Choosing a Course of Action

Many kinds of plants and animals live in pine stands in the southeastern United States (Martin et al. 1993a,b). A livelihood for all endemic species is enhanced by a variety of habitats, each changing in time and space. Habitats are classified as stands categorized by forest type, age, and area classes. Yet no definitive statements can be made about organizing forested landscapes for clustering baskets of benefits because we do not know how many kinds of species are in a forested landscape.

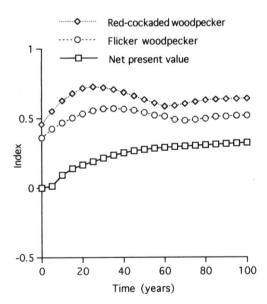

Figure 11.3   Landscape forestry, scheduled to favor RCWs and maintain positive cash flows, increases indices for RCWs to 0.64–0.7. Indices for flickers rise to 0.5–0.56. Indices for net present values rise to a positive 0.32.

For a relatively few organisms, we know how states of organization affect potential livelihood. For these organisms, such as flickers and RCWs, supplementary models are designed to suggest how different states of organization change an index. When normalized with indices for aesthetics, timber, fuelwood, cash flow, and biological diversity, managers are provided with information as a basis for making decisions. Choice of a course of action is a subjective decision made using mental models. Most decisions are tradeoffs in which no single benefit is maximum.

Tradeoffs for RCW

Some consequences, simulated for the Savannah River pine forests, are displayed in a bar-graph format to illustrate one way to compare outcomes. The four courses of action are arrayed from the lowest to the highest index for net present value for year 100. After 100 years, changes in age classes are approaching steady-state rates and indices are relatively stable (Fig. 11.4).

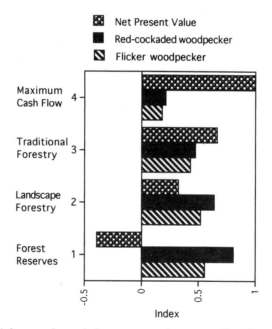

Figure 11.4   A bar graph can help managers choose a policy that results in acceptable tradeoffs between cash flows and habitats. With a policy for forest reserves, cash flows are a negative 0.43 in year 100 and indices for RCWs and flickers are positive 0.81 and 0.56 respectively. When the policy is for maximum cash flows, the index for net present value is 1.0, for RCWs 0.21, and for flickers 0.20. Outcomes for traditional and landscape forestry are examples of policies to provide positive cash flows and improved habitats.

Between the two extreme courses of action, called forest reserves and maximum cash flow, lies a continuum of different mixes of benefits. Landscape forestry offers a way to simulate a number of options between traditional forestry and forest reserves. The question is: How much are consumers willing to pay in incentives and higher prices for fewer wood products in return for more stands of old pines? An important point is that the final choice of a course of action is subjectively made by mental models of managers and other interested parties.

12

LANDSCAPE FORESTRY AND PUBLIC POLICY

Governments use public policies to direct and influence conservation and use of forested landscapes for benefits assumed to accrue to society. Policies are implemented with incentives, regulations, and constraints designed to influence the behavior of large numbers of people (Beer 1966, 1975; Hecht 1993; USDA 1983, 1993; Newman and Wear 1993). Laws and regulations are beyond the scope of this book. However, an important observation is that public policy influences changes in states of organization of forested landscapes that are in multiple ownerships (USDA 1983, 1993). This chapter examines use of landscape forestry methods to help design public policies before a proposal is implemented.

USE OF LANDSCAPE FORESTRY METHODS

Most approaches to designing public policies use traditional forestry and consider incentives and regulations for changing the structure, regeneration, and harvest of stands (USDA 1983, 1993; USDA Forest Service 1988). An important consequence, rarely included in public policies, is how a proposal might change states of organization of forested landscapes that are in multiple ownerships.

A Proposal

The proposal is to use incentives to change states of organization of pine forests to enhance the potential livelihood for the red-cockaded woodpecker (RCW). Concern is to enhance nesting habitats by increasing amounts of pine stands in old age classes. Since old stands of pine are important for nesting (Chapter 11), the proposal is to reduce the cost of capital to private landowners (Chapter 8) as an incentive for landowners to conserve some fraction of their pine forest in old stands. For this illustration, the proposal is kept relatively simple in order to emphasize landscape forestry methods rather than policy.

Choosing an Area for Simulation

A first step is to locate a large forested landscape where RCWs are present, where there are many pine forests in multiple ownerships, and where the proposal might change the potential livelihood of RCWs. The area selected covers 21 counties in southeastern North Carolina. This area contains many pine stands in multiple ownerships, and RCWs are present. Knowledge about numbers and locations of RCWs are not essential because the primary concern is how the proposed incentive program would change states of organization of the forests and thus RCW nesting habitats. A supposition is that increased nesting habitat will increase numbers of RCW colonies.

The area includes the city of Wilmington and the counties of Bladen, Brunswick, Columbus, Cumberland, Duplin, Green, Harnett, Hoke, Johnson, Jones, Lee, Lenoir, Moore, New Hanover, Onslow, Pender, Richmond, Robeson, Sampson, Scotland, and Wayne. The total land area is 3,382,908 ha. Forested landscapes are in many different kinds of ownerships and occupy 2,126,049 ha. Agricultural lands are declining but continue to occupy 908,680 ha. Urban lands include legal boundaries of cities and towns; suburban areas developed for residential, industrial, and recreational purposes; school yards, cemeteries, roads, railroads, airports, beaches, power lines, and other rights-of-way; and any lands converted from forest to urban uses. Urban lands are increasing and now occupy 348,178 ha (Cost 1974; Tansey 1986; Johnson 1990).

Lands in large forested landscapes continually shift from one to another use. Shifts in land use from forest to agriculture and back to forest may take as little as 1–3 decades. Lands retired from agriculture may stay in forest for 3–5 decades. However, shifts of agricultural and forestlands to urban uses tend to stay in urban uses for long periods of time (Cost 1974; Tansey 1986; Johnson 1990). Changes in land use over the past 38 years suggest that forested landscapes can be expected to occupy 60 percent or more of this landscape for several decades (Table 12.1).

Economic development and public policies encourage a growing population to occupy urban rather than rural areas. This shift in population increases opportunities for timber production, habitats, aesthetics, and biological diversity in rural areas.

Forested Landscapes in Urban Communities

Much of the land converted to urban uses (Table 12.1) will be planted to stands of trees, maintained as natural stands to protect water impoundments and streams, and managed as green space to conserve aesthetics and habitats. In many urban communities, fingers of forest stands traverse streets and extend into rural forested landscapes. These corridors are travel lanes for many herbaceous, shrub, and animal species that adapt to urban environments.

Landscape methods, principles, and theorems apply to forested landscapes in urban areas (Chapter 9). States of organization of parks, street trees, trees around houses, and other structures determine productions of benefits. Aesthetics, habitats, biological diversity, and, for some urban communities, fuelwood and timber are produced as consequences of states of organization of urban stands. Benefits of importance to urban communities include reductions of energy costs related to the shade of streets, sidewalks, and houses and the deflection of winds; delays in storm-water runoff, reduced erosion, and traps for water-carried dirt and oils from streets and roads; and traps for airborne particulates and chemicals common to urban communities. Stands are used in urban communities to organize playgrounds and outdoor classrooms, screen industrial areas, and enhance uses of parks.

An example of organizing forested landscapes in urban communities is beyond the scope of this book.

The Forested Landscape Situation

Inventories of the forests in 1983 and 1990 document changes in forest stands by 10-year age classes and by major forest types (Cost 1974; Tansey 1984; Johnson 1990). The data do not indicate causes for changes over the 7-year period (Table 12.2).

The 0–9 age class includes harvested lands waiting to be regenerated, retired agricultural lands being converted to forests, lands considered in need of planting, and some lands incapable of growing commercial timber. Age class 1–10 includes stands 1–10 years old. All stands in 1–10-year age classes are considered fully established forests.

TABLE 12.1   Proportions of Total Area in Three Major Classes of Land Use, Water Excluded, in 21 Counties in Southeastern North Carolina. (Cost 1974; Tansey 1984; Johnson 1990)

Date of inventory (years)	Kind of Land Use (percent)		
	Forests	Agriculture	Urban Uses
1952	0.66	0.30	0.04
1962	0.68	0.28	0.04
1973	0.65	0.27	0.08
1983	0.64	0.27	0.09
1990	0.63	0.27	0.10

Distributions of land among age classes reflect many activities that result in harvest of stands. Inventory data do not distinguish between harvesting to convert forestlands to urban and agricultural uses and harvesting to organize landscapes for timber, habitats, aesthetics, and other values. Most timber removals are assumed to be for structuring stands for timber production.

Many pine stands originated after retirement of lands from agriculture. Natural regeneration and plantations of pine are established on both retired agricultural lands and on forestlands after timber is harvested. Many harvested pine stands are replaced naturally with stands of hardwoods. The shift from pine to hardwood stands is well documented in forest inventories (Boyce and Knight 1979, 1980; Boyce et al. 1986).

Initial states of organization are used in a core model, to simulate future states of organization (Chapter 5). Alternative trends for the next 100 years are examined in relation to suppositions about how public policies might alter cash flows and potential livelihood of RCWs and flicker woodpeckers.

The characteristics of RCW and flicker woodpeckers are described in Chapter 11. Potential livelihoods for these woodpeckers have no direct market value to landowners.

The Question

The challenge is to design a model that will simulate changes in states of forest organization in relation to a public policy to subsidize the conservation

TABLE 12.2   Distribution of Pine and Hardwood Forests in 1983 and 1990 for 21 Counties in Southeastern North Carolina by Age Classes. (Cost 1974; Tansey 1984; Johnson 1990)

Age class (years)	Pine Forests Date of Inventory		Hardwood Forests Date of Inventory	
	1983	1990	1983	1990
	(thousands ha)			
0–0.9	134.5	78.3	259.4	285.9
1–10	169.0	192.7	141.8	231.3
11–20	212.2	166.6	90.6	79.5
21–30	155.2	173.8	59.4	47.5
31–40	128.9	112.7	75.7	69.5
41–50	108.1	90.9	131.5	102.6
51–60	77.0	80.3	126.3	120.7
61–70	30.3	33.7	74.2	86.6
71–80	6.9	13.5	46.6	58.4
81–90	4.2	5.2	99.3	89.6
Totals	1026.3	947.7	1104.8	1171.6

of old stands of pine. Evaluation of the proposal is to be based on supplementary models to examine differences in cash flows for landowners and potential livelihoods for RCWs and flicker woodpeckers. Cash flows are indicative of sales and productions of timber. The primary concern is increasing the livelihood for RCWs. The potential livelihood of flicker woodpeckers is indicative of the presence of young age classes, which are habitats for many species of plants and animals.

The Design

Forest inventory reports provide information about the harvest of timber by age classes for 1983 and 1990 (Tansey 1984; Johnson 1990). This information is used in combination with inventories for the 10-year age classes (Table 12.1) to develop the model. Design of the model is similar to the CRAG models (Chapter 5). One important change is to assign rates of rotation to every age class from which timber removals occur. After the model is constructed, rates of harvest, measured by rotation period, are adjusted to mimic average changes between the 1983 and 1990 inventories. This procedure does not validate the model because the method assumes straight-line changes between 1983 and 1990. Curved changes possibly occurred, but there are no data to indicate the form of the curves.

The model includes net rates of change in land use from 1983 to 1990 (Table 12.2), net rates of regeneration of harvested lands and retired agricultural lands, and net rates of conversion of pine to hardwood stands. An important assumption is that public policy does influence the behavior of large numbers of landowners, and responses to policy are as expected. For example, there is considerable evidence that larger numbers of landowners are taking advantage of incentive programs designed to convert erodable agricultural lands to forestlands (USDA 1983, 1993; USDA Forest Service 1988).

Construction and Simulations

Construction of the model is essentially the same as described for the CRAG models (Chapter 5). Changes are made in many equations to adapt the model to a large forested landscape and to contribute to answering the question. Net conversion of forestlands to urban uses is estimated to be 0.0005085 of total forestlands per year. This rate of conversion of forestlands is assumed to be the same for all policies. Outcomes are considered for four simulations, called cash flow, traditional forestry, landscape forestry, and RCW incentive.

Cash-Flow Forestry—A Basis for Comparison

Maximum cash flow is estimated with an assumption that forested landscapes in all 21 counties are managed for maximum, sustained flows of cash. This simulation is to establish a basis for comparison with other options. Harvest schedules are not constrained, as in Chapter 11, to sustain the initial habitat index for RCWs. With this policy, all pine stands are managed with a rotation period of 35 years and all hardwood stands with a rotation of 75 years (Fig. 12.1).

The potential livelihood for RCW declines to a very low value, about 0.1 of maximum potential. The livelihood for flickers is about 0.43. Net present values rise to an index value of 1 in year 100. The estimated net present value is $1.05 billion, which is the basis for normalizing all other estimates of net present value.

Simulated net present values are based on a cost of capital of 8 percent and an assumed reinvestment rate of 8 percent. Reinvestment rates are rarely as large as the cost of capital, but, in absence of better information, equal rates are used. I estimate stumpage prices and cost for management from many sources.

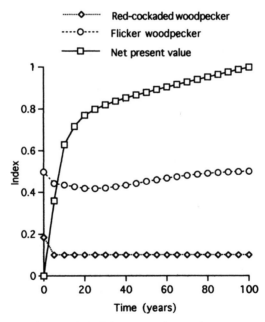

Figure 12.1 A basis is established for comparing options by assuming that all pine stands are harvested at age 35 and hardwood stands at age 75. If all forested landscapes in the 21 counties were managed for maximum sustained flows of cash, indices for net present value would be 1.0 in year 100 because cash flow for this year is used to normalize all net present values for this assumption. Habitat indices for RCWs decline to 0.1 and for flickers to 0.43. These values provide a base for comparing outcomes for different public policies.

Traditional Forestry

The assumption is that forestry practices reflected in inventories from 1983 to 1990 represent traditional forestry. Landowners are taking advantage of subsidies for planting pines (USDA 1983). Simulations extend recorded practices 100 years into the future. Because there are many landowners, simulation of the inventory trends from 1983 to 1990 appear as superimposed rotations. Trends in rates of harvest from age classes older than 30 years for the period 1983–1990 are documented in Table 12.3.

For purposes of comparing different simulations, initial net present values are assumed to be 0. Net present values are normalized with the value $1.05 billion, which is the maximum net present value for cash-flow forestry. Outcomes for traditional forestry are displayed in Fig. 12.2.

The initial index for the livelihood of RCWs is about 0.18 of the maximum habitat potential. Traditional forestry retains this index value close to the initial value. The index for the livelihood of flickers is between 0.42 and 0.46, which is a little below the initial value of 0.49. Net present values rise rapidly to a maximum index of 0.82 in year 100.

Simulations for traditional forestry is an extension of inventory trends recorded from 1983 to 1990. Outcomes support assertions that landowners manage forested landscapes in their best interest and simultaneously provide large amounts of raw material for the economy (Vardaman 1989). There is evidence that nonindustrial private owners, for whatever reason, capture significant nonmarket benefits, and the benefits, such as habitat for RCW, are reflected in their production behavior (Newman and Wear 1993).

Landscape Forestry

The initial inventory constrains habitat for RCWs because a relatively small proportion of pine stands are older than 70 years (Table 12.2). The policy for

TABLE 12.3 Rotation Ages and Fractions Rotating Through Ages for Pine and Hardwood Forests to Simulate Changes from 1983 to 1990 for 21 Counties in Southeastern North Carolina

| Age class | Rotation | Fraction Rotating: | |
| | | Pines | Hardwoods |
(years)		(percent of forest type)	
31–40	35	0.30	0.00
41–50	45	0.30	0.00
51–60	55	0.25	0.00
61–70	65	0.08	0.20
71–80	75	0.04	0.30
81–90	85	0.02	0.40
90+	95	0.01	0.10

landscape forestry is to change this initial state of organization toward a state that provides nesting and feeding habitats for RCW. The procedure is to use superimposed rotations to produce cash flow with short rotations and nesting habitats with longer rotations. Rotations of 30 percent of the pine types are set at 35 years of age for cash flow and for feeding areas for RCW. The remaining 70 percent of the pines are rotated through 95 years to provide nesting habitats for RCWs. Rotations of 30 percent of hardwood stands is set at 75 years to add to cash flow and increase harvested areas for flickers. The remaining 70 percent of hardwoods is harvested at 95 years of age to provide nesting habitats for flickers. The maximum potential livelihood for RCWs is constrained because 55 percent of the landscape is in hardwood forests that are unsuitable for RCWs (Table 12.2). With this limitation, landscape forestry increases the livelihood of RCWs to an index value of about 0.7 (Fig. 12.3).

The livelihood for flickers is increased to about 0.54. However, net present values are 0.45. Reduction of cash flows from 0.82 to 0.45 in exchange for enhanced livelihood for RCW is not likely to be acceptable to thousands of landowners who have been receiving higher returns for conserving forested landscapes. Imposing laws, constraints, and regulations is costly and likely to be met with considerable resistance. An alternative is to develop an RCW

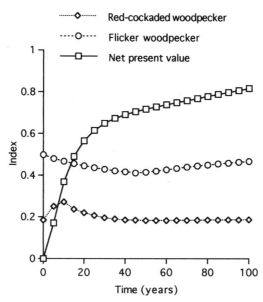

Figure 12.2   The assumption is that forestry practices reflected in inventories from 1983 to 1990 represent traditional forestry. Harvest rates are selected to retain indices for RCWs and flicker woodpeckers near current values. Index values in year 100 are 0.82 for net present values, 0.20 for RCWs, and 0.47 for flickers.

incentive program that compensates landowners for maintaining a part of their forest in old stands.

RCW Incentive

Net cash flow for traditional forestry is about 36 percent greater than for landscape forestry (Figs. 12.2, 12.3). A question is how an incentive program can encourage large numbers of landowners to delay harvest of 70 percent of their forest stands for 40 years. Reduction in cost of capital, as described in Chapter 8, is the option considered here. There are many ways to implement the incentive. The concern here is how to simulate some of the consequences.

Cash-flow forestry, traditional forestry, and landscape forestry are each simulated with an 8 percent cost of capital. The landscape forestry model is modified to simulate net present values with cost of capital set at 4 percent, which produces net present values approximating those for cash-flow forestry. This change offers an incentive that may attract many landowners to conserve 70 percent of their forest to 95 years of age. The low-cost loans are paid off

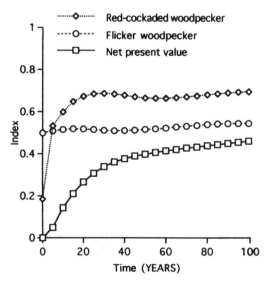

Figure 12.3   An incentive program is proposed to encourage landowners to schedule rates of timber harvest to favor nesting habitats for RCWs. A simulation of consequences suggests that the potential livelihood for RCWs is raised to an index value of 0.7 when incentives raise cash flows to amounts approximately equal to those of traditional forestry. Index values for net present values are 0.45 and those for flicker are 0.54.

as old stands are harvested. In effect, old stands become collateral for low-cost loans.

One consequence of subsidizing the cost of capital for old stands could be a livelihood for RCWs of 0.6–0.8 (Fig. 12.3). Some other consequences include increased public debt traded for livelihood of RCWs, increased or decreased cash flow in communities affected by the loans, and reduced harvest of timber to support the economy.

Current forestry in the 21 counties provides an average annual harvest of about 5.2 million m³ of pines and 2.6 million m³ of hardwoods. With landscape forestry, the harvest would decline to about 3.4 million m³ of pine and 2.1 million m³ of hardwoods. An RCW incentive program in most of the range of RCWs would reduce production of timber for houses, paper, and other goods at a time when demands are increasing (Ulrich 1990).

Public Policy Choices

Four scenarios are arrayed from the lowest to the highest index for RCWs and plotted with normalized indices for net present values in year 100 (Fig. 12.4).

One choice for a public policy could be to continue with traditional forestry, which provides many goods, services, and effects and retains the current livelihood for RCWs. However, attitudes and votes of the population may want the index for RCW livelihood increased (Fig. 12.3). If attitudes and votes demand government action, an option could be to find a level of subsidy between those for traditional and incentive forestry, possibly near the landscape forestry indices. The incentive would increase amounts of old pine stands and possibly increase numbers of RCWs. This action would compensate landowners for conserving a fraction of pine stands in age classes beyond ages for optimal cash flow.

Use of wood products would decline with an incentive program because of reduced harvest of timber. Incentive forestry would compensate landowners but would maintain timber harvest at levels indicated for landscape forestry. A consequence could be reduced jobs and manufacturing of wood-based products.

A third government option is to conserve RCW on public lands and permit all private landowners to continue with traditional forestry. This illustration considers only net present values to landowners. For public lands, models are modified to determine cost and benefits of these options to consumers and taxpayers. Such an analysis is beyond the scope of this chapter.

PUBLIC INCENTIVES CHANGE FORESTED LANDSCAPES

Since about 1940, large numbers of landowners have taken advantage of public incentives to regenerate pines on millions of hectares of lands in the South

(USDA 1983, 1993; USDA Forest Service 1988). Thirteen southern states, including Texas, Florida, Virginia, Kentucky, Missouri, and Arkansas, planted about 590,576 ha in 1988. Declining incentive programs reduced the area planted in 1990 to 381,287 ha (Vise 1991). Several analyses suggest that nonindustrial private landowners may incorporate nonmarket values in their mental models, but these owners apparently perceive economic gains, including public incentives, and act accordingly.

Without incentives, landowners limit investments in forestry practices. One constraint may be a perceived high risk of investments in forests that do not repay investments for many decades. Incentives reduce the risk of long-term investments and compensate landowners for producing benefits with no market values. Public policies can use incentives to change rates of planting, forest types, and rates of harvest. These changes in states of organization of forested landscapes affect national-economy, nonmarket values, such as habitats for RCW, aesthetics, and biological diversity.

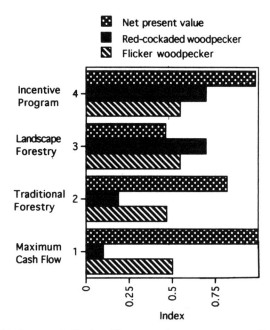

Figure 12.4   This bar-graph display illustrates the consequences of an incentive program to conserve stands of pines to old ages. Simulations suggest that an incentive program could increase potential livelihood for RCWs from about 0.2 for traditional forestry to about 0.7 for incentive forestry. Index values for flicker would increase from 0.47 for traditional forestry to 0.54 for incentive forestry. Indices for net cash flow to land owners would increase from 0.82 for traditional forestry to 0.98 because of government subsidies.

An Example from a Mountain Landscape

In the 21 mountain counties of western North Carolina, incentive programs encourage landowners to plant erodable soils to trees. This change in land use greatly reduces soil erosion, improves water quality, improves habitats, and enhances scenic views. Other assistance and incentive programs contribute to increased production of forest benefits (Farrish et al. 1993).

During the 35-year period, 1955–1990, harvest of trees for timber and other uses totaled more than 100 million m^3 (Cost 1975; Craver 1985; Johnson 1991). Yet volumes of timber in live hardwood trees doubled and volumes in pines increased 86 percent (Table 4.2). Growth in timber volumes came from growth of sprouts and seedlings following clear-cutting of the forest between 1880 and 1920 (Boyce and McClure 1975, 1978; Peterson 1968). Nonindustrial private forests (NIPF) cover 71.1 percent of the 1,773,979 ha of forestland in these 21 counties. Public lands, mostly national forests, cover 26.3 percent, and forests owned by forest industries cover 2.6 percent.

The inventory data suggest that NIPF owners in the 21 mountain counties benefit from assistance and incentive programs to conserve a diversity of forest conditions and to market timber from their lands.

An Example from a Piedmont Landscape

In the 18 Piedmont counties of western South Carolina, total area in forests increased from 1,701,300 ha in 1958 to 1,845,652 ha in 1993 (Snyder 1978; Tansey 1986; Brown 1993). Public policies are contributing to this shift of highly erodable agricultural lands to forest plantations of pine.

The variety of conditions on private forested lands, which cover half of all lands in these 18 counties, are important for providing habitats, aesthetics, timber, fuel, and biological diversity for millions of people who do not own land. Public policy, operating through assistance and incentives, influence decisions of many landowners and changes states of organization of forested landscapes. These kinds of aggregate changes are reducing soil erosion, improving water quality, increasing timber production, improving habitats, and enhancing scenic views (Table 12.4).

During the 35-year period, annual harvest of trees for timber and other uses increased from 3.9 million m^3 in 1958 to 7.5 million m^3 in 1993. Total harvest exceeded 200 million m^3 (Snyder 1978; Tansey 1986; Brown 1993). Yet volumes of timber in live hardwood trees increased 83 percent, and volumes in pines increased 63 percent. Growth in timber volumes comes from the growth of trees in both natural stands and plantations. Nonindustrial private forests (NIPF) cover 75.5 percent of the forested landscape in these 18 counties. Public lands, mostly national forests, cover 9.32 percent, and forests owned by forest industries cover 15.21 percent.

Aggregate Benefits from Multiple Ownerships

An important observation is that multiple owners are changing states of organization of forested landscapes and changing mixes of benefits produced. Each regional landscape produces an aggregate mix of benefits as a result of the owners' perceptions of how their particular portions of the forested landscape contribute to their self-interest. Since positive cash flow is essential for paying taxes and other costs for owning lands, sales of timber at young ages to produce cash are more important than sales at old ages to provide habitats for RCWs (Vardaman 1989; Newman and Wear 1993). A few landowners may use funds from other sources to pay for conserving some stands to old ages (Tables 4.2, 12.2, 12.4).

Organization of these large landscapes by actions of multiple owners results in significant productions of aesthetics, habitats, and biological diversity (Figs. 12.2, 12.4). The data do not indicate an altruistic concern for using landscape forestry to trade timber and cash flow for nonmarket values (Fig. 12.3).

States of organization of landscapes in multiple ownerships are changed by public policies (Boyce and Knight 1979, 1980; Boyce et al. 1986). Public policies seem to be most effective when landowners and consumers perceive that a policy serves their self-interest. For example, incentive programs to increase woody raw materials for society; reduce erosion; and enhance habitats, aesthetics, and biological diversity, are successful (Tables 4.2, 12.2, 12.4).

The opportunity, illustrated in this chapter, is to use landscape forestry methods to simulate consequences in the aggregate for landscapes in multiple ownerships before implementation of proposed policies. Simulated outcomes increase insights about the system. Decisions to use, not use, or modify a policy are made using the mental models of those persons responsible for public policies.

TABLE 12.4   Merchantable Volumes of Timber in Live Trees for the 35-Year Period 1958–1993 in 18 Piedmont Counties in Western South Carolina. (Snyder 1978; Tansey 1986; Brown 1993)

Year	Softwoods	Hardwoods	Total
	(million m^3)		
1958	55.6	55.1	110.7
1967	69.1	64.7	133.8
1977	104.4	94.5	198.9
1986	93.6	99.7	193.3
1993	90.5	101.0	191.5

13

EMERGING CONSUMER DEMANDS

Use and conservation of forested landscapes change as new demands emerge from consumers. Landscape forestry offers a way for landowners, managers, and retailers to interact with consumers to define emerging demands and to examine the consequences of changing states of organization of forested landscapes to fulfill demands. "Certification" and "sustainability" seem to be emerging demands that could bring important changes in how forested landscapes are used and conserved (Journal of Forestry 1993; Forest Farmer 1994).

This chapter illustrates the use of landscape forestry procedures to examine consequences that may result from fulfilling one or more emerging consumer demands. *Certification* and *sustainability* are used in the illustrations because these words signal emerging consumer demands.

CONSUMERS DIRECT USES OF FORESTED LANDSCAPES

Purchases of paper, wooden products, fuelwood, and hunting rights encourage landowners to organize landscapes to produce products for markets. Recent information suggests that some consumers throughout the world want forested landscapes organized to provide aesthetics, habitats for all organisms, and conservation of biological diversity. If compensated for their investments, landowners organize their forested landscapes to jointly produce combinations of legal and biologically possible benefits demanded by consumers (Chapters 10–12).

Aesthetics, habitats, and biological diversity have no market values but carry a cost for production (Chapters 11, 12). Since markets for fuelwood and timber incidentally increase productions of aesthetics, habitats, and biological diversity, consumers who want these incidental benefits search for alternative ways to encourage production. One tactic is to encourage governments to pass laws, such as the Endangered Species Act of 1973, to require landowners to provide desired, nonmarket benefits (Chapter 11). In addition to these actions, some consumers seem willing to accept fewer goods in the marketplace, pay higher market prices, and increase taxes in return for aesthetics, habitats, and biological diversity (Chapter 12). These emerging demands are suggested in the phrases "certification of forest" and "certification of forest products."

An Emerging Consumer Demand—Certification

Consumers view certification as a way to discriminate against forest products that are not "environmentally friendly." Certification is viewed by retailers as a way to sell more wood products. Environmentalists see certification as a way to produce nonmarket benefits. Forest managers view certification as a way to justify traditional forestry practices. A number of retail stores are offering certified wood products to their customers. Several independent companies are established as certifies of "environmentally friendly" forest and forest products. Some people see certification as a way to decrease conflicts over forest practices and help preserve the environment. Certification companies have formed a Forest Stewardship Council to oversee certification standards and practices (Journal of Forestry 1993; Forest Farmer 1994).

During periods of emergence, new consumers may have no generally accepted procedures for different people to follow with an expectation that all would agree or disagree on measurements within an acceptable error of estimate.

Emerging standards for certification include approval of written management plans, tenure and use rights for indigenous people, community rights and relations, optimized benefits from forested landscapes, environmental impacts, plans for monitoring and assessment of social and environmental impacts, and use of natural regeneration to replace tree plantations (Egan 1994; Ellefson 1993; Huggett 1993; Rosenberg et al. 1993; Tangley 1988; Journal of Forestry 1993; Forest Farmer 1994; Kessler et al. 1992; Swanson and Franklin 1992; Franklin 1993b; Alper 1993; Lippke and Oliver 1993; Peterson 1993).

Natural Forest versus Plantations

Mental models for sustainability contain assumptions that reduced human intervention into natural events result in forested landscapes providing desirable, if not optimal, aesthetics, habitats, and biological diversity. These assumptions are reflected in concerns for a land stewardship philosophy in which naturally regenerated forests are more desirable than planted forests (Kessler et al. 1992; Swanson and Franklin 1992; National Research Council

1986; Norse 1990). The emerging certification standard to shift traditional use of plantations to naturally regenerated forest is operational. The presence or absence of plantations and the consequences of shifting from plantations to naturally regenerated stands are measured by different people with consistently similar results.

A LANDSCAPE FORESTRY ANALYSIS

This illustration uses landscape forestry procedures to simulate some consequences of imposing a certification standard that encourages landowners to shift from plantations to naturally regenerated forests. The analysis simulates the consequences of producing benefits with traditional forestry in a landscape containing plantations. Models are designed to simulate changes in the same landscape when landscape forestry is used and when a scenario called *certified forestry* is used. The first step is to select a forested landscape with a high percentage of forest in plantations.

The Situation

A 35-county area in southeastern Georgia is a forested landscape with many pine plantations. Investments in both natural forest and in plantations of pine result from increased consumer demands for lumber, plywood, veneer, paper, paperboard, and fuelwood (Ulrich 1990). Southeastern Georgia provides a favorable environment for producing timber in combination with aesthetics, habitats, and biological diversity. A combination of economic, social, and political circumstances brings investments in pine plantations and in natural forest to fulfill consumer demands.

Between 1945 and 1960, large areas of agricultural land was retired and permitted to seed naturally to pine forests. Some of these lands were planted to pines. Over the past 40 years, planting of harvested pinelands and lands formerly in agriculture increased. During this 40-year period, rates of natural succession from pinelands to hardwood stands increased (Boyce 1975a; Boyce and Knight 1979, 1980). A 1988 inventory documents increasing rates of planting pines from 40–50 years ago to the present (Table 13.1).

The definition for NMS ("no manageable stand") is based on counting numbers of trees present and determining whether the number is too small to form a closed sunlit canopy at a future time (Johnson 1988). Lands in this classification are being regenerated, and new lands are being added to this classification as stands are harvested and as natural events, such as storms, fires, and insects, damage stands. Only lands classified as commercial forestland are included in this analysis.

All classes of landowners are responding to consumer demands for products produced from plantations and natural stands. These responses are in-

TABLE 13.1   Areas of Commercial Forestland by Forest Type and Age Class in 1988 for 35 Counties in Southeastern Georgia. (Johnson 1988; Sheffield 1982)

Age class (years)	All Types	Pine, Planted	Pine, Natural	Hardwood, Natural
		(thousands ha)		
0–10	685.5	516.8	29.9	138.7
11–20	354.6	269.1	23.3	62.3
21–30	330.6	189.2	57.6	84.7
31–40	272.3	34.6	145.2	92.5
41–50	248.2	5.7	105.8	136.7
51–60	183.4		68.0	115.3
61–70	104.9		37.2	76.6
71–80	57.1		3.1	53.9
81+	82.3		2.0	80.2
NMS[a]	592.5	15.0	156.6	420.9
Totals	2911.4	1030.4	628.8	1252.2

[a]NMS, no manageable stand.

dicated by the presence of pine plantations in all classes of ownership (Table 13.2).

Forest industries own and lease 38.5 percent of the commercial forestlands. More than half, 56.2 percent, are owned by farmers, individuals other than farm operators, and corporations excluding lands owned and leased by forest industries. About 5.2 percent of lands are in some form of public ownership, such as Blackbeard Island National Wildlife Refuge, Cumberland Island National Park, Okefenokee Swamp, and Wolf Island (Martin et al. 1993a). Some public lands are owned by the state of Georgia. No lands in southeastern Georgia are managed by USDA Forest Service.

TABLE 13.2   Areas of Commercial Forestland by Class of Ownership and Forest Type for 35 Counties in Southeastern Georgia in 1988. (Johnson 1988; Sheffield 1982)

Class of Ownership	Pine, Planted	Pine, Natural	Hardwood, Natural
	(percent of total)		
Industry[a]	21.7	4.0	12.8
Private	13.4	14.7	28.1
Public	0.3	2.8	2.1
Totals	35.4	21.5	43.0

[a]The industry class includes some leased lands.

From these 35 counties, demands for softwood timber, mostly pine, are as high as 9.5 thousand m³/year and for hardwoods as much as 11.6 thousand m³/year (Johnson 1988). Multiple landowners seem to be responding to these demands and are providing fuelwood and timber in relation to market prices. Schedules of harvest and regeneration rates are increasing growing stock volumes for pines and hardwoods (Table 13.3).

From 1960 to 1988, the area of commercial forestlands decreased because many forested lands were converted to urban developments and forest reserves (Johnson 1988; Sheffield 1982).

Examination of inventory data (Tables 13.1–13.3) suggests that potentials for timber harvest of both softwoods and hardwoods are larger for the next 30 years than for the past 30 years. Pine plantations are just beginning to grow into ages 25–35, which are ages for harvesting to produce large flows of timber and cash. Of course, the actual rates of harvest are likely to depend more on demands of consumers than on potentials for harvesting. An important observation is that a variety of private owners, including forest industries, are responding to market demands and are making investments to sustain flows of timber for 30 and more years into the future.

A second observation is that if returns on investments and incentive programs are large enough, many landowners and managers can be expected to change states of organization of landscapes to capture flows of solar energy for different baskets of benefits (Chapters 11, 12). A third observation is that new directions must be congruent with the four theorems (Chapter 9) if productions are to be sustained into the distant future.

Simulation with Traditional Forestry

A supposition is that traditional forestry over the past 40 years is responsible for current states of organization of the forested landscape (Tables 13.1–13.3). Distributions of land among age classes suggest rotation ages. Apparently, many natural pine stands are harvested between 41 and 50 years of age. Many hardwood stands are harvested in the age classes 61–70 and 71–80 years.

TABLE 13.3   Change in Growing Stock Volumes for Trees 12 cm dbh from a 30-cm Stump to a 12-cm Top for 35 Counties in Southeastern Georgia. (Johnson 1988; Sheffield 1982)

Year	Softwood	Hardwood	Total
	(thousands m³)		
1960	1247	671	1918
1971	1268	760	2029
1981	1391	898	2288
1988	1380	933	2313

Most pine plantations seem to be harvested in the 31–40 year age class. These rotation ages are used to simulate the potential harvest of timber and changes in states of organization from 1988 to 50 years into the future. Estimates of timber volumes for stands of different ages and types are from McClure and Knight (1984). I estimated prices from many sources for the purpose of displaying relative, not exact, market prices. Net present values are normalized by dividing by $4.2 billion, which is the maximum estimate for year 50.

An assumption for the model is that the three forest types are being moved toward a sustained state for the selected rotations (Chapters 5, 6). Conversions of former agricultural lands, now in natural pine stands, will decline to very low levels after about 5 years. Some natural pine stands will continue to naturally shift to oak-pine and then to hardwood stands. The simulation is from the 1988 inventory to 50 years later.

Supplementary models (Chapter 6) calculate normalized indices for cash flow, volumes of timber available for harvest, and percentages of forested landscape in different age classes. An assumption is that enhanced aesthetics, habitats, and biological diversity are indicated by increased amounts of hardwood stands more than 100 years old and pine stands more than 70 years old. Old age classes are used because old stands are important for nesting and feeding by many kinds of organisms. Age classes less than 10 years old are present in relatively large amounts for all three scenarios. Since the models contain negative feedback loops to move the landscape toward a sustained steady state, the presence of both old and young aged stands indicates that intermediate age classes are present (Chapter 9). A dispersion of age classes from seedlings to old age by forest types contributes to a variety of habitats, which contributes to aesthetics and biological diversity.

Simulation with Landscape Forestry

All pine plantations are conserved by replanting after harvest. Sixty percent of the plantations are harvested at about 30 years of age, and 40 percent are harvested at about 40 years of age. These superimposed rotations provide pulpwood and large trees for solid wood products.

Landscape forestry uses superimposed rotations to assure the presence of natural stands from seedlings to old-growth ages. For this illustration, half of the hardwood stands are harvested at about 75 years of age and half are harvested at 180 years of age. This harvest schedule increases habitats containing trees with cavities, dead trees, and areas with small-tree falls and canopy gaps. All hardwood stands are regenerated naturally. Conversions of hardwood stands to plantations is estimated to be 2 percent of the harvested areas. This rate represents plantings of areas that failed to naturally regenerate for whatever reason.

Half of the natural pine stands are harvested at about 40 years of age, and half are harvested at 100 years of age. This harvest schedule increases habitats for animals that use pine stands older than 40 years. Sixty-five percent of the harvested areas are regenerated naturally to natural pines and mixtures of pines and hardwoods. Conversions to plantations continues at the rate of 35 percent of the harvested areas.

Simulation with Certification Forestry

Emerging demands are for certification of products harvested from natural stands rather than from plantations. An assumption is that if landowners experience declining markets for wood from plantations and increasing markets for wood certified as produced from natural stands, harvested plantations will be regenerated naturally to pines and hardwoods rather than planted. This scenario is simulated by modifying the model for landscape forestry.

For certification forestry, superimposed rotations are the same as for landscape forestry. No conversions to plantations are permitted. However, natural regeneration of pine stands results in about 40 percent of the harvested areas naturally succeeding to hardwood stands and 60 percent remaining in natural pine classifications. For certification forestry, 98 percent of the harvested plantations are regenerated naturally to pines and about 2 percent are planted to pine because some landowners will continue to use plantations. Reduction of pine plantations to a small fraction of the landscape is the primary difference between landscape forestry and certification forestry.

Simulated Effects on Cash Flow

With traditional forestry and current market prices, estimated net present value in 50 years is about $4.2 billion. This number is used to normalize all estimates of net present values (Table 13.4). All net present values are assumed to be 0 at time 0. All regeneration costs, continuing costs, costs of capital, and operating costs are assumed to be the same for all scenarios. Stumpage prices are assumed to be the same for all three scenarios.

TABLE 13.4   Normalized Indices for Cash Flow Simulated Over 50 Years for Three Scenarios for a 35-County Area in Southeastern Georgia

From 1988 (years)	Normalized Index		
	Traditional Forestry	Landscape Forestry	Certification Forestry
0	0	0	0
10	0.56	0.20	0.06
20	0.74	0.36	0.11
30	0.80	0.49	0.14
40	0.95	0.58	0.17
50	1.00	0.64	0.18

Differences in cash flow for the three scenarios are due to differences in volumes and kinds of timber sold. Largest net returns are received for timber sold from plantations at about age 25–30 years. Landscape forestry uses superimposed rotations to provide some areas in old stands. Long discount periods for these old stands reduce cash flow (Chapter 8). Superimposed rotations are retained for certification forestry. However, liquidation of plantations shifts sales of pine timber to natural stands, which have longer rotations and less volumes per hectare than plantations. The result is reduced cash flows, which become negative after about 60 years.

If liquidation of plantations becomes a standard for certification, simulated net present values suggest that market prices for wood products may have to be raised 5 or more (1.00/0.18) times current prices to compensate landowners at rates equivalent to traditional forestry. For landscape forestry, prices may have to be raised 1.5 or more (1.00/0.64) times current prices to pay for aesthetics, habitats, and biological diversity associated with old stands (Table 13.4).

Simulated Effects on Timber Products

Simulation models contain negative feedback loops that constrain harvests to achieve steady-state distributions of age classes for each policy. Some variability in outcomes is related to the unequal distributions of land among age classes in the initial inventory (Table 13.1). With traditional forestry, initial rates of harvest of natural pine and hardwood are relatively high because stands older than rotation periods are available for liquidation (Table 13.5).

With traditional forestry, harvest of timber from plantations increases over time as stands planted during the past 30 years are harvested. If this policy is continued, most timber harvested after the next 20 years will come from plantations.

Landscape forestry uses superimposed rotations to grow some old stands. These longer rotations reduce total volumes of timber harvested by about 3 percent. By year 50 the volume harvested from pine plantations with landscape forestry is 42 million board feet less than with traditional forestry. For natural pines the reduction is 3 million board feet. With landscape forestry the volume harvested from hardwood stands increases by 20 million board feet. The net reduction in volume for using landscape forestry is 25 million board feet (Tables 13.5–13.6).

Landscape forestry conserves the initial area in plantations and continues to convert land formerly in agriculture to plantations. Many areas in natural pines are continuing to succeed to hardwood stands. Most of the hardwood stands remaining after year 50 are near streams and other areas where hardwoods are better suited for natural regeneration than pines.

If a certification standard requires harvested plantations to be naturally regenerated, existing plantations would continue to provide large volumes of timber for more than 30 years (Table 13.7).

TABLE 13.5   Simulated Volumes of Timber for Annual Harvests in Selected Years from Pine Plantations, Natural Pine Stands, and Natural Hardwood Stands if Traditional Forestry is Continued Over 50 Years for a 35-County Area in Southeastern Georgia

From 1988 (years)	Pine, Planted	Pine, Natural	Hardwood, Natural
	(millions board feet, International scale)		
0	306	578	1477
10	396	173	237
20	548	154	184
30	570	140	158
40	589	127	173
50	604	115	203

With certification forestry, increases in harvest from natural stands would begin to increase after about 20 years. However, these increases are not large enough to offset reduced harvest rates from plantations (Table 13.7). By year 50, total volumes harvested are 274 million board feet (922 − 648) less than with traditional forestry and 249 million board feet (897 − 648) less than for landscape forestry. These differences assume most landowners will respond to certification standards and regenerate harvested plantations to natural pine and hardwood stands.

Simulated Effects on Old Stands

With certification forestry, smaller volumes of timber are produced at higher costs than with traditional and landscape forestry. What consumers will re-

TABLE 13.6   Simulated Volumes of Timber for Annual Harvests in Selected Years from Pine Plantations, Natural Pine Stands, and Natural Hardwood Stands if Landscape Forestry is Used Over 50 Years for a 35-County Area in Southeastern Georgia

From 1988 (years)	Pine, Planted	Pine, Natural	Hardwood, Natural
	(millions board feet, International scale)		
0	306	151	135
10	377	140	168
20	515	136	200
30	533	130	213
40	549	121	221
50	562	112	223

TABLE 13.7   Simulated Volumes of Timber for Annual Harvests in Selected Years from Pine Plantations, Natural Pine Stands, and Natural Hardwood Stands if Certification Forestry is Used Over 50 Years for a 35-County Area in Southeastern Georgia

From 1988 (years)	Pine, Planted	Pine, Natural	Hardwood, Natural
	(millions board feet, International scale)		
0	306	151	135
10	366	190	168
20	281	142	213
30	213	205	231
40	158	268	248
50	117	271	260

ceive by forgoing timber volumes and paying higher prices for timber products are more areas of natural stands in older age classes (Table 13.8).

Percentages of old stands after 50 years are about the same for landscape and certification forestry. This is because the same superimposed rotations are used for both scenarios. Fifty years is not long enough for old stands to develop. When simulations are made to cover more than 100 years, percentages of old stands are larger for certification than for landscape forestry. However, landscape forestry retains plantations and sustains a positive cash flow.

Use of Simulated Outcomes

Outcomes of the simulations are relative differences and are for the purpose of providing interested parties with increased insights into the dynamics of

TABLE 13.8   Percentages of Pine Stands Older than 70 Years and Percentages of Hardwood Stands Older than 100 Years Simulated Over 50 Years for Three Scenarios for a 35-County Area in Southeastern Georgia. Key is Pine/Hardwood.

From 1988 (years)	Traditional Forestry	Landscape Forestry	Certification Forestry
	(percent of all commercial forest lands)		
0	1.5/9.2	1.5/9.2	1.5/9.2
10	0.0/0.0	3.7/11.2	3.7/11.3
20	0.0/0.0	5.7/12.1	5.7/12.2
30	0.0/0.0	6.0/12.0	6.4/12.1
40	0.0/0.0	5.4/11.4	5.7/11.4
50	0.0/0.0	4.5/10.6	3.3/10.3

the system. Outcomes are not to be taken as predictions and should not be taken as the only basis for making choices. Outcomes provide information for mental models. Regardless of how one views outcomes of this illustration, final decisions are made using mental models.

My use of proposals to certify forested landscapes and products is fortuitous because this issue is emerging at the time this book is being written. The proposed standard of requiring products from natural stands is used because the presence or absence of plantations is operational. Without operational definitions, few people can make observations and arrive at consistent results, within the limits of statistical error.

FROM SUSTAINED YIELD TO SUSTAINABILITY

Sustainability is another emerging consumer demand. Some people believe, apparently, that the concept of *sustained yield* includes timber and excludes other forest benefits, such as aesthetics, habitats, and biological diversity (Journal of Forestry 1993; Forest Farmer 1994). Misconceptions such as this one seem to be deeply imbedded in many mental models. Situation statements are used in landscape forestry to help remove inaccuracies from analyses (Chapter 3).

The Situation for Sustained Yield

A very old and appealing idea is to manage forested landscapes for the sustained yields of benefits. For many decades, managers have not been compensated for sustained yields of benefits that carry no market values. Yet the concept of sustained yield does include all forest benefits (Evelyn 1664; LeMaster et al. 1982; Journal of Forestry 1993).

In 1890, foresters proposed to sustain the productivity of soils rather than forests. Forests were considered crops, products of the soil. The goal of management was to sustain productivity of the soil because crops could be changed as consumer demands changed. The soil was to be sustained by shifting eroded agricultural land to forest. After a rotation of trees, the land would be returned to agriculture. In this way, soil fertility was to be conserved and used to provide sustained yields of forest benefits, food, clothing, and items yet to be demanded by society (Fernow 1891).

In the 1890s, some people considered private ownership of woodlands to be the bane of sustainable forestry. Sawmill operators were viewed as destructive agents who took only the most valuable trees and intentionally kindled fires to destroy the refuse timber, flowering plants, animal habitats, and aesthetics. A proposal was made to sustain the growth of forest by utilizing mature and marketable products produced by a proper rotation of valuable trees. This was to be achieved with cooperative forestry, which would be directed by governments and would be beneficial to communities and individuals alike. Several people expressed desires for sustaining a variety of habitats, aesthetics, spring flowers, and scenic views. Another view was to take the crop of trees made by nature and apply systematic forest management to sustain regularly producing conditions (James 1897).

Some foresters proposed bringing about an even distribution of land among all age classes younger than the age for harvest. This was the concept included in many plans for traditional forestry (Clutter et al. 1983; Smith 1986). Sustained yield of timber was based on organizing land areas into age classes such that a younger age class was always available to replace the harvested age class (Figs. 4.7 and 5.2).

Forestlands have rarely been distributed equally among age classes. Some people have taken this discrepancy as an indication of the failure of sustained-yield concepts (LeMaster et al. 1982). Reasons for this discrepancy are many. Sometimes an owner increases sales to take advantage of good markets or decreases sales in hopes of better future markets. Sometimes fire, storms, and other natural events disturb land areas by age classes. Sometimes the land has not been owned long enough to bring about an equal distribution of land areas among age classes (Tables 4.1, 13.1). Sometimes political events direct managers of public lands to deviate from a sustained-yield policy (LeMaster et al. 1982). Events of these kinds change amounts of timber available for harvest and bring drastic changes in future policies (USDA Forest Service 1992a). A change in policy does not destroy the concept of *sustained yield* for benefits that have operational definitions, such as timber, fuelwood, and game animals. Other benefits, when operationally defined, can be included in managerial actions to sustain yields.

Many authors have opposed devoting resources to sustain yields of benefits that may not be valuable tomorrow (LeMaster et al. 1982; Rosenberg et al. 1993). A classic example of this situation is the proposal to sustain yields of wood blocks for use in wagon hubs. In 1889, Martin Conrad (1889) made a strong case for conserving all natural stands of Osage orange trees and establishing large plantations of this tree in Illinois and other states to support future demands for wooden hubs for wagons. In the 1800s, Osage orange was the best wood available for wagon hubs. Soon after 1900, axle grease made metal bearings more useful than wooden hubs. By the 1920s, railroads replaced wagons. Today, airplanes and trucks have replaced railroads. This is one of many examples of continual changes in consumer demands as technical, social, political, and economic events change over time. One can find evidence to argue that substitutions negate efforts to restrain use of resources for purposes of sustaining future yields. Arguments continue (Rosenberg et al. 1993), yet the idea of sustained yield seems stronger today than in past years.

After 100 years, mental models of sustained yield seem to be widespread and to include many new phrases and expressions. "Sustainable forest" seems appealing because the words suggest continuous production and use of forest. The words suggest that a nation's forest resources are not diminishing. The idea seems appealing as an ethic for using natural resources today and si-multaneously conserving potential productivity for future generations. "Sus-tainable use" implies meeting the needs of the present without compromising the ability of future generations to fulfill demands (Rosenberg et al. 1993). When the USDA Forest Service informed all employees of a shift to ecosys-tem management, social and ethical reasons occupied more space in the mem-orandum than biological and economic reasons (USDA Forest Service 1992a). Sustained yield is described by some people as an article of faith in human-kind's ability to manage natural resources to sustain life and as an obligation of individuals to provide for future generations (Rumsey and Duerr 1975).

Mental models of sustained yield seem to reflect deep-seated linkages of individuals with social and biological values (Lee 1982). These linkages are reflected in numerous publications from professional and environmental in-stitutions. A few examples from a very long list includes animals and plants that exhibit beauty in form and appearance (Ackery and Vane-Wright 1984), old-growth forests (Franklin 1993a), endangered species (Tear et al. 1993), scenic values, recreation and aesthetics (Cordell and Hendee 1982), land-scapes (Sample 1992), wildlife, biological diversity, timber, fuelwood, cash flow, and many other items of interest to users of forested landscapes (Probst and Crow 1991; Soule 1986; Norris 1993; Harris 1984; Forman and Godron 1986). For professional managers, these mental models are important for in-dicating what consumers want from forested landscapes and how these wants are to be obtained (Schneider 1993; Egan 1993a,b). In the United States, more than 16 million consumers contribute money to environmental organizations in hopes the organizations will influence managers, owners, and governments to manage forested landscapes for sustained yield of various kinds of benefits (Hendee and Pitstick 1992).

Sustained yields of benefits are determined by states of organization (Chap-ter 9, Theorem 4). Every forested landscape irreversibly changes from state to state over time (Theorems 2, 3). Over the past 20,000 years and possibly longer, humans have searched, directed, and altered states of organization of forested landscapes to fulfill personal desires (Bowler 1992). In today's world, personal desires are related to or driven by cash flows, which provide incen-tives for landowners and managers to organize landscapes for the capture of solar energy in forms that can be marketed. States of organization desired by landowners and managers are determined by consumers, whose demands are expressed in markets for forest products and in votes to support or change governments and government actions. Benefits without markets are produced incident to organizing landscapes for marketable benefits, by government ac-tions, by concerned individuals and by nonprofit organizations. Yet states of organization of lands in public ownerships are directed to reflect desires of consumers. States of organization of lands owned by nonprofit foundations are organized to reflect the desires of those who donate funds or work toward obtaining gifts for purchase and management of the lands.

The situation is that benefits from forested landscapes are sustained over time by the aggregate actions of all people who use paper, sit in wooden chairs, live in houses containing wood, walk in wildernesses, fish in forested streams, and do other things that demand forest benefits. For hundreds and possibly thousands of years, benefits have been sustained because humans have tools, knowledge, and desires to culture crops for food and fiber, landscapes for beauty and forests for wood and other benefits (Gomez-Pompa and Kaus 1992; Lewontin 1993). The aggregate result of humanity's actions is to sustain yields of benefits desired by consumers. The results are reflected in inventories of forested landscapes that measure distributions of stands by forest type, age, and area classes (Tables 4.1, 13.1).

The Situation for Sustainability

Definitions for sustainability continue to emerge. Most proposed definitions do not give different people procedures for measuring and arriving at consistent answers about sustained flows of benefits from a forested landscape (Forest Farmer 1994; Journal of Forestry 1993). If states of organization (Tables 4.1, 12.2, 13.1) are used as measures of relative rates of sustained yields of selected benefits (Figs. 4.8, 4.10, 4.12, Tables 13.4–13.8), then sustainability can be viewed as plans for maintaining a desired state of organization into the distant future. Performance can be monitored in terms of inventories, which are defined with well-known operational procedures. The emerging question seems to be: How are forested landscapes to be organized to sustain flows of benefits when consumers cannot agree on a desired basket of benefits?

Consumers of forest benefits are scientists, fishermen, soldiers, environmentalists, politicians, shopkeepers, and readers of this book. Possibly every human consumes some kind of forest benefit. Most Westerners, for example, write on paper, read magazines, and sit in wooden chairs. Very few people view these actions as signals transported through markets, vendors, and manufacturers to forest managers. Signals from consumers are translated by landowners and forest managers into policies for organizing forested landscapes (Fig. 3.1). If compensation is acceptable, forested landscapes are organized to fulfill demands (Chapters 4, 12).

Consumer demands come through markets, as for southeastern Georgia. Demands bring public ownership of forested landscapes, as for the Craggy Mountains. Demands appear as laws and regulations, as for red-cockaded woodpeckers. Regardless of how imposed, demands are fulfilled, ultimately, by consumers compensating landowners and managers, public and private, to organize forested landscapes to produce baskets of benefits in the aggregate. Forested landscapes are organized in response to consumer demands for some or all of the thousands of benefits classified as aesthetics, habitats, fuelwood, timber, and biological diversity (Chapter 1). Consumers pay for benefits from forested landscapes with purchases of goods and services, incentive programs, salaries to regulators and government officials, and market benefits forgone for the sake of maintaining or improving aesthetics, habitats, and biological diversity.

An answer to the question of how forested landscapes are to be organized for sustainability varies with each forested landscape. No generalized answer can be given for all landscapes. Historical inventories suggest that landscapes are organized to fulfill policies that emerge from economic, social, and political situations (Chapters 4, 8, 11, 12). Bowler (1992) documents economic, social, and political situations occurring over the last several hundred years and relates changes in demands to use and conservation of forested landscapes. Every generation seems to change the way it wants to live. Every different lifestyle changes demands for fuel, clothing, shelter, and other items that bring about rearrangement of forested landscapes.

After thousands of years, some forested landscapes have been changed to grasslands, some to badly eroded mountainsides, and some to deserts. Agriculture, urban developments, transportation corridors, water impoundments, and airports continue to be the primary reasons for deforestation (Table 12.1), not harvest of timber to organize landscapes. In the last 300 years, traditional forestry practices have increased standing volumes of timber, amounts of timber harvested, and potentials for increased harvest in the future (FAO 1993; Tables 4.2, 10.2, 12.4, 13.3). Landscape forestry offers a way to trade some timber production for enhanced aesthetics, habitats, and biological diversity. The missing link is adequate compensation to landowners and managers to divert some solar energy from fuelwood and timber.

Emergence of fears about deteriorating environments seems likely to change some policies for organizing forested landscapes. To many people, harvesting timber is viewed as deforestation and destruction of habitats, aesthetics, and biological diversity. Yet harvest of trees is the only practical and economically efficient way to rearrange forested landscapes to support livelihoods for growing populations and simultaneously to enhance aesthetics, habitats, and biological diversity (D. M. Smith 1977; Chapters 2–12).

Fears about deteriorating environments, sustainability, biological diversity, and forest destruction lead to mental models (McKibben 1989) that conflict with models for scheduling harvests of stands to organize forested landscapes for combinations of benefits (Figs. 4.10, 4.12, 11.3, 12.3). For more than a hundred years, special-interest groups have struggled to dominate the way forested landscapes are organized. The complex of different mental models (Hendee and Pitstick 1992), called environmentalism (Bowler 1992), seems to thrive on battling against some kind of environmental deterioration. One prevalent mental model is that changed environments, forested landscapes, habitats, and past conditions of biological diversity can be restored to past states. The principles of irreversibility and continuity (Chapter 9) tell us there is no way to reverse growth from young to old age, no way to restore a rotten egg to a state that will hatch a chicken. There is no way to reverse change in biological systems. Our opportunities are to reorganize forested landscapes from existing states, step by step, toward states of organization that provide desired baskets of benefits (Theorems 1–4). We must look to the future for continually changing mixes of benefits, brought about as states of organization change, and attempt to direct states of change to fulfill policies.

Another prevalent mental model is that a desired benefit from forested landscapes can be tossed into a basket of aggregated benefits as one tosses items into a grocery cart. The reality is that tradeoffs are essential. Every change in a state of organization changes the mix of benefits in an aggregated basket. Solar energy is partitioned among items in the basket. Another reality is that investment in producing one kind of benefit, such as timber, does not prohibit productions of incidental benefits, such as habitats. What determines mixes in baskets of benefits is the state of organization of the landscape at any given moment of time. It is this relationship (Theorem 4) that offers opportunities to reintroduce into management of forested landscapes a sense of unity that is lost in the fragmentation of cultural practices into disciplines and demands into special-interest categories.

Environmentalism and environmental sciences represent an artificial classification of special-interest groups and disciplines that are linked by self-declarations of concern over the environment. Strong differences of opinion prevent a sense of unity of purpose. Universities offer courses in environmental management, each presenting very different contents, in departments and schools of law, medicine, psychology, sociology, economics, biology, geology, forestry, wildlife management, and business. The professional fragmentation of science, especially in the biological arena, limits opportunities to develop a discipline of ecology and a profession of environmental management. Bowler (1992) provides historical evidence that differences between special-interest groups will persist and change over time. An important point made by Bowler is that debates, perpetuated by the fragmented demands of environmental organizations, provide conflicting information that prevents any single group from convincing policy makers their position is the only possible way to save humanity from extinction.

In the absence of compensation for sustaining productions of baskets of benefits that include enhanced aesthetics, habitats, and biological diversity, landowners and managers are left with the question of how forested landscapes are to be organized. The only consistent and reliable signals available are demands from markets for fuelwood, timber, and sometimes hunting, fishing, and recreation rights. From these signals, owners and governments develop policies for organizing forested landscapes. Regardless of the kind of policy (Fig. 3.1) presented to managers, this book provides ways to simulate and evaluate consequences before taking an action.

Landscape forestry reintroduces into management procedures a sense of unity that is lost in the fragmentation of cultural practices into disciplines and practices of special interests. The procedures use superimposed rotations to divert portions of solar energy from productions of fuelwood and timber to many other items in the basket of benefits. It is a way to examine the use and conservation of forested landscapes as systems of interlocking natural events, demands of consumers, and directed rearrangements of forested landscapes. Landscape forestry is the way for managers to rearrange forested landscapes to support lifestyles desired and funded by most consumers.

APPENDIX

The appendix provides readers familiar with DYNAMO or STELLA with some macros and relationships found to be useful in building many landscape forestry models. Macros and some other parts of the CRAG models are useful as building blocks for other models, such as RED1 (Chapter 11). However, when models are modified or existing macros are used, suppositions and white boxes should be carefully examined for congruence with new situations.

Some of the macros used in the CRAG models can be used with little or no change in most landscape models. Changes for adapting the macros to different situations include linking the macros to other modules, changing constants for delays within age classes, changing table functions, adjusting stumpage prices for different kinds of timber, determining discount and re-investment rates, and inserting equations for cash inflows and outflows.

Primary control for simulated outcomes is the rotation period or periods for superimposed rotations and fractions rotating for superimposed rotations (Chapters 5, 6). Sizes of canopy openings are used in supplementary models to simulate habitats, aesthetics, kinds of regeneration, and growth rates of seedlings and sprouts. Kinds of regeneration, natural or planted, determine how macros are linked for conversion of types, costs for regeneration, and lengths of delays to regenerate harvested areas.

Equations are presented here in DYNAMO format. All equations are readily translated into STELLA. No equations for constants and for obvious calculations are presented. See the manuals that come with the appropriate software.

MACRO GRO

```
MACRO GRO(HAB,DELY,EQX,SUIN)
```

HAB is the land area in this age class (ha).

DELY is the delay, the time for sunlit trees to pass through this age class (years).

EQX is the equilibrium area in this age class if timber is harvested. EQX is set at 0 when no timber is harvested. See Chapter 6.

SUIN is the rate of succession into this age class.

This macro calculates rates of succession from one to another age class and calculates mortality from selected age classes. When the rate of succession into this age class is 0, succession out-liquidates the age class over the period DELY. If HAB is 0 and land begins to flow into this age class, no succession out occurs until after the period DELY. Succession out of this age class is a positive feedback loop. Rates of succession are determined by amounts of land in the age class and the delay period DELY.

Equations for GRO

```
A   GRO.K=(MAX(0,(HAB.K-EQX.K))/MAX(DT,$DLS.K))*$DSW.K
        Succession out of this age class (ha/year).
A   $DLS.K=SMOOTH($DLI.K,1)
        Smoothed divisor for DELY (years).
N   $DLS.K=DELY+1
        Initial smoothed divisor for delay (years).
A   $DLI.K=FIFZE((MAX(-1,($DLS.K-1))),DELY,/\
    (MAX((SUIN.KL-1),0)))
        Adjusted DELY for succession to next age class
        (years).
A   DSW.K=STEP(1,$STIM.K)
        Switch to turn succession on and off
        (dimensionless).
A   $STIM.K=FIFZE((DELY+TIME.K),$SST.K,(MAX((HAB.K-1),0)))
        Calculation of switch for succession (years).
A   $SST.K=SMOOTH($STIM.K,1)
        Smoothed switch (years).
N   $SST=0
        Initial switch time (years).
MEND
```

Use of GRO

The illustrated use is for CRAG-2 and CRAG-3, age class A1, upland hardwoods (Table 4.1; Figs. 5.1–5.3). A description of this age class is given in Chapter 6 (Fig. 6.1). Macro GRO is used in age classes A1–CC1, A2–CC2, and A3–CC3. No timber is harvested from these age classes. In the model CRAG-1, Macro GRO is used in all age classes because no timber is harvested with CRAG-1.

```
NOTE  Age class A1, upland hardwoods, age 1-10 years.
L A1.K=A1.J+DT *(REG1.KJ-SUAA1.JK)
      Area in age class A1 (ha).
N A1=IA1    Initial area in A1 (ha).
R SUAA1.KL=GRO(A1.K,DGR1,Z,REG1.KL)
      Succession to next age class (ha/year).
```

A1 is the area in this age class (ha).

DT is differential time (years) (Chapter 6).

REG1 is the rate of regeneration to this age class (ha/year).

SUAA is the rate of succession to the next age class (ha/year).

DGR1 is the delay period for this age class, which is 10 years.

Z is 0 for equilibrium, EQX, in age classes from which no timber is harvested.

MACRO HAR

```
MACRO HAR(SALES,TLQ)
```

HAR is the harvest rate for accumulated sales (ha/year).

SALES is the amount of timber sold and waiting for harvest (ha).

TLQ is the time for liquidation of this age class.

This macro schedules the harvest of standing timber that is sold and waiting to be harvested according to a sales agreement. TLQ acts as a switch to turn on liquidation when managers consider accumulated stands in this age class to be surplus (Chapters 4, 5, Figs. 4.7, 5.2).

Equations for HAR

```
A HAR.K=FIFZE((SALES.K/DRT),$DLSS.K,TLQ)
      Harvest rate (ha/year).
A $DLSS.K=SALES.K/MAX(DT,$DLS.K)
      Liquidation sales rate (ha/year).
L $DLS.K=$DLS.J+DT *(-$DDLS.JK)
      Divisor for liquidation sales (years).
N $DLS=DRT+1    Initial value of liquidation divisor
  (years).
```

```
R  $DDLS.KL=FIFGE(1,0,TIME.K,TLQ)
      Switch for changing liquidation divisor
      (dimensionless).
MEND
```

DRT is a constant. It is the delay period for the purchaser to remove purchased timber.

Use of HAR

The use of HAR is illustrated in the next section for the macro SEL.

MACRO SEL

```
MACRO SEL(CLASS,DCL,TSF,CEQ,TIN,FLR,FLOWX,TLX,TLN,SELOX,TOT)
```

SEL is the sell rate for this age class (ha/year).

CLASS is the land area in this age class (ha).

DCL is the delay period for this age class (years).

TSF is the table for sell policy (Fig. 6.5).

CEQ is the equilibrium for this age class (ha).

TIN is the succession into this age class (ha/year).

FLR is the flow rate for this age class (ha/year).

FLOWX is the flow rate for this forest type (ha/year).

TLX is the time to liquidate this age class (years). When TLX is 0, no liquidation occurs.

TLN is the time to liquidate the next-oldest age class (years).

SELOX is sales of older age classes (ha/year).

TOT is the succession out of this age class (ha/year).

This macro is used in age classes from which timber is harvested. In CRAG-2 and CRAG-3, macro SEL is used in age classes D1-O1, D2-O2 and D3-O3. This macro is not used in CRAG-1. SEL calculates rates of sale to bring about steady-state rates of change in the age classes. When this age class is older than the oldest age for harvesting timber, this and older age classes are liquidated over a time period specified by values for TLX. When timber harvests from older age classes fulfill harvest rates for a steady-state flow rate, no harvest is from this age class. When harvests from older age classes are less than steady-state rates, differences are made up from this age class. Harvests are scheduled to bring the forested landscape to a steady-state condition as soon as possible with minimum oscillations in land areas among age classes.

Equations for SEL

```
A  SEL.K=FIFZE($SL.K,$LIQ.K,TLX)
       The sell rate for liquidation or to bring about
       steady state (ha/year).
A  SL.K=MIN($PSEL.K,$HRQ.K)
       The sell rate for steady state (ha/year).
A  $LIQ.K=CLASS.K/MAX(DT,$DLS.K)
       Liquidation of age class in TLX years (ha/year).
L  $DLS.K=$DLS.J+DT*(-$DDLS.JK)
       The delay divisor for liquidation (years).
N  $DLS=TLX    Initial time to liquidate age class
   (years).
R  $DDLS.KL=FIFZE(0,1,TLX)
       The switch for delay divisor (dimensionless)
A  PSEL.K=FLR.K*TABHL(TSF,$CV.K,0,5,.5)
       The policy for sell rate (ha/year) (Fig. 6.5).
A  $CV.K=CLASS.K/MAX(1,CEQ.K)
       The coverage for sell policy (dimensionless)
       (Fig. 6.5).
A  $HRQ.K=FIFGE(0,(FLOWX.K-SELOX.K),SELOX.K,FLOWX.K)
       The harvest required relative to older age classes
       (ha/year).
R  TOT.KL=$SUC.K*FIFZE(1,0,TLN)
       The succession out of age class (ha/year).
A  $SUC.K=GRO(CLASS.K,DCL,CEQ.K,TIN.K)
       Succession out of age class with harvest for
       steady state. A switch in TOT turns this equation
       off when this age class is being liquidated
       (ha/year).
MEND
```

Use of SEL

The illustration is for age class E1 (Fig. 6.4), CRAG-2, and CRAG-3 (Figs. 5.2, 5.3).

```
NOTE  Age class E1, upland hardwoods, age 81-90 years.
L  E1.K=E1.J+DT*(SUE1.JK-SLE1.JK-SUEE1.JK)
       Area in E1 (ha/year).
N  E1=IE1    Initial inventory for E1 (ha).
```

```
R  SLE1.KL=SEL(E1.K,DGR1,TSL1,EQE1.K,SUE1.K,/\
   FLE1.K,FLOW1.K,TLE1,TLEE1,SEEO1.K,SUEE1.KL)
        Sell schedule for E1 (ha/year).
L  ASE1.K=ASE1.J+DT*(SLE1.JK-E1X.JK)
        Accumulated sales from E1 waiting to be harvested
        (ha).
N  ASE1=IASE1    Initial accumulated sales (ha).
R  E1X.KL=HAR(ASE1.K,TLE1)
        Harvest rate from E1 accumulated sales (ha/year).
```

E1 is the land area in this age class (ha).

SUE1 is succession into this age class (ha/year).

SLE1 is the sell schedule (ha/year).

SUEE1 is succession out of this age class (ha/year) when harvest is to bring about steady-state rates of change. Succession is turned off when this age class is being liquidated.

SLE1 is the sell schedule (ha/year).

DGR1 is the delay period for this age class, a constant (years).

TSL1 is the sell policy, a white box (Fig. 6.5).

EQE1 is the equilibrium for this age class (ha).

FLE1 is the flow rate for this age class (ha/year) (Fig. 6.4).

FLOW1 is the flow rate for this type (ha/year) (Fig. 6.4).

TLE1 is the time to liquidate E1, a constant (years).

TLEE1 is the time to liquidate the next-oldest age class, a constant (years).

SEEO1 is sales of older age classes (ha/year).

SOME RELATIONSHIPS FOR THE CRAG MODELS

Table functions are used to establish sell policies for each forest type (Fig. 6.5). Yield tables and sale prices for timber by age classes are table functions (manuals; Richardson and Pugh 1981).

Inflows of cash are calculated as yields of timber multiplied by sales prices. Additions include leases for hunting, fishing, recreation rights, and incentives to produce nonmarketable benefits.

Flow rates of land for an age class from which timber is harvested are calculated as the area of the forest type multiplied by the fraction harvested from this age class. This product is divided by harvest age for this age class. Flow rates for a forest type are the sum of the flow rates of age classes from which timber is harvested.

The area of a forest type is calculated as the sum of all age classes for the type plus accumulated sales waiting to be harvested.

Conversion rates are calculated as fractions of land converted from one to another type at the time of harvest. For natural conversions, for example, of pine to oak-pine to hardwood stands, the fractions are those experienced by measurements and observations.

Regeneration rates are lands available for regeneration divided by the amount of time required to establish seedlings naturally or by planting.

Cash-flow indicators use the conventional mathematics of finance equations (Fleischer 1984; Clark et al. 1979). Equations are written to include net present values, net cash flow, profitability index, equivalent annual rents, and internal rates of return.

A debug test for core models is made by setting all conversion rates to zero and plotting or printing land areas in each forest type for 50–100 years. Values simulated should equal initial values for all simulated times. Any deviations indicate errors in one or more equations.

SUPPLEMENTARY MODELS

Supplementary models use information, such as changes in areas of age classes, to calculate benefits such as timber harvested, cash flow, aesthetics, habitats, and biological diversity. Outcomes of supplementary models are normalized from -1 to $+1$ or from 0 to $+1$. Normalized indices permit plots of outcomes with different units of measure. Decisions are based on relative differences and not on forecast values. Indices can be changed by changing rates of timber harvest, sizes of canopy openings, and kinds of regeneration. An example is the calculation of the biological diversity for spiders.

Biological Diversity of Spiders

Three guilds of spiders are recognized to occur in hardwood forests. Biological diversity is enhanced by increasing proportions of a forested landscape in hardwood forest types and by maintaining a distribution of age classes from 1 year to old ages over time and space. Such a distribution is operationally measured as proportions of total area in the landscape in hardwood types, proportions of area in seedling age classes, and proportions of area in old age classes over time. The presence or absence of seedling and old age classes over time is indicative of the presence or absence of all intermediate age classes (Fig. 6.2). Biological diversity is related to distributions of habitats, indicated by forest types, age classes, and sizes of openings, distributed over space and time. A relatively simple supplementary model indicates potential livelihood for each guild of spiders and, in the aggregate, biological diversity.

Equations for the Biological Diversity of Spiders

NOTE Biological Diversity of Spiders in Hardwood
     Forests
A SPID.K=SMOOTH∧
  (EXP(LOGN(SDSP.K*MTSP.K*INSP.K)/3),SPIDA)
       The index for biological diversity, SPID, is an
       exponential average of 3 decimal values for the
       three guilds of spiders, SDSP, MTSP, and INSP.
       The index is smoothed over a period of time
       that is required for spiders to self-organize for
       changed habitat conditions, SPIDA (Chapter 3).
A SDSP.K=HOS.K*TABHL(TSSP,PSEH.K,0,.1,.01)
       The index for seedling spiders, SDSP, is a func-
       tion of the proportion of area in hardwood
       seedling habitats, PSEH, adjusted for size of
       canopy openings, HOS. PSEH is calculated in the
       core model as the area in regeneration and in
       age classes less than 5 years old divided by
       the total area of hardwood forests in the for-
       ested landscape.
T TSSP=.1,.1,.2,.4,.5,.6,.7,.8,.85,.9,.95
       The table for relationship between spiders and
       seedling habitats (Fig. 5.6).
A HOS.K=TABHL(THOS,ASO.K,.1,5.5,.9)
       The adjustment for size of canopy openings,
       HOS, is a function of the average size of
       openings less than 5.5 ha, ASO. The average
       size of canopy openings is calculated in the
       core model as a normal distribution of sizes
       around an average size that is established by
       policy.
T THOS=.1,.45,.65,.8,.9,.95,1
       The table for adjustment to sizes of canopy
       openings.
A MTSP.K=TABHL(TMSP,MTHS.K,0,1,.1)
       The index for mature timber spiders, MTSP, is
       a function of the proportion of area in mature
       timber stands older than 80 years in hardwood
       types. MTHS is calculated in the core model.
T TMSP=.01,.2,.4,.7,.9,.92,.95,.98,.99,1,1
       The table for the relationship between spiders
       and mature timber stands (Fig. 5.5).

```
A  INSP.K=TABHL(TINS,PHDW.K,0,1,.1)
       The index for spiders indifferent to age classes
       of hardwood stands, INSP, is a function of the
       proportion of area in hardwood stands, PHDW.
       The proportion of area in hardwood stands is
       calculated in the core model.
T  TINS=0.5,.1,.15,.25,.4,.7,.85,.9,.95,.98,1
       The table for the relationship between indiffer-
       ent spiders and the proportion of area in hard-
       wood forest types.
C  SPIDA=3
       The time for spiders to self-organize after a
       habitat change (years).
```

Use of Biological Diversity Equations

Functional indices for biological diversity are not useful to managers (Boyce and Cost 1978; Preston 1960; Pielou 1977; Ludwig and Reynods 1988). Procedures presented here are operational for managers in that undesirable indices can be adjusted by changing rates of timber harvest, sizes of canopy openings formed, and kinds of regeneration encouraged. The estimation of biological diversity using simulation models simulates changes over time, which, by the principle of continuity, is essential. The relationships between states of organization of forested landscapes and biological diversity are explicitly displayed for scrutiny by interested parties. More important, the operational procedures can be repeated by others and adjusted to fit new and different situations (Figs. 5.5, 5.6).

REFERENCES

Ackery, P. R., and R. I. Vane-Wright. 1984. Milkweed butterflies, their cladistics and biology. Ithaca, NY: Cornell Univ. Press.

Adams, D. L., and G. W. Barrett. 1976. Stress effects on bird-species diversity within mature forest ecosystems. Am. Midl. Nat. 96(1):179–194.

Allen, T. F. H., and T. B. Starr. 1982. Hierarchy: perspectives for ecological complexity. Chicago: Univ. of Chicago Press.

Alper, J. 1993. Protecting the environment with the power of the market. Science 260: 1884–1885.

Andrewartha, H. G., and L. C. Birch. 1954. The distribution and abundance of animals. Chicago: Univ. of Chicago Press.

Aresta, Michele, and Giorgio Forti. 1986. Carbon dioxide as a source of carbon. NATO ASI Series, Series C, Mathematical and Physical Sciences, Vol. 206. Boston: D. Reidel Publishing Co.

Armstrong, J. S. 1985. Long-range forecasting. New York: John Wiley & Sons.

Art, H. W., and F. H. Bormann. 1993. The dictionary of ecology and environmental science. New York: Henry Holt and Co.

Ashby, W. R. 1973. An introdution to cybernetics. London: Chapman and Hall and Univ. Paperbacks.

Avery, T. E., and H. E. Burkhart. 1983. Forest measurements. New York: McGraw-Hill Book Co.

Bachiel, A. 1992. Expectations of a changing nation—the public. In Proc. Soc. Am. For. Natl. Convention, Richmond, VA, Oct. 25–28, 1992. Bethesda, MA: Society of American Foresters, pp. 7–14.

Bacon, W. R., and J. Dell. 1985. National forest landscape management. Vol. 2, chap. 6: Fire. Agric. Handb. 608. Washington, DC: USDA Forest Service.

Bailey, J. A. 1984. Principles of wildlife management. New York: John Wiley & Sons.

Bailey, R. G. 1988. Ecogeographic analysis: a guide to the ecological division of land for resource management. Misc. Publ. 1465. Washington, DC: USDA Forest Service.

Bailey, R. G. 1989. Explanatory supplement to Ecoregions Map of the Continents. Environ. Conserv. 16(4):307–310.

Baker, F. S. 1923. Notes on the composition of even aged stands. J. For. 21:712–717.

Barnes, B. V., K. S. Pregitzer, T. A. Spies, and V. H. Spooner. 1982. Ecological forest site classification. J. For. 80(8):493–498.

Bass, R. D. 1978. Ninety six: the struggle for the South Carolina back country. Lexington, SC: The Sandlapper Store.

Baumol, W. J., and W. E. Oates. 1989. The theory of environmental policy. New York: Cambridge Univ. Press.

Becht, G. 1974. Systems theory, the key to holism and reductionism. BioScience 24: 569–579.

Beck, D. E. 1978. Growth and yield of white pine. In Proc.: Symp. for the Management of Pines of the Interior South. Tech. Publ. SA-TP2:72–90. Atlanta, GA: USDA Forest Service, Southeastern Area State and Private Forestry.

Beer, S. 1966. Decision and control: the meaning of operational research cybernetics. New York: John Wiley & Sons.

Beer, S. 1975. Platform for change. New York: John Wiley & Sons.

Begon, M., and M. Mortimer. 1986. Population ecology. Sunderland, MA: Sinauer Assoc.

Belsky, A. J., and Canham, C. D. 1994. Forest gaps and isolated savanna trees. Bioscience 44(2):77–84.

Benjamin, A. C. 1955. Operationism. Springfield, IL: Thomas Books.

Birdsey, R. A. 1992. Carbon storage and accumulation in United States forest ecosystems. Gen. Tech. Rep. WO-59. Washington, DC: USDA Forest Service.

Blackmon, B. G. 1992. Ecosystem management in forestry and natural resource education programs. In Proc. Soc. Am. For. Natl. Convent. Richmond, VA, Oct. 25–28, 1992. Bethesda, MD: Society of American Foresters, pp. 456–458.

Bowler, P. J. 1992. The Norton history of the environmental sciences. New York: W. W. Norton & Co.

Boyce, S. G. 1951. Plant succession in a thinned loblolly pine stand in a Piedmont county. M.S. Thesis. Raleigh, NC: North Carolina State Univ., School of Forest Resources

Boyce, S. G. 1954. The salt spray community. Ecol. Monogr. 24:29–67.

Boyce, S. G. 1955. Unpublished data from the Yellow-jacket Ridge cutting practice plots in the Vinton Furnace Experimental Forest. Delaware, OH: USDA Forest Service, Northeastern Forest Experiment Station.

Boyce, S. G. 1975a. How to double the harvest of loblolly and slash pine timber. J. For. 73:761–766.

Boyce, S. G. 1975b. The use of bole surface in the estimation of woodland production. Philos. Trans. R. Soc. Lond. Ser. B. 271(911):139–148.

Boyce, S. G. 1977. Management of eastern hardwood forests for multiple benefits (DYNAST-MB). Res. Pap. SE-168. Asheville, NC: USDA Forest Service, Southeastern Forest Experiment Station.

Boyce, S. G. 1978. Theory for new directions in forest management. Res. Pap. SE-193. Asheville, NC: USDA Forest Service, Southeastern Forest Experiment Station.

Boyce, S. G. 1985. Forestry Decisions. Gen. Tech. Rep. SE-35. Asheville, NC: USDA Forest Service, Southeastern Forest Experiment Station.

Boyce, S. G. 1986. Organizing a forest for multiple use. In Proc. of a Conf. on the Northern Hardwood Resource: Management and Potential. Michigan Technological Univ., Houghton, August 18–20, pp. 268–290.

Boyce, S. G., and W. S. McNab. 1994. Management of forested landscapes. J. For. 92(1):27–32.

Boyce, S. G., and J. P. McClure. 1975. Capture of the biological potential for yellow poplar timber. In Proc. of the 3rd Annu. Hardwood Symp., Hardwood Research Council, Cashiers, NC, May 1975, pp. 134–144.

Boyce, S. G., and J. P. McClure. 1978. The harvest of yellow poplar timber can be doubled. In Marketing and Utilization of Yellow poplar, Proc. of Symp., Univ. of Tennessee, Knoxville, March 21–22, 1978, pp. 18–31.

Boyce, S. G., and H. A. Knight. 1979. Prospective ingrowth of southern pine beyond 1980. Res. Pap. SE-200. Asheville, NC: USDA Forest Service, Southeastern Forest Experiment Station.

Boyce, S. G., and H. A. Knight. 1980. Prospective ingrowth of southern hardwoods beyond 1980. Res. Pap. SE-203. Asheville, NC: USDA Forest Service, Southeastern Forest Experiment Station.

Boyce, S. G., and N. D. Cost. 1978. Forest diversity—new concepts and applications. Res. Pap. SE-194. Asheville, NC: USDA Forest Service, Southeastern Forest Experiment Station.

Boyce, S. G., E. C. Burkhart, R. Kellison, and D. VanLear. 1986. Silviculture. III. The South. J. For. 84(6):41–48.

Bridgman, P. W. 1927. The logic of modern physics. New York: Macmillan Publishing Co.

Brown, M. J. 1993. Forest statistics for the piedmont of South Carolina. 1993. Res. Bull. SE-138. Asheville, NC: USDA Forest Service, Southeastern Forest Experiment Station.

Bruce, R. C., and S. G. Boyce. 1984. Measurements of diversity on the Nantahala National Forest. In J. L. and J. H. Cooley, eds. Proc. of Symp.: Natural Diversity in Forest Ecosystems. Institute of Ecology, Univ. of Georgia, Athens, Nov. 29–Dec. 1, 1982, pp. 71–85.

Bruner, J. S. 1960. The process of education. Cambridge, MA: Harvard Univ. Press.

Buckner, C. A., and D. J. Shure. 1985. The response of *Peromyscus* to forest opening size in the Southern Appalachian Mountains. J. Mammal. 66(2):299–307.

Buford, M. A., comp. 1991. Proceedings of the 1991 symposium on systems analysis in forest resources, Charleston, SC, March 3–6. Gen. Tech. Rep. SE-74. Asheville, NC: USDA Forest Service, Southeastern Forest Experiment Station.

Bull, E. L., and R. S. Holthausen, 1993. Habitat use and management of pileated woodpeckers in northeastern Oregon. J. Wildl. Manage. 57(2):335–345.

Buongiorno, J., and J. K. Gilless. 1987. Forest management and economics. New York: MacMillian Publishing Co.

Burns, R. M., ed. 1983. Silvicultural systems for the major forest types of the United States. Agric. Handb. 445. Washington, DC: USDA Forest Service.

Burns, R. M., ed. 1989. The silvicultural basis for silvicultural and management decisions in the National Forest System. Gen. Tech. Rep. WO-55. Washington, DC: USDA Forest Service.

Burns, R. M., and B. H. Honkala, eds. 1990. Silvics of North America. Vol. 1, Conifers; Vol. 2, Hardwoods. Agric. Handb. 654. Washington, DC: USDA Forest Service.

Carmean, W. H., and S. G. Boyce. 1973. Hardwood log quality in relation to site quality. Res. Pap. NC-103. St. Paul, MN: USDA Forest Service. North Central Forest Experiment Station.

Clark, G. B., and S. G. Boyce. 1964. Yellow poplar seed remains viable in the forest litter. J. For. 62(8): 564–567.

Clark, J. J, T. J. Hinderlang, and R. E. Pritchard. 1979. Capital budgeting: planning and control of capital expenditures. Englewood Cliffs, NJ: Prentice-Hall.

Cliff, E. P. 1962. Multiple-use management on the National Forest of the United States. In Proc., 5th World Forestry Congr., Seattle, WA, August 29–September 10, 1960. 1:173–181.

Clinton, B. D., L. R. Boring, and W. T. Swank. 1993. Canopy gap characteristics and drought influences in oak forests of the Coweeta Basin. Ecology 74(5):1551–1558.

Clutter, J. L., J. C. Fortson, L. V. Pienarr, G. H. Brister, and R. L. Bailey. 1983. Timber management: a quantitative approach. New York: John Wiley & Sons.

Conner, R. N. 1979a. Seasonal changes in woodpecker foraging patterns. Auk 98:562–570.

Conner, R. N. 1979b. Minimum standards and forest wildlife management. Wildl. Soc. Bull. 7:293–296.

Conner, R. N. 1980. Foraging habitats of woodpeckers in southwestern Virginia. J. Field Ornithol. 51:119–127.

Conner, R. N., and C. S. Adkisson. 1975. Effects of clearcutting on the diversity of breeding birds. J. For. 73:781–785.

Conner, R. N., R. G. Hooper, H. S. Crawford, and H. S. Mosby. 1975. Woodpecker nesting habitat in cut and uncut woodlands in Virginia. J. Wildl. Manage. 39(1): 144–150.

Conner, R. N., J. W. Via, and I. D. Prather. 1979. Effects of pine-oak clearcutting on winter and breeding birds in southwestern Virginia. Wilson Bull. 91(2):301–316.

Conrad, M. 1889. Forestry and national welfare. In Proc. Am. For. Cong., Atlanta, GA, Dec. 1888. Washington, DC: American Forestry Association, p. 43–50.

Cordell, H. K., and J. C. Hendee. 1982. Renewable resources recreation in the United States: supply, demand, and critical policy issues. Rep. on the 1980 Conf. on Renewable Natural Resources. Washington, DC: American Forestry Association.

Cost, N. D. 1974. Forest statistics for the southern coastal plain of North Carolina, 1973. Res. Bull. SE-26. Asheville, NC: USDA Forest Service, Southeastern Forest Experiment Station.

Cost, N. D. 1975. Forest statistics for the mountains of North Carolina, 1974. Res. Bull. SE-31. Asheville, NC: USDA Forest Service, Southeastern Forest Experiment Station.

Coyle, F. A. 1981. Effects of clearcutting on the spider community of a southern Appalachian Forest. J. Arachnol. 9:285–298.

Craver, G. C. 1985. Forest statistics for the mountains of North Carolina, 1984. Res. Bull. SE-77. Asheville, NC: USDA Forest Service, Southeastern Forest Experiment Station.

Cruikshank, J. W. 1941. Forest resources of the mountain region of North Carolina. Forest Survey release 7. Asheville, NC: USDA Forest Service, Appalachian Forest Experiment Station.

Davis, L. S., and K. N. Johnson. 1987. Forest management. New York: McGraw-Hill Book Co.

Delcourt, P. A., H. R. Delcourt, D. F. Morse, and P. A. Morse. 1993. History, evolution and organization of vegetation and human culture. In W. H. Martin, S. G. Boyce, and H. C. Echternacht, eds., 1983. Biodiversity of the southeastern United States: lowland terrestrial communities. New York: John Wiley & Sons, pp. 47–80.

Della-Bianca, L. 1983. Sixty years of stand development in a Southern Appalachian cove-hardwood stand. For. Ecol. Manage. 5:229–241.

Denning, P. J. 1988. Blindness in designing intelligent systems. The science of computing. Am. Sci. 76:118–120.

Diaz, Luis F., George M. Savage, and Clarence G. Golueke. 1982. Resource recovery from municipal solid wastes. Boca Raton, FL: CRC Press.

Diaz, N., and D. Apostol. 1992. Forest landscape analysis and design. R6 ECO-TP-043-92. Portland, OR: USDA Forest Service, Pacific Northwest Region.

Dickison, G. J. 1980. Composition and stand dynamics of an old growth upper cove hardwood forest in Walker Cove Research Natural Area, Pisgah National Forest, NC. M.S. Thesis. Durham, NC: Duke Univ.

Douglas, J. E. 1983. The potential for water yield augmentation from forest management in the Eastern United States. Water Resourc. Bull. 19(3):351–358.

Duerr, W. A. 1949. The economic problems of forestry in the Appalachian Region. Cambridge, MA: Harvard University Press.

Duerr, W. A., D. E. Teeguarden, N. B. Christiansen, and S. Guttenberg. 1979. Forest resource management. Philadelphia: W. B. Saunders Co.

Egan, T. 1993a. Upheaval in the forests. New York Times, Natl. Ed., Sec. A, pp. 1, 9, July 2, 1993.

Egan, T. 1993b. Land deal leaves Montana logged and hurt. New York Times, Natl. Ed., Sec. A, pp. 1, 7, Oct. 19, 1993.

Egan, T. 1994. Tight logging limit set in Northwest. New York Times, Natl. Ed., Sec. A, p. 8, Feb. 24, 1994.

Ehrlich, P. R., and A. H. Ehrlich. 1990. The population explosion. New York: Simon & Schuster.

Ellefson, P. V. 1993. Politics and policymaking: a teaching challenge in forestry. J. For. 91(3):24–27.

Elton, C. 1949. Population interspersion: an essay on animal community patterns. J. Ecol. 37(1–23):19, 28, 444, 497, 523, 580, 648.

Engelberg, J., and L. L. Boyarsky. 1979. The noncybernetic nature of ecosystems. Am. Nat. 114(3):317–324.

Evans, G. C. 1976. A sack of uncut diamonds: the study of ecosystems and the future resources of mankind. J. Ecol. 64(1):1–39.

Evelyn, J. 1664. Sylva, or a discourse of forest trees and propagation of timber in His Majesty's Dominions. London: Royal Society of London.

Everard, J. E. 1971. Metric conversion tables and factors for forestry. For. Comm. Booklet 30. London: Her Majesty's Stationery Office.

FAO. 1993. Forest products, statistics 1980–1991. Rome: Food and Agricultural Organization of the United Nations.

Farrish, K. W., J. C. Adams, and C. V. Thompson. 1993. Soil conservation practices on clearcut forestlands in Louisiana. J. Soil Water Conserv. 48(2):136–139.

Fernow, B. E. 1891. The forest as a national resource. In Proc. Am. For. Assoc., Washington, DC, 1891. Washington, DC: American Forestry Association, pp. 36–53.

Fernow, B. E. 1893. Timber as a crop. In Proc. Am. For. Congr., Chicago, Oct. 1893. Washington, DC: American Forestry Association, 10:142–147.

Flebbe, P. A., and C. A. Dolloff. 1991. Habitat structure and woody debris in Southern Appalachian wilderness streams. Proc. Annu. Conf. Southeast. Assoc. Fish Wildl. Agencies 45:444–450.

Fleischer, G. A. 1984. Engineering economy. Monterey, CA: Brooks/Cole Engineering.

Forest Farmer. 1994. Certifying forest sustainability. For. Farmer 53(1):22–23.

Forman, R. T. T., and M. Gordon. 1981. Patches and structural components for a landscape ecology. BioScience 31(10):733–740.

Forman, R. T. T., and M. Gordon. 1986. Landscape ecology. New York: John Wiley & Sons.

Forrester, J. W. 1961. Industrial dynamics. Cambridge, MA: MIT Press.

Franklin, J. F. 1993a. Lessons from old growth. J. For. 91(12):10–13.

Franklin, J. F. 1993b. Preserving biodiversity: species, ecosystems, or landscapes. Ecol. Appl. 3(2):202–205.

Franklin, J. F., and T. A. Spies. 1991. Ecological definitions of old-growth Douglas-fir forests. In L. F. Ruggiero et al., eds., Wildlife and vegetation of unmanaged Douglas-fir forests. Gen. Tech. Rep. PNW-GTR 285. Portland OR: USDA Forest Service, Pacific Northwest Station, pp. 61–69.

Franklin, J. F., K. Cromack, Jr., W. Denison, A. McKee, C. Maser, J. Sedell, F. Swanson, and G. Juday. 1981. Ecological characteristics of old-growth Douglas-fir forests. Gen. Tech. Rep. PNW-GTR-118. Portland, WA: USDA Forest Service.

Frothingham, E. H. 1917. Ecology and silviculture in the southern Appalachians: old cuttings as a guide to future practice. Paper presented at meeting of the Ecol. Soc. Am., New York, 1916, J. For. 15:343–349.

Frothingham, E. H. 1931. Timber growing and logging practice in the Southern Appalachian Region. Tech. Bull. 250. Washington, DC: USDA Forest Service.

Gaffey, M. J. 1993. Forging an asteroid-meteorite link. Science 260:167–168.

Gauch, H. G. Jr. 1993. Prediction, parsimony and noise. Am. Sci. 81(5):468–478.

Getz, W. M., and R. G. Haight. 1989. Population harvesting. Princeton: Princeton Univ. Press.

Gilbert, F. F., K. A. Blatner, M. S. Carroll, R. L. Richmond, and B. A. Zamora. 1993. Integrated forest resources education: one response to the challenge. J. For. 91(3): 17–22.

Gleason, H. A. 1939. The individualistic concept of the plant association. Am. Midl. Nat. 21:92–110.

Gomez-Pompa, A., and A. Kaus. 1992. Taming the wilderness myth. BioScience 42(4): 271–279.

Goodman, B. 1993. Drugs and people threaten diversity in Andean Forests. Science 261:293.

Gunter, J. E., and H. L. Haney Jr. 1984. Essentials of forestry investment analysis. Corvallis, OR: Oregon State Univ. Bookstores.

Hagen, J. B. 1992. An entangled bank. The origins of ecosystem ecology. New Brunswick, NJ: Rutgers Univ. Press.

Halls, L. K. 1978. Effect of timber harvesting on wildlife, wildlife habitat and recreation values. In Proc. of a Symp.: Complete Tree Utilization of Southern Pine. Madison, WI: For. Prod. Res. Soc. pp. 108–114.

Hansen, A. J., and F. di Castri, eds. 1992. Landscape boundaries: consequences for biotic diversity and ecological flows. New York: Springer-Verlag.

Hansen, A. J., T. A. Spies, F. J. Swanson, and J. L. Ohmann. 1991. Conserving biodiversity in managed forests. BioScience 41(6):382–392.

Hansen, A. J., S. L. Garman, and B. Marks. 1993. An approach for managing vertebrate diversity across multiple-use landscapes. Ecol. Appl. 3(3):481–496.

Hansen, H. C. 1962. Dictionary of ecology. New York: Philosophical Library.

Harmon, M. E., W. K. Ferrell, and J. F. Franklin. 1990. Effects on carbon storage of conversion of old growth forests to young forests. Science 247: 699–702.

Harris, L. D. 1984. The fragmented forest. Chicago: Univ. of Chicago Press.

Hecht, S. B. 1993. The logic of livestock and deforestation in Amazonia. Bioscience 43(10):687–695.

Hendee, J. C., and R. C. Pitstick. 1992. The growth of environmental and conservation-related organization: 1980–1991. Renewable Resour. J. 10(2):6–11.

Hill, K., and A. M. Hurtado. 1989. Hunter-gatherers of the new world. Am. Sci. 77(5): 436–443.

Holbrook, H. L. 1974. A system for wildlife habitat management on southern national forests. Wildlife Soc. Bull. 2(3):119–123.

Holland, M. M., P. G. Risser, and R. J. Naiman, eds. 1991. Ecotones: the role of landscape boundaries in the management and restoration of changing environments. New York: Chapman and Hall.

Hornbeck, J. W., and W. T. Swank. 1992. Watershed ecosystem analysis as a basis for multiple-use management of eastern forests. Ecol. Appl. 2(3):238–247.

Horridge, G. A. 1977. Mechanistic teleology and explanation in neurology. BioScience 27:725–732.

Hosner, J. F. 1993. Meeting demands for breadth and depth: a two-tiered approach. J. For. 91(3):15–16.

Hoyt, S. F. 1957. The ecology of the pileated woodpecker. Ecology 38:246–256.

Huggett, R. J. 1993. Modelling the human impact on nature. Oxford: Oxford Univ. Press.

Hunter, M. D., T. Ohgushi, and P. W. Price. 1992. Effects of resource distribution on animal-plant interactions. San Diego: Academic Press.

Hunter, M. L. Jr. 1990. Wildlife, forests and forestry. Englewood Cliffs, NJ: Prentice Hall.

Jacob, F. 1977. Evolution and tinkering. Science 196(4295):1161–1166.

James, G. B. 1897. Co-operative forestry. Proc. Am. For. Assoc., Brooklyn, NY, 1894. Washington, DC: American Forestry Association 11:169–173.

Jamison, A. 1993. A tale of two brothers. Book reviews. Science 261:497–498.

Johnson, T. G. 1988. Forest statistics for southeast Georgia, 1988. Res. Bull. SE-104. Asheville, NC: USDA Forest Service, Southeastern Forest Experiment Station.

Johnson, T. G. 1990. Forest statistics for the coastal plain of North Carolina, 1990. Res. Bull. SE-111. Asheville, NC: USDA Forest Service, Southeastern Forest Experiment Station.

Johnson, T. G. 1991. Forest statistics for the mountains of North Carolina, 1990. Res. Bull. SE-118. Asheville, NC: USDA Forest Service, Southeastern Forest Experiment Station.

Jolley, H. E. 1969. The Blue Ridge Parkway. Knoxville, TN: Univ. of Tennessee Press.

Josephy, A. M., ed. 1991. America in 1492. New York: Vintage Books.

Journal of Forestry. 1993. Certifying sustainable forest products: a roundtable discussion. J For. 91(11):33–38.

Kahneman, D., P. Slovic, and A. Tversky, eds. 1982. Judgement under uncertainty: heuristics and biases. Cambridge, England: Cambridge Univ. Press.

Kauffman, S. A. 1993. The origins of order. New York: Oxford Univ. Press.

Kelly, J. F., P. M. Sandra, and D. M. Leslie, Jr. 1993. Habitat associations of red-cockaded woodpecker cavity trees in an old-growth forest of Oklahoma. J. Wildl. Manage. 57(1):122–128.

Kennedy, P. 1993. Preparing for the twenty-first century. New York: Random House.

Kepner, C. H., and B. B. Trego. 1965, The rational manager. New York: McGraw-Hill Book Co.

Kershaw, J. A., C. D. Oliver, and T. M. Hinckley. 1993. Effect of harvest of old growth Douglas-fir stands and subsequent management on carbon dioxide levels in the atmosphere. J. Sustainable For. 1(1):61–71.

Kessler, W. B., H. Salwasser, C. W. Cartwright Jr., and J. A. Caplan. 1992. New perspectives for sustainable natural resources management. Ecol. Appl. 2(3):221–225.

Koch, P. 1984. Utilization of hardwoods growing on southern pine sites. Agric. Handb. 605. Washington, DC: USDA Forest Service.

Koshland, D. E. 1977. A response regulator model in a simple sensory system. Science 196:1055–1063.

Lee, R. G. 1982. The classical sustained yield concept: content and philosophical origins. In Sustained Yield, Proc. of a Symp., Spokane, WA, April 27–28, 1982. Pullman: Washington State Univ., Cooperative Extension Service, pp. 1–10.

LeMaster, D.C., D.M. Baumgartner, and D. Adams, eds. 1982. Sustained Yield, Proc. of a Symp., Spokane, WA, April 27–28, 1982. Pullman: Washington State Univ., Cooperative Extension Service, pp. 1–144.

Leopold, A. 1933. Game management. New York: Charles Scribner's Sons.

Levy, H. 1932. The universe of science. London: Knopf.

Lewin, Roger. 1988. Pattern and process in extinctions. Science 241:26.

Lewontin, R. C. 1993. The doctine of DNA. St. Ives, England: Penguin Books.

Likens, G. E., F. H. Bormann, R. S. Pierce, J. S. Eaton, and N. M. Johnson. 1977. Biogeochemistry of a forested ecosystem. New York: Springer-Verlag.

Lippke, B., and C. D. Oliver. 1993. Managing for multiple values. J. For. 91(12):14–18.

Litton, R. B. Jr. 1984. Visual vulnerability of the landscape: control of visual quality. Res. Pap. WO-39. Washington, DC: USDA Forest Service.

Lohrey, R. E. 1987. Site index curves for direct-seeded slash pines in Louisiana. South. J. Appl. For. 11:15–16.

Loomis, J. B. 1993. Integrated public lands management. New York: Columbia Univ. Press.

Lorimer, C. G. 1980. Age structure and disturbance history of a southern Appalachian virgin forest. Ecology 61:1169–1184.

Lorimer, C. G., and L. E. Frelich. 1994. Natural disturbance regimes in old-growth northern hardwoods. J. For. 92(1):34–38.

Lucas, O. W. R. 1991. The design of forest landscapes. New York: Oxford Univ. Press.

Ludwig, D., R. Hilborn, and C. Walters. 1993. Uncertainty, resource exploitation, and conservation: lessons from history. Science 260:17, 36.

Ludwig, J. A., and J. F. Reynolds. 1988. Statistical ecology. New York: John Wiley & Sons.

Machin, K. E. 1964. Feedback theory and its application to biological systems. In G. M. Hughes, ed., Homeostasis and feedback mechanisms. New York: Academic Press, pp. 421–445.

MacLean, C. D., J. L. Ohmann, and P. M. Bassett. 1991. Preliminary timber resource statistics for the Olympic Peninsula, Washington. Res. Bull. PNW-RB-178. Portland, OR: USDA Forest Service, Pacific Northwest Research Station.

Mann, C. C., and M. L. Plummer. 1993. The high cost of biodiversity. Science 260: 1868–1871.

Marcin, T. C. 1993. Demographic change. J. For. 91(11):39–45.

Marsh, G. P. 1964. Man and nature. Cambridge, MA: Harvard Univ. Press.

Martin, A. C., H. S. Zim, and A. L. Nelson. 1951. American wildlife and plants: a guide to wildlife food habits. New York: McGraw-Hill Book Co.; unabridged ed. published in 1961 by Dover Publications, New York.

Martin, W. H., S. G. Boyce, and H. C. Echternacht. 1993a. Biodiversity of the southeastern United States: lowland terrestrial communities. New York: John Wiley & Sons.

Martin, W. H., S. G. Boyce, and H. C. Echternacht. 1993b. Biodiversity of the southeastern United States: upland terrestrial communities. New York: John Wiley & Sons.

Matthews, J. D. 1991. Silvicultural systems. New York: Oxford Univ. Press.

McArdle, R. E. 1962. The concept of multiple use of forest and associated lands—its values and limitations: Keynote address. Proc., 5th World For. Congr., Seattle, WA, August 29–September 10, 1960. 1:143–145.

McClure, J. P., and H. A. Knight. 1984. Empirical yields of timber and forest biomass in the southeastern United States. Res. Pap. SE-245. Asheville, NC: USDA Forest Service, Southeastern Forest Experiment Station.

McDonnell, M. J., and S. T. A. Pickett. 1993. Humans as components of ecosystems. New York: Springer-Verlag.

McFarlane. 1992. A stillness in the pines. New York: W. W. Norton & Co.

McKibben, W. 1989. The end of nature. New York: Random House.

McNab, W. Henry. 1987. Rationale for a multifactor forest site classification system for the southern Appalachians. In R. R. Hay, F. W. Woods, H. DeSelm, eds. In Proc. of the 6th Cent. Hardwood For. Conf., Feb. 24–26, 1987. Knoxville, TN: Univ. of Tennessee Dept. of Forestry, Wildlife and Fisheries, pp. 283–294.

McNab, W. H. 1991. Land classification in the Blue Ridge Province: state-of-the-science report. In D. L. Mengel, and D. T. Tew, eds. Proc. of Symp.: Ecological Land Classification: applications to identify the productive potential of southern forests. Gen. Tech. Rep. SE-68. Asheville, NC: USDA Forest Service, Southeastern Forest Experiment Station.

Meadows, D. H., D. L. Meadows, and J. Randers. 1992. Beyond the limits. Post Mills, VT: Chelsea Green Publishing Co.

Mengel, D. L., and D. T. Tew, eds. 1991. Ecological land classification: applications to identify the productive potential of southern forests. Proc. of a Symp., Charlotte, NC, January 7–9, 1991. Gen. Tech. Rep. SE-68. Asheville, NC: USDA Forest Service, Southeastern Forest Experiment Station.

Merz, R. W., and S. G. Boyce. 1956. Age of oak "seedlings." J. For. 54:774–775.

Miles, R. 1967. Forestry in the English landscape. London: Faber and Faber.

Munns, E. N., T. G. Hoerner, and V. A. Clements. 1949. Converting factors and tables of equivalents used in forestry. Misc. Publ. 225, revised. Washington, DC: USDA Forest Service.

Murdy, W. H. 1975. Anthropocentrism: a modern version. Science 187:1168–1172.

Naiman, R. J., H. DeCamps, and M. Pollock. 1993. The role of riparian corridors in maintaining regional biodiversity. Ecol. Appl. 3(2):209–212.

National Research Council. 1986. Ecological knowledge and environmental problem-solving. Washington, DC: National Academy Press.

Newman, D. H., and D. N. Wear. 1993. Production economics of private forestry: a comparison of industrial and nonindustrial forest owners. Am. J. Agric. Econ. 75: 674–684.

Nixon, C. M., M. W. McClain, and R. W. Donohoe. 1980. Effects of clear-cutting on gray squirrels. J. Wildl. Manage. 44(2):403–412.

Norman, D. A. 1981. Perspectives on cognitive science. Norwood, NJ: Ablex Publishing Corp.

Norris, L. A. 1993. Sustaining long-term health and productivity. J. For. 91(7):32–35.

Norse, E. A. 1990. Ancient forests of the Pacific Northwest. Washington, DC: Island Press.

Odum, E. P. 1983. Basic ecology. New York: Saunders College Publishers.

Okada, K., and K. Shimura. 1990. Reversible root tip rotation in *Arabidopsis* seedlings induced by obstacle-touching stimulus. Science 250:274–276.

Oliver, C. D. 1992. A landscape approach: achieving and maintaining biodiversity and economic productivity. J. For. 90(9):20–25.

Oliver, C. D., and B. C. Larson. 1990. Forest stand dynamics. New York: McGraw-Hill Book Co.

Oliver, C. D., D. R. Berg, D. R. Larsen, and K. L. O'Hara. 1992. Integrating management tools, ecological knowledge and silviculture. In R. J. Naiman, ed. Watershed management. New York: Springer-Verlag.

O'Hara, K. L., and C. D. Oliver. 1992. Silviculture: achieving new objectives through stand and landscape management. Western Wildlands pp. 28–33.

O'Neill, R. V., D. L. DeAngelis, J. B. Waide, and T. G. H. Allen. 1986. A hierarchical concept of the ecosystem. Princeton, NJ: Princeton Univ. Press.

Oreskes, N., K. Shrader-Frechette, and K. Belitz. 1994. Verification, validation, and confirmation of numerical models in the earth sciences. Science 263:641–646.

Payne, C. J. M. Bowker, and A. C. Reed. 1992. The economic value of wilderness. In Proc. of Natl. Conf. on the Value of Wilderness, Jackson, WY, May 8–11, 1991. Asheville, NC: USDA Forest Service, Southeastern Forest Experiment Station.

Peet, R. K. 1974. The measurement of species diversity. Annu. Rev. Ecol. System. 5: 285–307.

Peterson, D. W. 1968. Pisgah working circle, plan period 1969–1978. Files, National Forests in North Carolina. Asheville, NC: USDA Forest Service.

Peterson, J. 1993. Today's forestry graduates: an exodus of elephant drivers. J. For. 91(3):12–14.

Phillips, D. L., and D. J. Shure. 1990. Patch-size effects on early succession in southern Appalachian forests. Ecology 71(1):204–212.

Pickett, S. T. A., and P. S. White. 1985. The ecology of natural disturbance and patch dynamics. Orlando, FL: Academic Press.

Pielou, E. C. 1977. Mathematical ecology. New York: John Wiley & Sons.

Post, W. M., T. H. Peng, W. R. Emanual, A. W. King, V. H. Dale, and D. L. DeAngelis. 1990. The global carbon cycle. Am. Sci. 78:310–326.

Preston, F. W. 1960. Time and space and the variation of species. Ecology 41:611–627.

Probst, J. R., and T. R. Crow. 1991. Integrating biological diversity and resource management. J. For. 89:12–17.

Radford, A. E., H. E. Ahles, and C. R. Bell. 1968. Manual of the vascular flora of the Carolinas. Chapel Hill: Univ. of North Carolina Press.

Raines, H., ed. 1993. Aid for owls, trees and loggers. Editorial. New York Times, Natl. Ed., Sec. A, p. 10, July 3, 1993.

Richardson, G. P., and A. L. Pugh III. 1981. Introduction to system dynamics modeling with DYNAMO. Cambridge, MA: MIT Press.

Risser, P. G., J. R. Karr, and R. T. T. Forman. 1984. Landscape ecology: directions and approaches. Spec. Publ. 2, Champaign, IL: Illinois Natural History Survey.

Roise, J., J. Chung, R. Lancia, and M. Lennartz. 1990. Red-cockaded woodpecker habitat and timber management production possibilities, South. J. Appl. For. 14(1): 6–12.

Rosenberg, A. A., M. J. Fogarty, M. P. Sissenwine, J. R. Beddington, and J. G. Shepherd. 1993. Achieving sustainable use of renewable resources. Science 262:828–829.

Roughgarden, J. R., R. M. May, and S. A. Lavin. 1989. Perspectives in ecological theory. Princeton, NJ: Princeton Univ. Press.

Rowe, J. S. 1991. Forests as landscape ecosystems, implications for their regionalization and classification. In D. L. Mengel and D. T. Tew, eds. Proc. Symp.: Ecological Land Classification: applications to identify the productive potential of southern forests. Gen. Tech. Rep. SE-68. Asheville, NC: USDA Forest Service, Southeastern Forest Experiment Station, pp. 3–8.

Rumsey, F., and W. A. Duerr. 1975. Social sciences in forestry: a book of readings. Philadelphia: W. B. Saunders Co.

Runkle, J. R. 1981. Gap regeneration in some old-growth forests of eastern North America. Ecology 62:1041–1051.

Runkle, J. R. 1982. Patterns of disturbance in some old-growth mesic forests of the eastern United States. Ecology 62:1533–1546.

Sample, V. A. 1992. Building partnerships for ecosystem management on forest and range lands of mixed ownerships. In R. N. Staebler, ed. Proc. Soc. Am. For. Natl. Convent. Richmond, VA, Oct. 25–28, 1992. Society of American Foresters, pp. 456–458.

Sander, I. L., and F. B. Clark. 1971. Reproduction of upland hardwood forests in the Central States. Agric. Handb. 405. Washington, DC: USDA Forest Service.

Schenk, C. A. 1897. Forest Finance. Proceeding of the American Forestry Association, Special meetings at Asheville, NC, and Nashville, TN, September 17–22, 1897. Am. For. Assoc. 12:124–133.

Schenck, C. A. 1974. The birth of forestry in America, Biltmore Forest School 1898–1913. Ovid Butler, ed. Santa Cruz, CA: Forest History Society and Appalachian Consortium.

Schneider, K. 1993. Remedies take shape in Northwest timber fight. New York Times, Natl. Ed., Sec. A, p. 7, June 19, 1993.

Schniewind, A. P. 1989. Concise encyclopedia of wood and wood-based materials. Cambridge, MA: Pergamon Press–MIT Press.

Schnur, G. L. 1937. Yield, stand and volume tables for even-aged upland oak forests. Tech. Bull. 560. Washington, DC: USDA Forest Service.

Schobert, Harold H. 1990. The chemistry of hydrocarbon fuels. London: Butterworths.

Schwarzkopf, S. K. 1985. A history of Mt. Mitchell and the Black Mountains. Raleigh, NC: Div. of Archives and History, N. C. Dep. of Cultural Resources.

Sedell, J. R., and F. J. Swanson. 1984. Ecological characteristics in old-growth forests in the Pacific Northwest. In W. R. Meehan, T. R. Merrell Jr., and T. A. Hanley, eds., Fish and wildlife relationships in old-growth forests. Morehead City, NC: American Institute of Fishery Research Biologists, pp. 9–16.

Senge, P. M. 1990. The fifth discipline. New York: Doubleday Currency.

Sharitz, R. R., L. R. Boring, D. H. Van Lear, and J. E. Pinder III. 1992. Integrating ecological concepts with natural resource management of southern forests. Ecol. Appl. 2(3):226–237.

Shaw, J. H. 1985. Introduction to wildlife management. New York: McGraw-Hill Book Co.

Sheffield, R. M. 1982. Forest statistics for southeast Georgia, 1981. Resour. Bull. SE-63. Asheville, NC: USDA Forest Service, Southeastern Forest Experiment Station.

Sheffield, R. M., and M. T. Thompson. 1992. Hurricane Hugo, effects on South Carolina's forest resources. Res. Pap. SE-284. Asheville, NC: USDA Forest Service, Southeastern Forest Experiment Station.

Shorrocks, B., and I. R. Swingland, eds. 1990. Living in a patchy environment. New York: Oxford Univ. Press.

Shure, D. J., and D. L. Phillips. 1987. Litter fall patterns within different-sized disturbance patches in a Southern Appalachian Mountain Forest. Am. Midl. Nat. 118(2):348–357.

Shure, D. J., and D. L. Phillips. 1991. Patch size of forest openings and arthropod populations. Oecologia 86:325–334.

Shure, D. J., and L. A. Wilson. 1993. Patch-size effects on plant phenolics in successional openings of the Southern Appalachians. Ecology 74(1):55–67.

Slobodkin, L. B. 1975. Comments from a biologist to a mathematician. In S. A. Levin, eds., Ecosystem Analysis and Prediction. Proc. SIAM-SIMS Conf., Alta, UT, July 1–5. Philadelphia: Society for Industrial and Applied Mathematics, 1975:318–329.

Smathers, G. A. 1982. Man as a factor in Southern Appalachian bald formation and illustrations of selected sites along the Blue Ridge Parkway in North Carolina. Res./Resour. Manage. Rep. SER-57. Atlanta, GA: USDI National Park Service, Southeastern Regional Office.

Smith, D. M. 1977. The scientific basis for timber harvesting practices. J. Washington Acad. Sci. 67(1):3–11.

Smith, D. M. 1986. The practice of silviculture, 8th ed. New York: John Wiley & Sons.

Smith, H. A. 1936. The need for common understanding. Editorial. J. For. 34(4):363–365; reprinted in 1989 J. For. 87(6):47–48.

Smith, P. G. 1993. Where to next? J. For. 91(3):3.

Snyder, N. L. 1978. Forest statistics for the piedmont of South Carolina. 1977. Res. Bull. SE-45. Asheville, NC: USDA Forest Service, Southeastern Forest Experiment Station.

Soule, M. E., ed. 1986. Conservation biology: the science of scarcity and diversity. Sunderland, MA: Sinauer Assoc.

Spaeth, J. N. 1928. Twenty years growth of a sprout hardwood forest in New York: a study of the effects of intermediate and reproduction cuttings. Bull. 465. Ithaca: New York (Cornell) Agricultural Experiment Station.

Spurr, S. H. 1979. Silviculture. Sci. Am. 240(2):76–91.

Steenberg, B. K. 1972. The crucial forestry issues of today's world as seen from FAO. Unasylva 104:5–9.

Stern, P. C. 1993. A second environmental science: human-environment interactions. Science 260:1897–1899.

Stone, R. 1993. Spotted owl plan kindles debate on salvage logging. Science 261:287.

Strom, R. W. 1985. Long term effects of timber management on herbaceous and woody understory vegetation in a second growth upland oak forest in southeastern Ohio. M.S. Thesis. Athens, OH: Ohio University, College of Arts and Sciences.

Swanson, F. J., and J. F. Franklin. 1992. New forestry principles from ecosystem analysis of Pacific Northwest forests. Ecol. Appl. 2(3):262–274.

Tammi, N. D., S. L. Paige, and S. G. Boyce. 1983. Management alternatives to meet old growth forest objectives: a North Carolina piedmont case. In Proc. Soc. Am. For. Natl. Mt., Portland, OR, Oct. 16–20, 1983. Bethesda, MD: Society of American Foresters, pp. 56–59.

Tangley, L. 1988. Research priorties for conservation. BioScience 38(7):444–448.

Tansey, J. B. 1984. Forest statistics for the southern coastal plain of North Carolina, 1983. Res. Bull. SE-72. Asheville, NC: USDA Forest Service, Southeastern Forest Experiment Station.

Tansey, J. B. 1986. Forest statistics for the piedmont of South Carolina. 1986. Res. Bull. SE-89. Asheville, NC: USDA Forest Service, Southeastern Forest Experiment Station.

Tansley, A. G. 1935. The use and abuse of vegetational concepts and terms. Ecology 16(3):284–307.

Tear, T. H., J. M. Scott, P. H. Hayward, and B. Griffith. 1993. Status and prospects for success of the Endangered Species Act: a look at recovery plans. Science 262: 976–977.

Terminology Committee. 1917. Forest terminology. J. For. 15:68–101.

Thomas, J. W. tech. ed. 1979. Wildlife habitats in managed forests: the Blue Mountains of Oregon and Washington. Agric. Handb. 553. Washington, DC: USDA Forest Service.

Thomas, J. W., and R. E. Radtke. 1989. Effects of timber management practices on forest wildlife management. In R. M. Burns, ed., The scientific basis for silvicultural and management decisions in the National Forest System. Gen. Tech. Rep. WO-55. Washington, DC: USDA Forest Service, pp. 107–117.

Uhl, C., K. Clark, N. Dezzeo, and P. Maquirino. 1988. Vegetation dynamics in Amazonian treefall gaps. Ecology 69:751–763.

Ulrich, A. H. 1990. U. S. timber production, trade, consumption, and price statistics 1960–1988. Misc. Publ. 1486. Washington, DC: USDA Forest Service.

USDA. 1983. Conversion of southern cropland to southern pine tree plantings. Office of Budget and Program Analysis. Washington, DC: USDA.

USDA. 1993. Natural resources, federal spending and resource performance 1940–1989. Office of Budget and Program Analysis. Washington, DC: USDA.

USDA Forest Service. 1983. The principal laws relating to Forest Service activities. Agric. Handb. 453. Washington, DC: USDA Forest Service.

USDA Forest Service. 1988. The South's fourth forest: alternatives for the future. For. Resour. Rep. 24. Washington, DC: USDA Forest Service.

USDA Forest Service. 1991a. Unpubl. records, Supervisor's Office, National Forests in North Carolina, Asheville.

USDA Forest Service. 1991b. National Forest System Land and Resource Management Planning. Federal Register 36 CFR, Part 219, Vol. 56, Feb. 15, 1991. Washington, DC.

USDA Forest Service. 1992a. Ecosystem management of the National Forest and Grasslands. Memorandum from the Chief of the Forest Service to Regional Foresters and Station Directors, June 4, 1992, file 1330-1, Washington, DC.

USDA Forest Service. 1992b. Taking an ecological approach to management. Proc. Natl. Workshop, Salt Lake City, UT, April 27–30, 1992. WO-WSA-3. Washington, DC: USDA Forest Service, Watershed and Air Management.

Vardaman, J. M. 1989. How to make money growing trees. New York: John Wiley & Sons.

Verner, J. M., L. Morrison, and C. J. Ralph, eds. 1986. Wildlife 2000: modeling habitat relationships of terrestrial vertebrates. Madison: Univ. of Wisconsin Press.

Vise, R. 1991. Without capital gains incentive reforestation decreases. For. Farmer 50(9):12–13.

Vitousek, P. M., and W. A. Reiners. 1975. Ecosystem succession and nutrient retention: a hypothesis. BioScience 25:376–381.

Wahlenberg, W. G. 1960. Loblolly pine. Durham, NC: Duke University, School of Forestry.

Waring, R. H., and W. H. Schlesinger. 1985. Forest Ecosystems, concepts and management. New York: Academic Press.

Warren, W. G. 1986. On the presentation of statistical analysis: reason or ritual. Can. J. For. Res. 16:1185–1191.

Weiss, H., M. A. Courty, W. Wetterstrom, F. Guichard, L. Senior, R. Meadow, and A. Curnow. 1993. The genesis and collapse of third millennium North Mesopotamian Civilization. Science 261:995–1004.

Wells, B. W. 1956. Origin of Southern Appalachian grass balds. Ecology 37:592.

Wenger, K. F., ed. 1984. Forestry handbook, 2nd ed. New York: John Wiley & Sons.

Whaley, R. S. 1993. Working partnerships: elements for success. J. For. 91(3):10–11.

Wiener, N. 1961. Cybernetics: or control and communication in the animal and the machine, 2nd ed. Cambridge, MA: MIT Press.

Wiener, N. 1967. The human use of human beings. New York: Avon Books.

Wilcox, B. A. 1987. Editorial. Conserv. Biol. 3:188–189.

Williams, M. 1989. Americans and their forests: a historical geography. New York: Cambridge Univ. Press.

Willison, G. L. 1981. Natural regeneration twenty years after clearcutting as affected by site and size of opening in southeastern Ohio. M.S. Thesis. Columbus, OH: Ohio State University.

Wilson, A. D., and D. J. Shure. 1993. Plant competition and nutrient limitation during early succession in the Southern Appalachian Mountains. Am. Midl. Nat. 129:1–9.

Wood, D. A. 1983. Foraging and colony habitat characteristics of the red-cockaded woodpecker in Oklahoma. In D. A. Wood, ed., Proc. Red-cockaded Woodpecker Symp. II. Tallahassee: Florida Game and Fresh Water Fish Commission.

Wood, G. W. 1990. The art and science of wildlife management. J. For. 88(3): 8–12.

Wood, G. W., L. J. Niles, R. N. Hendrick, J. R. Davie, and T. L. Grimes. 1985. Compatibility of even-aged timber management and red-cockaded woodpecker conservation. Wildl. Soc. Bull. 13(1):5–17.

INDEX